THE POETICS
OF STAGE SPACE

THE POETICS OF STAGE SPACE

The Theory and Process of Theatre Scene Design

BRUCE A. BERGNER

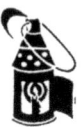

McFarland & Company, Inc., Publishers
Jefferson, North Carolina, and London

LIBRARY OF CONGRESS CATALOGUING-IN-PUBLICATION DATA

Bergner, Bruce A., 1962–
The poetics of stage space : the theory and process of theatre scene design / Bruce A. Bergner.
       p.   cm.
Includes bibliographical references and index.

ISBN 978-0-7864-7541-4
softcover : acid free paper ∞

1. Stage props—Design and construction.   2. Theaters—Stage-setting and scenery.   I. Title.
PN2091.S8B423 2013   792'.025—dc23   2013013758

BRITISH LIBRARY CATALOGUING DATA ARE AVAILABLE

© 2013 Bruce A. Bergner. All rights reserved

No part of this book may be reproduced or transmitted in any form or by any means, electronic or mechanical, including photocopying or recording, or by any information storage and retrieval system, without permission in writing from the publisher.

On the cover: model for *The Beggar's Opera* by John Gay, directed by Jeffrey Matthews, performed at Washington University's Edison Theatre, 1994, design by the author; background texture (iStockphoto/Thinkstock)

Manufactured in the United States of America

*McFarland & Company, Inc., Publishers
Box 611, Jefferson, North Carolina 28640
www.mcfarlandpub.com*

To Kim, Miles and Hallie:
my favorite compositions

Table of Contents

Preface	1
Introduction: Composition	4
Part One. Seeing	7
1. Fundamentals	9
2. The Theatre Artist	16
3. Physics	19
4. Geography	31
5. Geometry	45
6. Aesthetics	57
7. Music	74
8. History	81
9. The Connective Thread	88
Part Two. Knowing	93
10. The Soul of Space	95
11. The Anthropology of Space	114
12. Metaspatial Design	127
13. The Appraisal of Space	131
Part Three. Making	135
14. The Ritual of Making	137
15. Designing	147
Part Four. Being	163
Bibliography	167
Index	169

Preface

As a seasoned practitioner and teacher of theatre scene design (a subfield of stagecraft also known as set design, scenography, art direction, production design), I can say with some dismay that advanced-level books on the theory and concepts of stage design are rare. In 1941, Robert Edmond Jones published his masterpiece *The Dramatic Imagination*. This was the first time someone approached the subject of stage design from a staunchly philosophical angle. Since then, there has been a wealth of basic textbooks, cursory introductions to tools and techniques, profiles of famous designers and encyclopedias of design available to working professionals and students. But there are a select few recognized sources that unpack the nature of the stage design process and its medium.

This book aims to conduct such an exercise by focusing on the primary sculpting block of stage design, space. Space is an elusive concept seldom explored in theatre books. This is astounding because space is a central concern of the art form of theatre. Actors, directors, designers, artisans and audience are all directly impacted by its powers. I approach it with a deferential contemplation. As I do, I pick it apart and lay its diverse components out for the consideration of my audience.

In this presentation, I magnify the process of spatial design and its many considerations. This process is not exclusive to theatre. Architects, destination designers, interior designers, industrial designers, sculptors and myriad other creative individuals follow the principles of "making" explored in my book. That is why the book may reach beyond my specific field. It is an interdisciplinary effort in many ways. It is my hope to stretch beyond the domain of theatre and service a broader scope of kindred spirits.

As I proceed, I tell the spatial designer's story. Since I am one such individual, it is my story as well. Due to my nature, it would be impossible for me to segregate my own inspirations from the concepts in this book. As a result, I share a bit of myself in these pages.

This stands to reason because I harbor a passion for the subject. I am inspired by all of the things you might expect for a visual designer. For instance, colors are extremely vivid to me. That is due in part to a psychological peculiarity. I have a condition known as synesthesia. When I think of letters and numerals in my mind, I see them as colors. The colors are always the same for each letter and numeral and always have been the same. If I visualize a word or a group of numbers such as a calendar year (like "1962"), I see the mix of those colors in my mind, the same mix as if one were to stir up the individual pigments for each letter and make a mixed color. But, the first letter or numeral is dominant; it has more of a percentage of its pigment in the composed mix than the characters that follow.

So, color and I have a relationship. My rods and cones are hypersensitive. I do not only see a color, but through a color. I can almost "pixelate" it. I see what colors go into its making. They appear as tiny particles in the field of a color. A green field has little particles of blue and yellow. I can actually see them, if I look very closely. Rich colors radiate in my eyes and seem extraordinarily deep. It's as if they are made of copious dancing particles of radioactive pigment all boiling together in an enormous pot. Naturally, colors excite me.

I have a similar passion for space, and all that goes into it. I have grown to see space, the area where something exists, lives, moves and acts, as a deep and meaningful part of design and life itself. And I regard visual and spatial qualities as signifiers of something profound or revealing. Frankly, I spend a good deal of time contemplating all this.

And so, this book tells you what and how this designer thinks. I think about what kinds of worlds will best serve the stories we tell. I think of what the attributes of those worlds might be. I think about how the spaces of life are made and what connections they have to their cultures. This informs my own creations as I try to fabricate connections between my spatial designs and the culture of the staged story. The reader can expect to become acquainted with the fruits of that thinking.

And I've devoted some serious thought to the identity of those readers. In part, I direct this book at a figurative circle of people with whom I am associated or hope to be further associated. I describe them as follows with a nod to our "kinship." The book is directed at my "*siblings*" in theatre, my "*cousins*" in related design areas and my "*friends*" in the worlds of composition. Allow me to introduce them:

Siblings in theatre: I belong to this family. We are theatre people. These folks are part of a long history of what I affectionately call "freaks" (artists, authors, actors and audience) who together hold a mirror up to life and expose its truths — good and bad — via a live performance in an "appropriate" space. This book will help my siblings to better appreciate what is meant by "appropriate." "Freaks," by the way, is a term used with all good intentions. It refers to a variety of unusual and creatively passionate people who dwell on the margins of society and look in at mainstream life. I am one of those freaks, if you will.

The art form of theatre is populated with an abundance of curious individuals. And I can claim, from well over 25 years experience as a professional designer, that there is no concrete or standard method for stage design. As a result, creative folks in my field are always looking for new inspirations and approaches. In this book, I offer a fairly dense body of ideas, theories, suggestions, instructions and conclusions regarding the spirit of what we do and how we do it, without restricting invention through hard guidelines. With its new perspectives, its depth of observation and its spirit of fostering creativity, this work should advance the field of theatre.

Cousins in Design: These include architects, industrial designers, interior designers, furniture designers, etc. These folks share my creative blood, but are not part of my immediate creative family. We have mutual processes and products and we can speak the same language. I admire them because they, like me, are compelled to go to the drawing board and devise the perfect objects to suit their subjects. They have a drive. And that drive forces them to deeply and broadly pursue service to the aspects of life they hold dear. I encourage these cousins to "deeply and broadly pursue" by the principles I share here.

Friends in Composition: These include musicians, writers, inventors, etc. Design is a process to serve a need. Composition is a process of forming various parts into a logical whole. A finished composition expresses a message clearly with an impact that can be felt deeply. The composer, to achieve this, must be informed by a vast body of knowledge, as is the theatre artist: a composer of worlds. All composers will find an affinity in this book. It addresses their creative process, and if relevant, their collaborative process. I expect that my friends will find a kernel of inspiration in its pages.

And the Rest: Of course, this book serves all who show interest. It suggests a manner of understanding the worlds around us. It suggests a way in which we exist and a way we create what we live. It presents a model of how to look at and assess detail and it demonstrates what makes for effective design. In the process, it introduces a view of the theatre many might not know, that taken from the vantage point of a theatre artist.

* * *

I would like to acknowledge several inspiring individuals who were of great assistance in the development and completion of this project: Robert Neblett, Ph.D., Cecelia Pang, Ph.D., Lynn Nichols, Ph.D., Oliver Gerland, Ph.D., James Symons, Ph.D., Bud Coleman, Ph.D., Richard Devin, USAA 829, Alan Trumpler USAA 829, Jessica Munns, Rand Harmon, Ann M. Sullivan, David Cooperstein, AIA, and the staff of PGAV Destinations — Saint Louis.

Introduction: Composition

This book is about a process of creation, the making of worlds. More specifically, it addresses the craft of spatial design, an engine by which imagined worlds can be realized. This craft is my livelihood. I am a scene designer for the theatre. As a theatre artist who designs space, I have the privilege of creating worlds for stories to be told. And on these pages, I present a testament from my journey in that craft. When I work, I must interact with space on two levels. I must negotiate with dramatic space, the medium of my life's work; and I must investigate the "real" living spaces of human cultures to inform my work. They both have common purposes, similar evolutions and seem to speak to each other on a conceptual level. So it is natural that I address them in tandem in this book.

The primary focus of my design work is a matter of *composition*, a word I will refer to often. I am a composer of worlds. I put worlds together from component parts in order to serve a story being told on a stage. In this book, I expose the *beauty, truth and relevance* of composition as I know it. The *beauty* is the human will to form an orderly and meaningful "whole" from disparate parts. The *truth* is that the "whole" resonates with the song of its culture and its history. The *relevance* involves connecting the practice of composition with a better understanding of life and creativity. As such, I look at the creative life and the created life. And I do so via the subject of space. I then offer my assessment of what space should be and how it can interface with people. This makes up "the poetics of space."

In the spirit of composition, this book contains a central theme: that from many perspectives comes one understanding. From many, one. The Latin is "*E Pluribus Unum*," a phrase inscribed on much of American heraldry. Ultimately, that is what composition is all about. This book itself is a compositional process of bringing many ideas down to a single point.

In the process, I address the subject of space with a justifiable reverence. I realize that space is an abstract concept and a little hard to grasp. But it deserves some scrutiny, coupled with some reflective poetry, to escalate its relevance to another level. Space is the carving block of theatre design, architecture and other related fields. The block deserves serious consideration because it is underrepresented in the scholarly realm.

This is unfortunate, because space can be quite intriguing. It has a creation, an evolution, a life, and interacts with its tenants or inhabitants. It's like a living organism. It can have human-like traits, including spirit, body and personality, etc. As such, I approach space, whether to study it or design it, as anthropologists or scientists might approach their subjects. I try to read it, interpret it, find deep meanings and stories in it and carefully deconstruct its power and its relationship with human beings.

This is natural. Scene designers for the theatre are curious beasts of many interests. We must engage with space from many different angles on every project. We are similar to architects in that we must consider the values of space. But we differ from them in that all our designs are temporary and as such have a little more artistic freedom. As we conduct our creation, we explore the form, function and meaning of space. In this book, I share my discoveries from that endeavor, including a healthy dose on the spatial design process.

I am convinced that the designer's process of engaging with space expresses a larger idea. I write this book, in part, to illuminate that idea. The idea relies on the concept that there are four critical components or phases of spatial design. And I present the notion that these four components comprise a progression, or a process for life. These components are: *Seeing, Knowing, Making,* and *Being.*

I break down these four procedural phases via the scopes of space and spatial design. A rudimentary summary of the breakdown goes like this: *Seeing* helps us appreciate (to know). *Knowing* helps us create (to make). *Making* helps us serve our world (to be). And *being* is life. The book is structured with these four phases as sectional headings and follows the process in a linear fashion.

Part One (*Seeing*) explains the nature of how we observe physical space. The chapters in this section each approach space in the manner of a different academic discipline (theatre artists are famous for borrowing techniques, methods and vocabulary from other areas of study to conduct our work — this follows suit). For example, Chapter 3 examines the physical body of space, its surface features, in the manner of physics. Chapter 7 examines the expressive nature of space via the language and concepts of music.

Part One addresses how we, as designers, look at space: how we observe its qualities, construction, details and characteristics and how we can understand tangible space as a vital consideration in the practice of theatre design.

Part Two *(Knowing)* steps beyond the observation of material space and suggests "deeper ways of knowing." This is a section on interpreting and defining the meanings of space. It is a bit more suggestive and imaginative. But it does offer several examples and practical techniques for exploring space at a deeper, more personal level. Part Two asserts that spatial understanding (and spatial design) transcends the physical observations outlined in Part One. While Part One is about *describing* space, Part Two is concerned with *defining* space, interpreting its deeper meanings and powers.

Part Three *(Making)* moves the reader from the analysis of space covered in the first two sections to the exercise of creating space. It articulates the nature of the collaborative/creative process. By presenting creativity as a cultural ritual, it goes beyond instructing readers on how to conduct their work. It presents the vital connection between creativity and life. One theme in the book is the elevation of design as a noble and necessary function of cultural existence.

If Part One is about how we observe and describe space, and Part Two is about finding ways to know and define space, Part Three follows the linear progression and offers some direction on the creation of spatial worlds, the primary charge of theatre design. This is an advanced manual for the theatre collaborative process. But it also offers sage advice for all creative individuals regardless of field. Part Three concludes by expressing the "goals" of good stage/spatial design, the poetics of space.

Part Four *(Being)* is a brief conclusion that finds the soul of the book by connecting space to life. Space is not a static locale. It is in fact a living event. And designers, especially those in the theatre, create worlds for life to ensue. This reinforces the thesis (and structural progression) of the book: that first we learn to see, and from our sight comes curiosity. Curiosity leads us to wonder and contemplate. From that, we come to know the worlds around us. From deep knowledge, we can dare to create or make things. By making things, we foster being, or life. I am essentially concluding that the design process models a process for existence.

In all parts, I support my points with illustrative examples from practical design work, and design analysis from the field.

By unifying the progression of these parts with a theme of *composition*, I introduce the readers to *a way of understanding* long practiced by the culture of theatre artistry that I represent. We are composers of worlds who function collaboratively toward a concluding aim. And each of us is a composition of many viewpoints, backgrounds, talents and understandings, or what Lord Byron called "a sky of many colors." I have been one such composition since my raw beginnings.

So, it is through the multi-faceted lens of a theatre artist's eye that I bear witness. In my work I must be able to comprehend space with a diversified view. I begin by looking, in many different ways. When I look in proper ways, I begin to see things that spark my interest. My interest inspires me to study closer and begin to understand space. I begin to *know* it. From knowledge comes the capability to create. And creativity breeds life.

This book follows that course.

PART ONE

~

Seeing

When you write a book about space, it's a little hard to avoid sounding like a fan of the television series *Star Trek*. Space is, after all, the "final frontier." In the 1990s, the producers of that series created a spin-off show subtitled *Deep Space Nine*, implying correctly that space is quite vast. It also suggests that humans and their alien allies trek to the deepest regions of space, establishing outposts and staking claims to celestial territories. This is where I get into trouble. The very first thing I want to say here is that space is deep. Trekkies will confer and resoundingly accuse me of being puerile and obvious. And I would concur, if I were speaking of the enormity of cosmic space. But here, I am a bit more specific. By space, I refer to the designated areas where a person or a society exists, essentially their life-spaces. I believe that such areas deserve intricate consideration, a deep study if you will, especially by those who design spaces.

So, space is deep. The space where you live, work, play, love or function, is deep with detail, meaning and message. It is also deep in the structures of its composition. Very little is accidental. Those who are charged with composing new spaces should look deeply into existing spaces. They should strive to understand them, how they work, the stories they tell and the images they project. In other words, space-makers should "go deep" in their compositional exercises, because deep in space, you find a connection to the life of the dwellers. It is my aim to describe that depth and that connection.

In order to understand the connection of space to life, we must first be able to see space. The first section of this book is about describing what we see. I present the subject through the methodology of the theatre artist. Because I am a theatre designer, I can approach the subject and convey my ideas most naturally by using the experience, language and knowledge of my field. As you will see in the next two chapters, theatre is relentless in its pursuit of an effective reflection of life. And good theatre designers pursue well-informed spatial worlds for that reflection.

In our craft, theatre artists try earnestly to expose the connective thread between humanity and their world. We are a resourceful bunch. With notoriously low or non-existent budgets, we operate like Jacks and Janes of all trades, using every conceptual scrap and angle of approach within our grasp to devise our modest stage productions. Usually with a mix of enthusiasm and exhaustion, we try to pull together a show from a multitude of influences. In the process we communicate by using a hybrid language made of voices from many fields. It is as though we are, as an art form, a collective composition of varied understandings.

The composition of space (in the theatre and in life) is the fruit of this composition of understandings. And these understandings stem from what one sees. Part One demonstrates ways of seeing and describing space in the manner of numerous academic disciplines. In the theatre, we love to conduct this kind of intellectual adoption. The various manners of seeing I share in Part One merge together into a composition of observations that can clarify and illuminate the true nature of the "final frontier."

1
Fundamentals

It is best to begin a discussion about seeing space by establishing some fundamental definitions of terms. Since this is a book about space, I will begin there.

Space

Essentially, space is potential.

Being a practitioner of the performing arts, it is justifiable for me to use an example from the world of modern dance. In dance, the performance space is an empty box. It is the dark, open shell of the proscenium stage, surrounded only by lights and the curtains that define its perimeter. This empty box has the potential to take on a dynamic identity. The movement of performers in space dictates that identity. Space takes on character, meaning and life via the movement of humans (or some other animated object) within it. The art of dance relies on the spark of life that is generated by the injection of movement into space. The open space allows dance great potential.

If the space has distinctive attributes of its own, such as decorative walls or dimensional features, it still has potential. But, the potential is controlled by those attributes. The dynamic identity, character, meaning and life in the space are reactive to those attributes. The relationship becomes more complex and for those of us in theatre, more dramatic. In this scenario, the space needs a designer to compose its dramatic potential. Dramatic potential breeds dramatic action. The same logic holds true in architectural design. The attributes of an architectural space define its potential. The potential breeds the action of life therein.

Ultimately, space is an identifiable, dimensional "nothingness" with the potential to become a world. You must understand worlds to create worlds. And creating worlds is by design.

Design

Design is an action. The action is to compose a meaningful and purposeful entity from component parts. This means that design entails the action of composition, arranging a plurality into a logical and functional singularity. That sounds like a tall order, but it's all in a day's work. Design is also a process of honing to the essence and to the optimal efficiency of that entity. Designers must "get to the heart of the matter," with no waste and no gratuitous detail (unless the gratuitous detail is, in fact, essential to the purpose — and sometimes it is). Designers look to serve a purpose and address a need with their work. It is best to do so by chiseling the thing down to its basic form and function.

Design often attempts to generate something progressive and interesting to move the culture forward. I, for one, don't care much for repeating the past, unless it's an homage. Design resides on the leading edge of cultural evolution. Buildings, fashion, graphics, décor and devices are all propelled forward by the energy and agendas of their culture. In its form, a design defines a culture's style, its priorities, its desires and fears, dreams and nightmares. And in its function, it can rectify inefficiencies, solve problems and propagate industry. Design is the "ram's horn" of culture, an active heraldry with a forward thrust. Art operates in a similar way and this includes Theatre Art.

Theatre Art

Theatre is an art form that uses live performance to hold a mirror up to culture. Antonin Artaud, in his influential 1938 critical work *The Theatre and Its Double*, advances this. Artaud argues that theatre is more than a proper presentation of literature. It offers a sensory experience for its audience that may or may not be rooted in literature. It ignites feelings between humans, those who perform, those who perceive, and all who participate. In the end, it reproduces moments of life at various levels of distortion and diffusion. By this, it reminds us of who we are, where we belong and what we do. This can make us laugh, cry, wiggle uncomfortably in our seat and even shriek. Therefore, at its best, theatre art tells the truth.

Theatre is an art form that creates its work collaboratively. It is not a solo operation. There is no single easel artist, no lonely sculptor, and no isolated poet toiling in solitude. Its about teamwork, social interaction, gathering and dynamics. It can be about screaming and yelling too. Typically, it is a clumsy mash-up of odd individuals endeavoring blindly to invent what becomes a miraculously unified creative process. In that process, there are several distinctive and self-ordained "experts" each contributing their share to the character of the live performance.

Theatre presents an illusion of life in varied forms and styles, depending on the period of its making. The conditions of life in a particular theatrical movement's "home" culture dictate the variation. A culture of comfort might portray its characters as mannered and cartoony, drawn with bold lines and caricatures, making the facade override the flesh and bone beneath. A culture of want might render its characters as desperate and dusty souls in a layered collage of pathetically textured reality.

The illusion of life rises out of a core text, usually a script, written or conceived by an author who stands as a representative for the culture at a given point in time. The text is driven by its depictions, fueled by action and guided by storylines, morals or themes. It may spontaneously dance about like a reckless crackling of assorted fireworks, commanding attention and inspiring awe. It may confuse or confound as well. But, the standard is for theatre to represent its double for the betterment and enjoyment of those who purchase the tickets.

Human performers, who at their best surpass the faithful service of conservative rendition, deliver the text to its audience. This is where theatre and chamber music differ. Both are collaborative forms of performing art. But most chamber music dutifully honors the intentions of its original composers by loyal recreation. Theatre may remount old plays, even using historic acting methods. But it nearly always injects an aspect of the current into the mix. It simply cannot resist originality. Conceptual approaches to style, milieu and overall message are tuned to the context of the time. All of this creativity is conducted in an appropriate theatre space, one that is devised to best convey the core text by the Theatre Designer.

Theatre Design

Design for the Theatre is a collaborative and creative process that intends to make an essential and appropriate world where the performance of a text may live. This world is spatial. It depends on a housing, a place where it can be known. It may employ signifiers that brand it with the markings of its culture, its tenants or its central ideas. It may be flavored with atmosphere, mood and effects that transport the audience toward a temporary suspension of disbelief. But no matter what ingredients go into the pot, the stew must be prepared with an awareness of the tastes of the culture and with the nourishment of its original text preserved.

Theatre designers do not craft static space, as an "old-school" sculptor might. We are responsible for materializing a living world, a space that fosters life. And more importantly, we do not design pictures, but moments. We are to draft a dramatic event that tells a story, conveys a message or evokes a feeling. We become artists of occurrences. Each environmental trait should look the part, being visually apposite to the nature and style of the text. And it should supply the event with a motivational mechanism, helping to move the action forward. Architectural and interior designers hold comparable credos. They must serve their clients' demands for efficacy through form and function. Like theatre, the intent is to deliver an experience to the attendees. It is a spatial experience.

Theatre Space

The performance space is the vehicle of the event. A dramatic event usually offers a message to its attendees. The space is the vessel for the carriage of the message. To follow my comparisons to architecture, I will suggest that performance space is "architecture for moments." It is constructed to elevate the key moments in an event. These key moments are instances of high dramatic value in a story, such as revelations, redirections and resolutions. We design to heighten and reinforce the impact of these moments and then fill in the spaces in between with structures and traffic lanes that allow our performers to move into the moments fluidly.

After addressing the key moments, we need to unify the entirety of the space so that it becomes its own world. This is a world with enough credibility and believability to transport its audience into the rapture of the event. We create the world by utilizing a wide array of experiences and expertise, information gathered by a healthy curiosity and the willingness to try and err. As designers, we are obliged to understand the connections between humanity

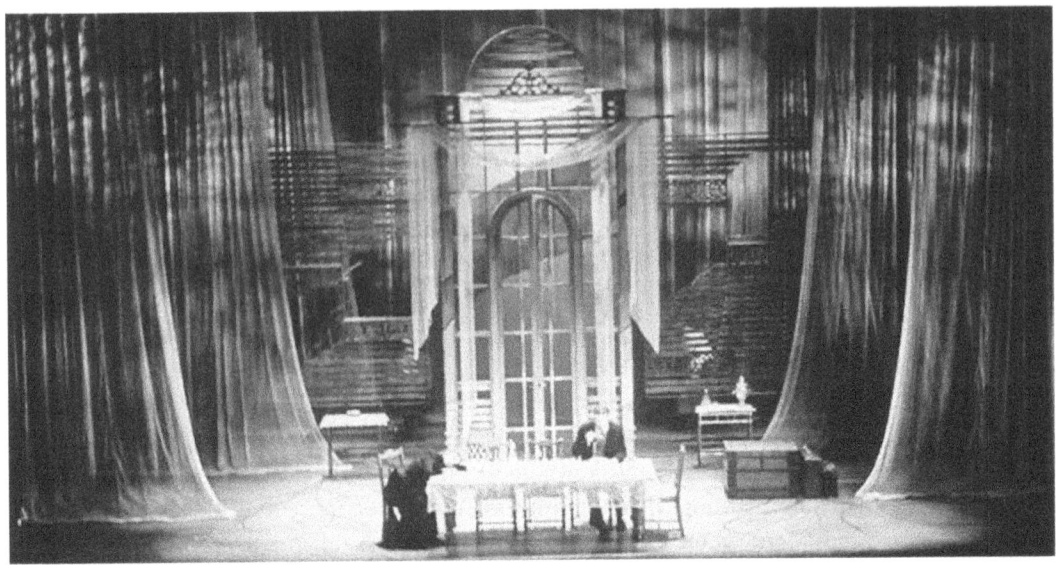

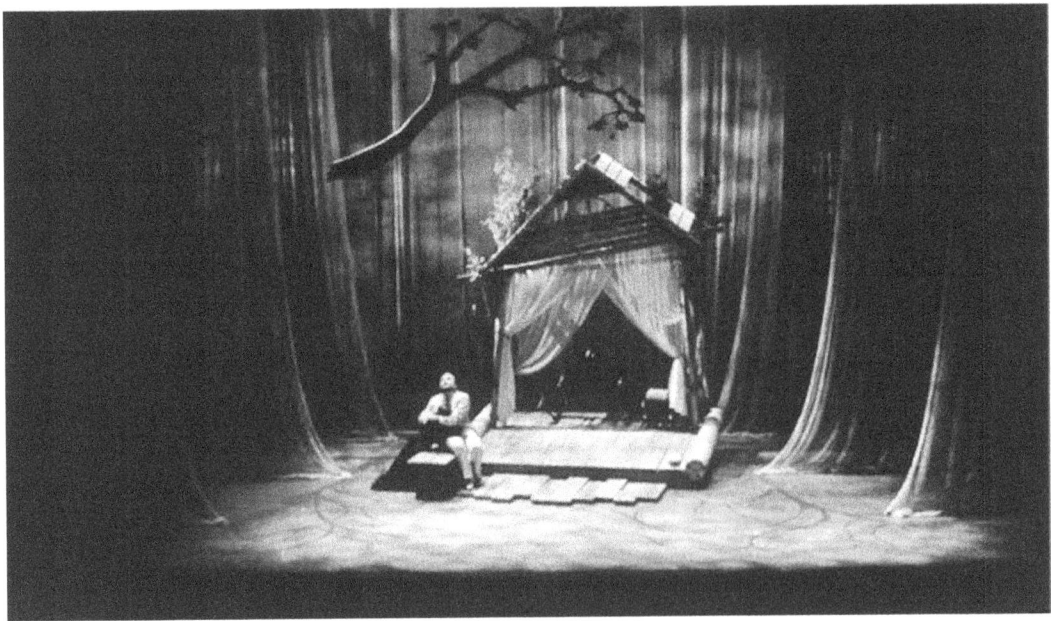

Top and above: A designed space reinforces key moments in a play. Production photographs from *The Seagull* by Anton Chekhov. Design by the author.

and its spatial worlds. And to better create these worlds, we master an appreciation of the Basic Forms of Space.

The Basic Forms of Space

There are a variety of archetypal forms of space. We see these repeatedly in life and on the theatre stage. They are connected to their tenant cultures, echo their origins and project into their futures. I will discuss a few below: the organic space, the circle, the square and the line. I will also address the distinctions of static and dynamic spatial forms. In my descriptions of the forms, I will identify how they manifest in theatre situations.

The Organic

This is the spatial design of nature. Humans do not intentionally formulate or scheme organic space. But we do have an impact on all aspects of nature, through pollution, construction and agriculture, etc. Avoidance of this is impossible. For the most part though, organic space is free to develop by its own propensity. We encounter this space when we encounter nature, on hikes and trail expeditions, on camping and hunting trips and the like. It is the jungle, the grove, the thicket, the clearing and the geological formation. And though it is not manmade (unless we attempt a replica) it is a spatial form designers should consider.

From a designer's standpoint, we might describe it as wandering and irregular, yet strangely logical. Scientists will insist that it is all well ordered, following the laws and patterns of nature. And landscape painters would concur that there is a beauty in its occult balance and asymmetry. Certain religious individuals might claim that organic space is designed by a higher power and others will advocate for its spiritual value. It has many readings.

For me, organic space relates to our own human nature. It possesses a beauty that at first scares us, appearing spooky and feral. With a bit of adaptation, we allow it to speak to us. It reminds us of our primitive roots. It forces us to confront our fears and find our way alone. It challenges us to grow and learn and to survive. And it promotes a personal spirit quest.

In the theatre, the common spatial arrangement most akin to the organic is environmental staging. Since the 1980s, theatre artists have tried to dissolve the cemented convention of a hard separation between audience and performance. They try to weave the action through the positions of the audience in a seamless fashion. This allows the action to wander free, organically flowing in an interactive dialogue with the participants in a staged event.

The Circle

The circular space represents the gathering, the communal place. This began as a space of ritual in early cultural developments. It represents the earliest form of the group dynamic, a place for storytelling and sharing. We hear of cave paintings that depict a central figure delivering a ritualistic reenactment of a hunt to a circle of fellow tribesmen. We have evidence of a tribal shaman in the center of a circle, perhaps by a fire, conducting a ritualistic dance for purposes of summoning the spiritual realm. These romantic images, seen with glowing color in television documentaries, help assert that the circle is a ritual space and one of the earliest inventions of sacred space. Its form is expressed at Stonehenge, on the Mandala, in Romanesque churches and by covens in parks at midnight on the solstice.

In the circle, we see each other across the space. There are no castes, no power hierarchies, and no cheap seats. The circle forces equality and affinity, one participant relating to another. It is intimate, immediate and unbroken. There is a sense of belonging and perhaps something magical, a bonding and a validation of each person's value.

The theatrical manifestation for this is in "arena" staging or "theatre-in-the-round" (where the audience views the action from all around a central playing space). The famous Swiss designer Adolphe Appia (1862–1928) invented the concept for this in the first half of the twentieth century. It caught on among consultants and architects and by the 1960s numerous in-the-round theatre facilities emerged in America and Europe. In these arenas, the audience focuses more on the actor, language and ideas than spectacle. It is always intimate and feels ceremonial.

The Square

I will include rectangles in this category. After all, rectangles are merely stretched squares. They are symmetrical and four sided, so they belong in the family.

This spatial form is definitely human-made. It is a construction of the civilized mind. I am convinced that the square space is humanity's original attempt at perfection, perfect corners and rigid symmetry, regulations and order. The Greeks even held a reverence for the "golden rectangle," a quadrilateral of "ideal" proportions and geometry. The square space opposes the wild wanderings of the organic. It is not nearly as spiritual and primordial as the circle. It is indicative of how we define reason, logic and technical mastery. It draws us out of the forest and into civility, out of instinct and into intellect. It finds beauty and truth in mechanical balance. It "cleans up" nature and offers a mathematical definition of reality.

A box emerges when the square extrudes. This affirms our compulsion to structuralize. Humans crave the frame. We wish to place ourselves in a neat box. Our governments, laws, systems and technology are all structured in some iteration of a box. To think "outside the box" is daring and radical. Theatre is equally compelled. Our most abundant architectural form is the proscenium stage, a stage that is distinguished by the rectangular portal that frames the playing area. And the proscenium favors the "box set."

The Line

This is also known as the path, the way, the sequenced space. The line implies a journey. And it implies a destination, a goal to reach. The line extends the spatial focal point. It features varying encounters, where visitors focus on the many things they pass, an ever-changing course with ever changing pictures. The visitors focus on the destination as well, following a lead toward an eventual payoff. This implies the existence of a guide. It does not wander free, as in the organic. It is not personal and solitary, for others have trod the path. It is a socially understood way.

A recent trend in playwriting involves an episodic style of writing that many call cinematic. Plays may have a series of short, abrupt scenes that bounce from locale to locale without pause or the luxury of scenic shifts. Staging cinematic theatre means that a scenic designer must conceive a fluid and linear progression that can easily and plausibly depict the flow of spatial worlds the scenes demand. He must create a clever and flexible spatial unit that morphs by some simple modulation. This allows a spatial line, even without a literal road.

The Static and the Dynamic

All spaces, even the seemingly fixed, become dynamic when a human enters or when we activate a story. I allude to this notion earlier in the chapter when I speak of modern dance. Many spaces are permanent and static in their footings. They may be constructed with no means of motion or tangible change. Most buildings exist in this category. But they can also be visually striking as they stand and can provide for an exhilarating dynamism by being a profound container or backdrop.

Moving and evolving spatial forms also exist and can transport the tenant, providing a kaleidoscopic regeneration. This is both virtuous and damning at times. Sometimes it is best to rest and soak in the world around you, allowing the space's profundity to sing its song without having to get up and move. There is such a thing as too much dynamic potential. So it is best to choose wisely when designing space. To help, I will share two points of thought:

1. That which is still is pondered and that which moves is experienced.
2. The still speaks a sentence and expects to be heard while the moving asks a question and expects an answer.

Summary

These forms repeat through time and place and take on variations, deviations, mixing and mutations. It is unlikely that you will encounter a pure and stand-alone example of any one of these forms. There will be aspects of the square in the line, the circle in the organic and so on. But one form will dominate and radiate its presence as the primary "spokes-form" for the space. These forms are understood by the definition of their makeup. That definition requires an engagement with the form, a complex examination. Being a theatre artist has taught me to relish the diversity of interpretations, approaches and processes that it takes to generate our art. And the part that I most appreciate is this complexity of consideration we conduct as we begin on our task.

2

The Theatre Artist

Composition is a practice that I attend to daily in my work. This is natural. So much of what I do involves the combining of diverse particles into an arrangement that has unity. I compose with doors and windows and hues and shades, etc. As I say in my introduction, the term composition, for me, means "from many, one" or "E Pluribus Unum." I will talk about that occasionally as I proceed in this book. It is the subject of my mantra and hugely important in the practice of theatre. In fact, my colleagues and I are compositions ourselves of a sort. I call this the composition of the theatre artist.

The nature of theatre is to create collaboratively. It is about many people making one event. Following that sentiment, the nature of the theatre artist is to contribute to the craft by considering many things in many ways to arrive at a single concept. Essentially, the theatre artist is a composition of many experiences and proficiencies focusing on the single goal of mounting a production.

A stage director merges her experiences with literature, physical movement, spacing, pacing and dramatic moments to mold the show. She is the mantle that holds the collaboration together. Among her proficiencies are the abilities to communicate and motivate effectively, to resolve inter-personal squabbles (these are frequent) and to hold the helm on course. It is not her responsibility to micro-manage or do all the chores herself. She depends on the others. But, she must bring the biggest bag of tricks to the table as she embarks on her effort.

The actor uses many studied methods and techniques and draws upon many internal and personal influences to develop a character. He may exercise his craft with the methods of Constantin Stanislavsky, Lee Strasburg, Sanford Meisner and the like. He may conduct preparations that make the layperson chuckle like barking or seething or assuming torturous body positions. He may also tap into his emotional memory and conjure events from childhood to remind him of the muscle twitch that comes before sobbing and the raised eyebrow that precedes a look of desire. He composes all of these things into a consistent portrayal.

A theatre company employs a dramaturg, also known as a literary manager, to conduct research on all aspects of the plays being presented. She is a resource for informing the art being created and is well versed in the history and criticism of dramatic literature. The dramaturg collects concrete and abstract research from many sources to compose a single understanding of the textual world of the show being produced. Hers is a composition of evidence that will confirm or dispute the inclinations of the developers of the production. She sets them straight.

The stage designer merges artistry, research, history, technology and raw experience in the creation of an appropriate, coherent, visual and visceral environment for a show. He composes this environment and is himself composed of collected ideas, visions, schemes, routines and habits. His charge is laid in concrete terms. It is contracted and clear: he will use his "inner composition" to conceive and document specifications for an outer composition, the physical world of the play.

The world of the play exists in a space. As a result, space is a vital consideration for theatre artists.

Directors shape the show by blocking their actors in space. This most often requires a completed spatial design, with specific entrances and exits, seating, paths for movement and other parameters all clearly documented before the rehearsals begin. Directors envision the movement patterns of the characters based on their relationships, the timing of the dialogue and the motivations of their movements. Then they position the actors scene by scene in a facsimile of the performance space, the rehearsal space.

Actors depend on the appropriate arrangement of space and its physical obstacles to bring their characters to life. Movement is a crucial part of the acting craft. The space and the movement must coincide. If the movement needs to be fluid and graceful, the space should be open, allowing grand crossing patterns of performers. If the movement is motivated by dramatic tension or wants to employ physical humor, the space should have obstacles to negotiate. A space may be raked (with a sloped floor), cluttered, faceted with various levels or be vastly empty. All of these qualities contribute to the manner of the movement.

Designers certainly shape the space. In fact, space is our first regard when we begin the theatre design process. Designers love it when others believe we are virtuous. On one hand we try to appear proactive, anticipating the problems we likely will face and have an impressive answer ready at our stead. But, more often than not, we must be reactive, dodging the harsh realities that are thrown at us like monkey wrenches of fate. One "wrench" is the reality of the given space, the permanent stage and house. We cannot tear down plaster proscenium arches or uproot concrete subfloors. That is, unless we are working on Broadway. Another reality is the script. We may have to contend with an author who has no concept of the laws of physics. I know one play that calls for balloons to fall and then rise up to the sky on cue with no visible means of support. That is a challenge. Then there are issues of budget and labor and all such unpleasantries.

I dare not leave out costume designers, stage lighting designers and sound designers in this discussion. They are equally virtuous and noble, proactive and reactive, and certainly part of the spatial discussion. So I celebrate them with this nod:

My fellow designers have a huge role in shaping space. With regards to costume, you can think of the silhouettes of eighteenth century gowns and how they resemble walking statues with enormous spheres of influence. These gowns certainly determine the sizes of doorways, etc. Think also of the motion of fabrics, with the rustling sleeves on 1930's dresses and the slinky stretch of spandex pants from the 1980's. They become part of the dynamics of the space. Lighting designers, on the other hand, will play with your mind. They reveal and conceal space with highlight and shadow as they wile away at the manipulation of perception. Sound designers must contend with space. The acoustics are rarely friendly and only by their own ingenuity can they resolve the problems with creative speaker placement, wireless microphones on every head and by bouncing the sound around the walls of the space like so many billiard balls.

But, for all of us, the main instigator to a show's design is the collective of characters in the play itself. Their lives impact our choices and the space becomes the projection of those lives. We can view the characters as a group and find in them the culture of the story. I believe that this is true of all space: The culture dictates the space and the space dictates the culture, architectural, natural and otherwise. As a result, all designers are bound to conduct intensive research toward an understanding of the culture and design accordingly.

Scene designers, specifically, create spaces by approaching the work, including research, from many angles targeting a unified spatial design. We do so with the aid of many informants. But, unlike a bureau of investigation, our informants are metaphysical. They reside in our working psyches and are influenced by an affinity we have with various disciplines of study. I share some ways that scene designers approach, view and describe space in the following six chapters. Each chapter addresses spatial design by assuming the theme of a different academic discipline. I expect that this discussion might illuminate *a way of seeing* space at large.

3
Physics

I admire physicist Stephen Hawking with awe. I have read two of his books and I'm still a little spellbound. He actually quotes Shakespeare in one of them, so I feel I should allude to his field in mine.

In this chapter, I discuss how designers consider the body of space. (Somewhat) like the physicist, we address and express the dimensionality of physical space analytically. In a sense, this is an analysis of a dimensional body. Space has countless features, and most are materially evident. These features are the things we look at, touch, smell, taste (rarely taste) and hear. Globally speaking, these are things we see, meaning things we clearly comprehend at face value. And I begin to discuss them in this chapter by describing our Hawking-esque approach to the physical and dimensional body.

Scene designers specify the dimensions of space via various graphic documents. These documents stand as our primary communicators. They tell everyone the real story, replete with excessive detail, specification and notation. The documents are seen by myriad talented and charismatic souls, including a few grumpy stage carpenters I know who prefer to clean their hunting rifles in the scenery shop during their many breaks (pardon my facetiousness). So, it is vital that these documents be carefully drawn to convey exactly what is intended ("if it's not on the page, it's not on the stage," say the gun-toting boys). What follows is an exhibition of the dimensions of space (as designers see it) and how they relate to our design documents.

The First Dimension—The Plan

I am referring here to what you see when you look down on a space from above. This is expressed by designers on the Ground Plan drawing, a top-view "map" of the space and its details. The first dimension is the plan, the layout and survey of space.

For me, this is the "brain" of space. In a way, it is the space's web-work, its circuitry and its nervous system. If a brain conducts transmissions of vital activity, so does the plan. A plan channels action, moves the organisms, regulates the dynamism and keeps the clock-work. A plan can process and direct the interaction of the tenants. The mindful placement of a chair with a calculated proximity to the entry door can have a profound impact on how the seated protagonist responds to an antagonist standing nearby.

In the theatre, this is most evident in works of realism. A play by Ibsen or O'Neill

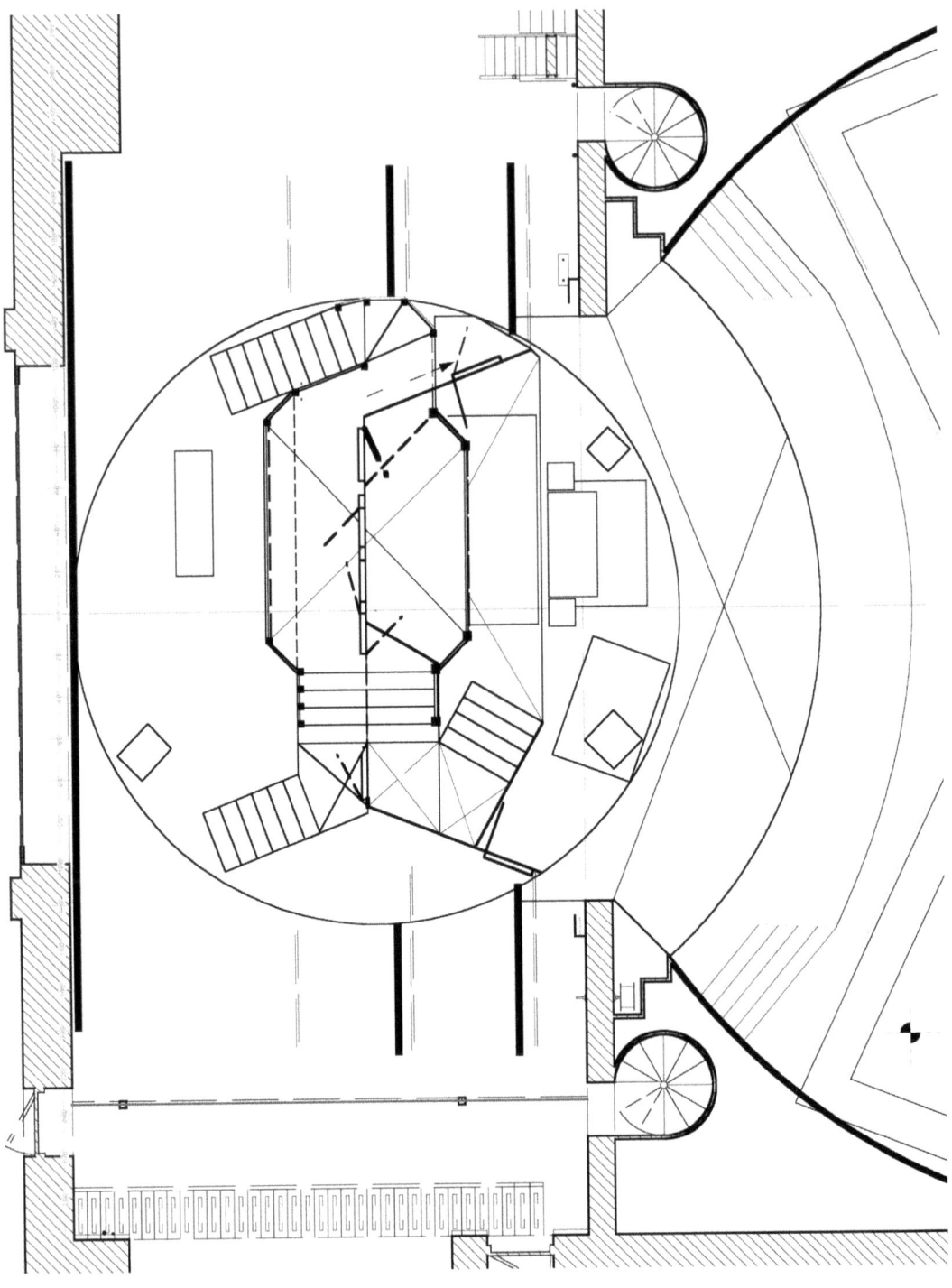

A ground plan is the map of the stage space showing the space from above. Ground plan by the author for *Noises Off* by Michael Frayn.

thrives upon the intimacy of an intelligently planned unit set. The doors, windows and seating devices must be mapped with a close dramaturgy, following the dynamic tensions, confrontations, elusions and embraces within the dialogue. In fact, the dialogue of a text's language should transfigure into a dialogue of spatial elements if the space is well designed.

The plan activates impulses. Action is rooted in its structure. It moves people. The manner of living is constructed by it. It creates and controls relationships. An example is my design for a production of Sam Shepard's *Buried Child*, set in a decrepit midwestern farmhouse. The position of old Dodge's favorite couch, turned away from the entry porch and distant from his wife Hallie's sanctuary upstairs, puts Dodge in a place of self-imposed alienation. All remnants of warmth and living, things Dodge might have once enjoyed, are pushed back. He cowers forward and away from them, facing only his ragged television set, with no more will to grasp sanity.

These kinds of things are not exclusive to the plans of theatre. The layout of spatial features, real or contrived, allows or denies human urges. Similar thoughts are tossed about by believers of Feng Shui and by visionary architects such as Philip Johnson and Frank Gehry. The plan makes decisions for the culture. It is the intellect of space.

The Second Dimension — The Elevation

Designers express the second dimension on the Front Elevation drawing, a mechanical front-view depiction showing the surface details. It is called an elevation because it elevates the plan, raising the frontal features so you can see how it will be.

The elevation is the face, the silhouette and the exposed epidermis of space. For all intents and purposes, it's the façade. A façade can be a bit of a falsehood. And I mean a false hood. The façade is incomplete; it conceals the something or the nothing behind it. In the theatre, some of our most popular forms include opera, ballet and the traditional book musical. Good or bad, this is proven by a glance at the attendance numbers of top-tier opera and ballet companies and commercial dinner theatres vs. those of non-traditional and experimental groups. One constant among these marketable forms is the presence of music, where performers can spontaneously "break into song."

Musical theatre pieces allow designers a diversion from the hard, slice-of-life reality that is so often the focus of our work. Musical works allow us to present rather than represent. We can hold up a façade, an incomplete and false reality that can dazzle and delight. In fact, that is exactly what is expected of us on these ventures. There is a joke in the theatre that if a commercial musical theatre producer catches you being earthy, real and dimensional in your designs, you'll be (metaphorically) "spanked on the behind like your mama never done." Standard book musicals flaunt their two-dimensional painterly drops and flats. The other frequent trait in musical forms is the presence of dance, or at least the presence of large choruses lumbering in and out of the wings. This kind of mass movement requires flat scenery because the access lanes must be so big.

But the elevation concerns more than painterly facades. The elevation is about The Look. The look carries identifiers and presents the space as an attracting object. Like sexual attraction, a space's look compels the audience, the buyer, or the victim. The elevation also carries the illusions of space. Theatre has long toyed with illusion. Scenic artists are adept at Trompe Loeil, a painting technique that "fools the eye" into believing the painted relief is real. Illusion is in the spirit of theatre. We enjoy mimicry and imitation. With these, we can better expose the truth of life. After all, the mirror is effective. That is why so many of us avoid it in retail stores but rush to it in our bathrooms, first thing in the morning.

The elevation can be the front wall of a space, the thing your face encounters. It can hold dimensional components, such as moldings and trim. Sometimes, the elevation can allow a window to the soul. That is, if you allow a window. And sometimes the elevation can provide a door to the truth. That is, if you provide a door. On a production of Jose Rivera's apocalyptic play *Marisol*, my co-creators and I feel that the play is about the disintegration of reliable systems such as religion, gender, and social structure. The design involves an enormous wall to represent these systems, an elevation of an archetypical space. The wall shatters as the play goes on and as it does, we begin to see the true (dimensional) nature of the characters evolve. The elevation of the *Marisol* set represents the meaning of the play.

The Third Dimension—The Section

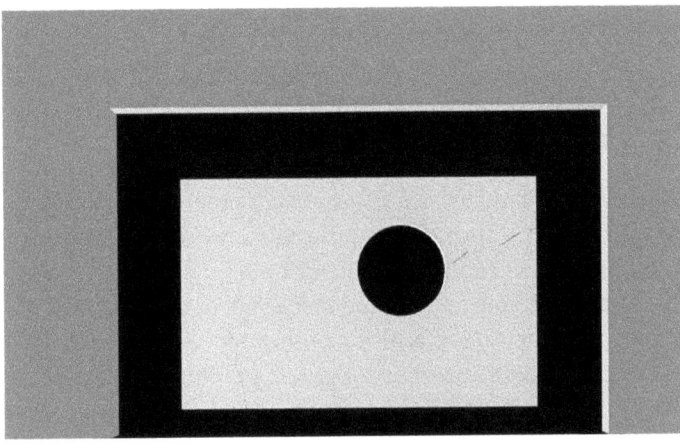

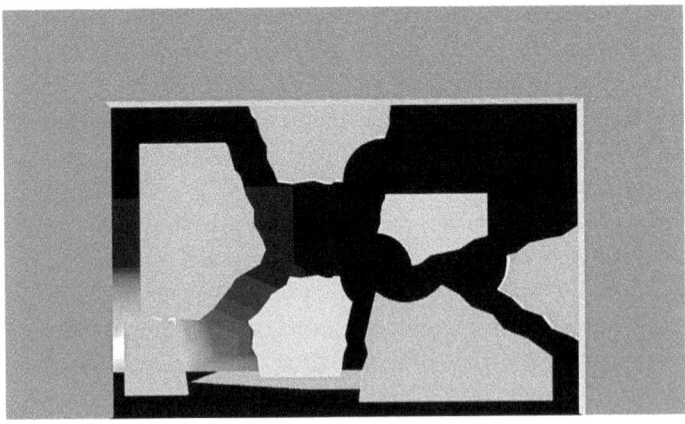

The Elevation drawing, a front view depiction, presents the façade or face of the space. Here are computer generated elevations of the set for *Marisol* by Jose Rivera. The wall shown at the top is whole, below it is disintegrating. These drawings tell the story of how the surface façade of a design works.

When I ask my students: what comes after the top and the front view? They quickly reply that the side view does. It's instinctive recognition. Spatial awareness is natural to our preceptors. The side view depicts the third dimension, depth. Designers express this dimension on the Side Section drawing, known by some as the cross-section, or simply The Section. A section drawing is basically a cutaway view. It shows more than the external side details. It also shows but the internal workings. There are many popular cross section views of buildings and ships that you can see in children's fact books.

The section view represents the interior of space exposed. It's about looking and going inside. I contend that seeing depth means seeing truth. Depth means revelation. When you look at the deep, inner-workings of something, the guts, and other things we'd rather not see, are revealed. In the theatre, we have this device called masking that we use to cover up those nasty bits. These are typically black velour curtains, or some other simple scenic items that mask off the backstage area with all of its garbage, cables, smoke machines and stagehands.

The section also reveals those things we deeply desire. It exposes that which the elevation cannot, or that which the elevation hides. It is about the hidden truth. We all have a hidden truth, a fear, a desire, a conscience and perhaps a demon. I believe that space does as well. Take a good, deep look and you will start to see it. The use of depth expresses a deeper part of the space's reality and avoids a pretense. The audience can discern depth when it is used wisely and in it they sense an air of significance about the action, a sense of the truth. The section drawing's purpose is to communicate this revelation.

Deep designs reveal emotions and the subconscious of the space's story, both the light and dark aspects. I will argue that no one writes stories with more attention to matters of light and dark than Shakespeare. He is regarded as "great" for more than his complex plots and eloquent phrases. There is great depth in his characters, often to the point of inner turmoil. An actor playing Tybalt, Hamlet or Lady Macbeth knows this intensive reach.

Designs for Shakespeare embrace depth as well, sometimes literally. My design for *Twelfth Night* uses a raked stage that extends from the front row of the audience to the backwall of the stage (and even beyond the backwall, into the loading area behind the stage). It is a design about a journey for the characters. They enter far upstage and slowly reveal their true natures as they come forward, like zooming into clarity in the manner of a camera. Shakespeare always offers a very three-dimensional rendering of the world and it is always a joy to support that kind of literature with a design that goes deep.

The section reveals dimensionality and relief, the modeled features of a design. These include things like sculptural motifs, bas-relief and moldings. Such deep relief in a design implies reality, realism, and tangible, accessible life. Tangible life is sensed, felt and interactive and is usually regarded with a serious consideration. And this is how the section differs from the elevation. While the elevation tends to celebrate the look or façade, the jovial and trivial, the section celebrates the guttural truth and the revelation of complexity. In this dimension, we shed the comfortable veneer and experience something akin to Saint John of the Cross' *Dark Night of the Soul*, a purging pilgrimage to the furthest reaches of inner truth. In there, we are like forensic scientists, analyzing the inner-workings, their process and product. The section teaches us a full understanding of material space and from there we can put it all together with the plan and elevation and appreciate a space's full surface impact.

The Fourth Dimension—The Model

After theatre designers and architects resolve the plan, elevation and section views of their designs, they normally move on to create a 3D model that represents the design in its entirety. Often, this is a fully realized, hard representation done to scale. It depicts the actual contours and shape of the design in miniature form. It usually includes realistic textures and colors and all of the nuances that one can muster. The construction of this model is exhaustive and relies on a keen resourcefulness, knowledge of art supplies and non-traditional

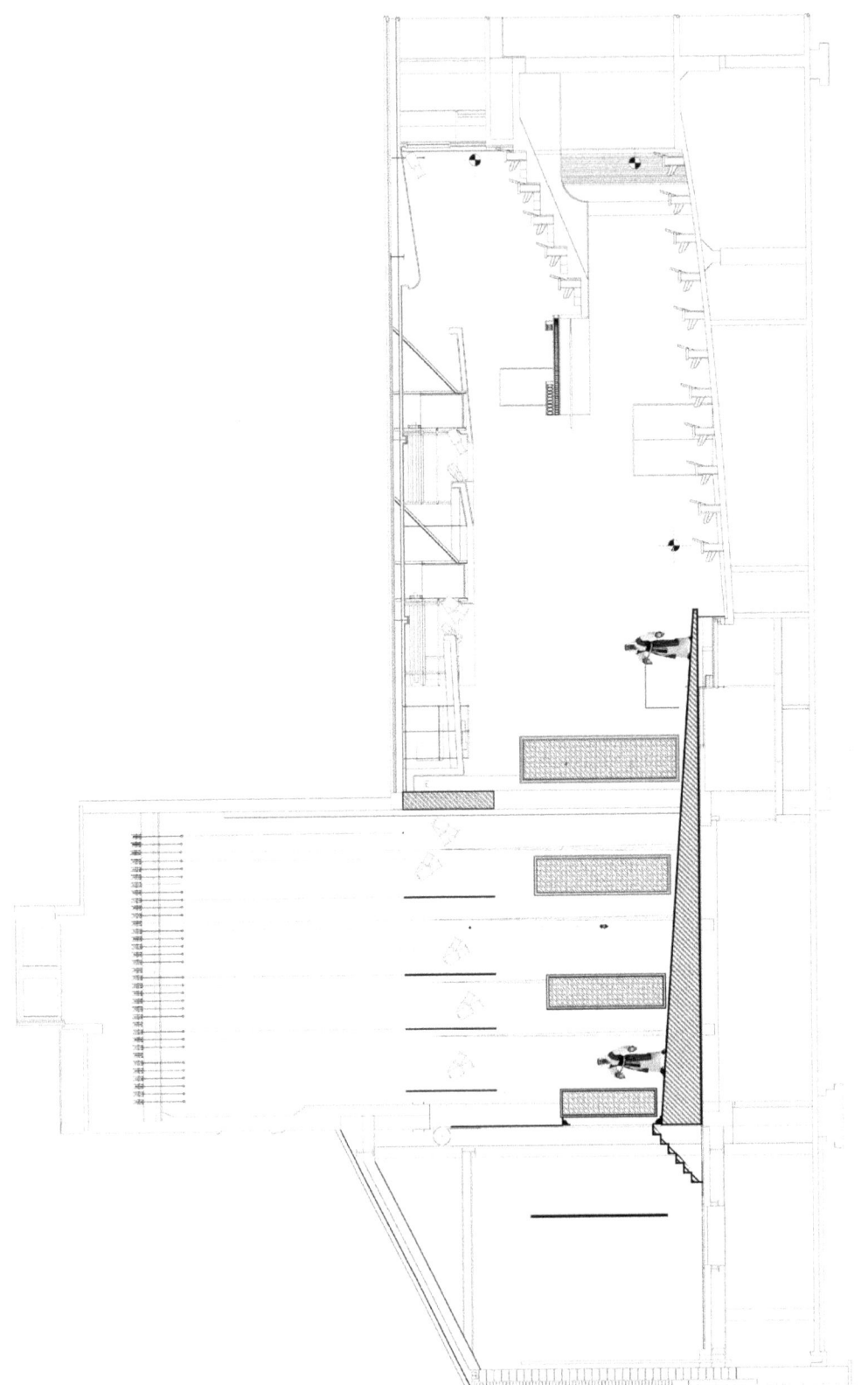

The side section drawing. The section depicts depth and the internal details of the space. Section for *Twelfth Night* by Shakespeare. Design by the author.

materials, and a delicate touch. In many cases, designers will opt to create digital models via CAD 3-D modeling programs. These programs will allow the viewer to virtually "walk-through" a space, rendered on the screen, and get a fairly accurate dimensional sense of its scope. Information from the plan, elevation and section must be entered into the program in order for the model to be constructed, so the process usually follows that linear path: resolve the plan, elevation and section and then move to making the model. It is also not unusual for a designer to first craft a rough "sketch-model" before working out the three views, so the process can, at times, be a bit circular.

The model is a very useful tool in the collaborative process. It communicates a concrete vision that can stimulate discussion and decision-making among the allied artists on a project. And it does so efficiently and concretely. The director, lighting designer, costume designer, sound designer and choreographer are the first to see the model once it is complete. With it, the collective can envision the potential of the design in action. It's like an amazing toy. It really catalyzes the imagination of a group of artists to a point where they begin to sense where the whole show is going. This means that the model really transcends its three dimensions. When regarded collaboratively, the model represents the whole spatial entity, including its outward influence and its direction. It tells us what the design is and where it is heading. When we see the model we read its intent. After the model will eventually come the full-scale construction, the full understanding, undivided and whole. The journey to this is a grand and progressive composition.

In the model, we can also appreciate the structure of space. We see its full working form, extending beyond the illusions and selective focus points of the individual graphic views. We appreciate how the structure might conduct itself. It might have the potential to rejuvenate and reshape itself. It may evolve organically and recompose itself via its use by its inhabitants. The interactive relationship of the spatial structure, the body of the space including all of its physical features, and those influential creatures within it, might result in a form of symbiotic spatial life. The model, like no other document, demonstrates this to the imaginative eye. It presents the space as a living organism. And so, the model must include a small, scaled human figure to show the impact and the relationship of the space to the inhabitant and vice versa.

To think of space as a living organism may seem outlandish and abstract. But this is a mentality that can elevate a designer's work from the ranks of the serviceable to those of the profound. If the designer can make a regular practice of visualizing the living potential, spatial evolution and the relationship of space and tenants, she can begin to formulate events rather than singular pictures, images and locales. This will yield a dynamism in the live performance, with immediacy and a purpose. And it can lead the field forward, an obligation of good art and design.

Too often, spatial design is about satisfying a craving for a certain look. In both theatre and architecture, there is a photographic record of famous, landmark designs that students of the practice strive to emulate. These are often held as ideals. And it is only natural that the human tendency to imitate that which it reveres will result in repeated attempts to capture the essential look, but not necessarily the contextual "life," of these ideal works. It's easy to see how this can stunt innovation. It does, however, build tradition as well and I acknowledge the merits of doing so. I believe that a balance of reverence and adventure is best. The reverence doesn't necessarily lead the adventure nor do the two reverse. The two move in tandem. And as they do, the true ideal is found in the expansion of the space's potential and its life. The nice thing about the model is that it forces the designer to confront, honestly, where the design is going. It tells the true tale.

So, the model is a storyteller and a fortuneteller as well. It predicts the life of the spatial organism. The life span (and a bit of the organism's afterlife) is discussed below.

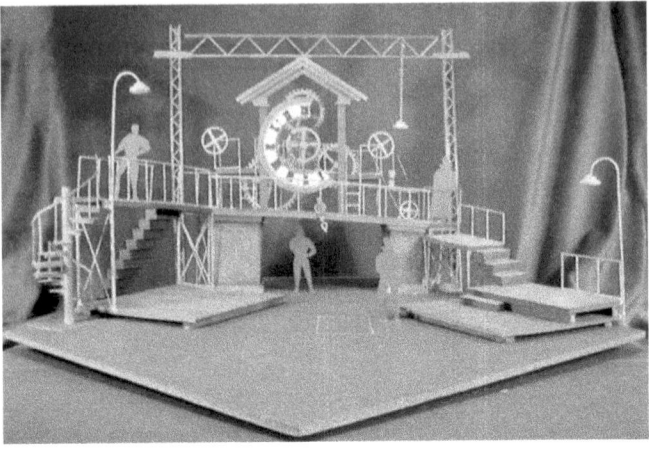

The scenic scale model. This model demonstrates potential use of the space. Model for *Hamlet* by Shakespeare. Design by the author.

Further On... — Perspective

There is another form of expression we use. And it represents another aspect of spatial design, the power of the perception of distance. More importantly, though, this form of expression speaks to the relationship of the designer, her work and the world. It speaks of the role of the creative mind in a world bound by traditional concepts of the divine. And it signifies a transitional moment in the perceptual understanding of the world in which we live. The form of expression that I speak of is Perspective.

A designer's scale model expresses the living potential of the spatial organism and the intent of the design. Perspective has another role. It suggests the eternity of space. It begins to convey a kernel of divinity in the space's potential, elevating its stature. It depicts realistically the vision of the design and demystifies the nature of knowing our world. Perspective offers a view. It is about the dialogue between observer and life. It allows a free regard and a free discussion. It encourages sight, knowledge, creation and life, all toward eternal potential.

Perspective is a functional expression by designers. More accurately, it is a tool we use. It involves a form of drawing, the perspective drawing. The perspective drawing could be a loose sketch or lavish illustration with exquisite detail, but it always is used as a communication device to represent a recognizable rendering of reality. It always begins with a deliberate and calculated line drawing that depicts a fairly realistic impression of familiar dimensionality, the way our eyes optically perceive depth and distance. Perspective is constructed in a mechanical, graphic process that uses an established vantage point and a vanishing point on the horizon. It captures the manner in which we perceive eternity, as focused, sharp and large in the foreground and fuzzy, smaller and having less visual contrast in the background.

We've all seen the drawing of a railroad track with the rails converging together and the ties getting smaller and fainter as they extend to the horizon. The horizon is a line that really suggests what is further on, beyond the immediate dimensions, as far as our eyes may

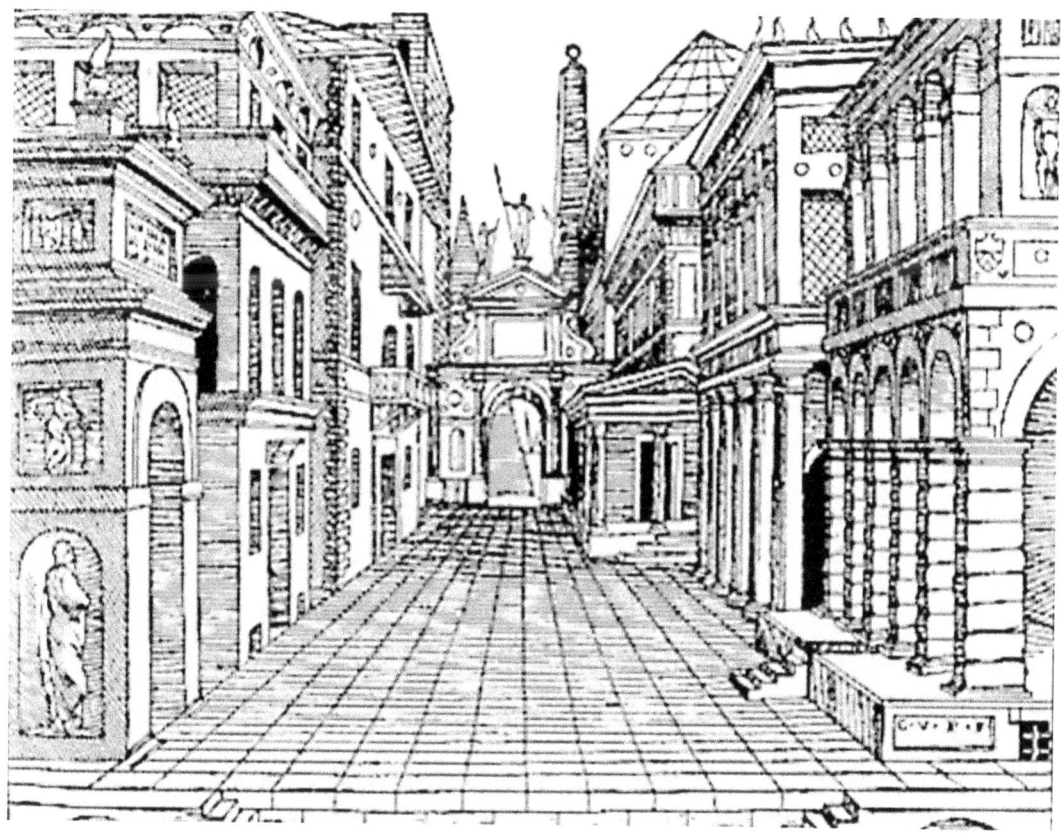

Perspective in design was ushered in during the Renaissance. Here, designer Sebastiano Serlio's famous "tragic" scene with the illusion of depth well-rendered.

see, but not as far as our imaginations may dream. The horizon line is not a boundary, but the temporary extent of a momentary limit, with a great deal of promise beyond. With regards to physics, perspective is about reaching beyond the tangible dimensions, it clues us into the fact that there is more beyond that which we see.

A graphic perspective arrangement may use a form of invented or manipulated perspective for effect. Designers often manipulate the impression of depth using "forced-perspective," or an exaggerated foreshortening of spatial details to create a sense of extreme depth or false depth. As she sketches out a space, the designer can establish a horizon line, and then adjust the placement of vanishing points on that line in such a way as to create an amplified sense of distance, similar to the bird's eye lens on a camera. The result is often a striking and sometimes disturbing visual effect.

Perspective in art and design stems back to its discovery by renaissance artists and has been an integral part of drawing, painting and stagecraft ever since. Theatre designs from the fifteenth and sixteenth centuries show an embrace of this "new" technical mastery. At this inaugural time, the proscenium theatre is reaching one of its historical high points. Artists are celebrating the notion of the proscenium arch being a living picture frame and the spectacle within the frame being a living painting, including extensive use of forced-perspective. These stage settings are called "vistas." The works of Italian designer/architect

Sebastiano Serlio (1475–1554) include "stock" (or reusable) designs for comic, tragic and idyllic plays that fit well into the vista space of the stage. The well-known English artist, Inigo Jones (1573–1652), brought this renaissance technique to the English stage via his masterful scenic painting, including collaborations with playwright Ben Jonson. The work of Serlio and Jones represents a period of advancement in spatial design that coincides with an advancement in humanism.

Perspective aligns with the Enlightenment. Through its illusory depiction of depth, it gives a sense of life and reality to a design and dares to express the potential of eternity. This is a significant departure from the primitive, flat-appearing paintings that stem from the middle ages. In a sense, perspective attempts to emulate the work of God, or to expose a trick of God and a trick of eternity. The conception of eternity relies on the perception of distances in space and time. The arrival of such concepts coincides with the rise of science and reason, of freedom of the mind.

In a way, perspective rejects the bondage of a domineering higher power. It rejects a reliance on incurious acceptance and the limited understanding of the depth of things. It rejects primitive renderings of reality. It elevates humanity. Therefore, it represents a liberation of humanity and a reconsideration of humanity's place in the universe. This signifies humanity's potential and celebrates the eternity of space, the eternity of *our* space, the space around us that we see and enjoy each day. With perspective, as a technique in art and a concept in life, we begin to see that the space around us extends and compels us to reach, to dare to sail to the horizon line without fearing a fall off the edge.

Forced perspective goes a step further. It manipulates reality for effect and dares to amplify on that which is eternal by mocking it, exaggerating it and distorting it. It gives the designer a profound charge. That is, it makes her the creator and manipulator of worlds, worlds to suit cultures and stories. I do not intend hubris here, as Hawking and his peers would not intend blasphemy when they proclaim their understanding of the entirety of the cosmos. I am reporting a historical transition. The dawn of mechanical perspective marks the embarkment of the designer into this a noble role. It marks the first time designers (who, being on the leading edge of culture, are followed eventually by the masses) grasp the potential of that which lies further on…

Time (The Event)—The Storyboard

The theatre production is a living work of art in both space and time. It is experienced, not just watched. As I discuss in Chapter 2, the art of live theatre is an art of occurrences. As we place ourselves into the occurrence, we find a connective tissue between the actor and ourselves, we engage with the mirror of life and respond as we feel we must. This creates a bond between the performer (in most cases, the storyteller) and us (the cultural participants in the ritual), as we enter the experience of the story. The storytelling is at the center of the experience as a shaman is at the center of ritual. This pseudo-shaman brings us to an understanding, a comprehension or a feeling. As this goes on, the space, the action in time, the atmosphere we experience, and the manner of our relationship to the performers all contribute to the impact and meaning of this thing we, in theatre, call The Dramatic Event.

I'll contend again that other designers and artists create events when they create practical objects. The industrial designer might devise a tool that allows one to quickly complete a task. And that efficiency, in turn, might allow us the time to move on to another task or even provoke an innovation. A musical instrument designer might create a device that can produce new sounds that can move people's emotions in new ways. An architect can create a corridor that leads us down a journey of reflection, an event that might lead us to make an important life choice, and take a turn that might lead us to unpredictable destinations.

The theatre designer, like a film director or an animation artist, documents the course of the event, the sequence of moments that make up the experience, in the design Storyboard. This is a design document that addresses motion. The previous documents address space exclusively. By contrast, the storyboard shows us the spatial motion and evolution that occurs as time, and the show, progresses. It acknowledges the arc of the play, the beginning middle and end. It is basically a series of sketches that depicts how a show flows from scene to scene. Essentially, it is a musical score for the design. The storyboard testifies to the journey of the space through time.

It is vital for a designer to consider that journey. It can have many formations. It may be an arc or a progression. It could be a rise, a fall or a dance. You can imagine the many types of dances these events might mimic. A story might be told with an increasing intensity that comes to a climax and releases itself. The story may also dart about from here to there and generate a spellbinding experience for the participants. The event isn't random. It is planned. We plan the physical locations in the space and we plan the way the space moves. This is the choreography of design.

The event, in whatever form it may take, is what is experienced. What is designed is the event. So, what is designed is the experience. If the medium of design is space, then space dictates experience. That is crucial so I'll say it again: *Space dictates experience.*

The storyboard communicates the experience, as it should occur in the space, in order for it to be realized. The process we usually take with such invention is to progress from dream to realization. This can only be achieved by clarity of vision. As physicists clearly predict the clockwork of the cosmos, celestial events and the general expanse of the universe, we as designers predict the journey of a living and shared experience. The kind of experience that we envision is the potential of the space.

Potential—The Rehearsal

In regards to physics, potential is a complicated matter. On one level, it refers to the stored energy that a body possesses relevant to its position in a force field. Space, as I've argued, is potential. It can, if designed thoughtfully, possess its own stored energy. With the force field of human life injecting and igniting it, space is capable of kinetic action. The space can take motion and a journey can ensue. The journey may reach for the eternity of our dreams and imagination. My comments in the sections above touch on this. The potential energy of space is developed into kinetic energy once the space is inhabited. There is no doubt that this is true in architecture and interior design. Such designers are obligated to their potential tenants. This also holds true in the theatre, an art form that is of, by and for the people.

Once a theatre design is conceived (with regards to both space and time), its vision must be maintained as the show is realized. That maintenance is conducted while the show rehearses. The rehearsal is held in a specific rehearsal space that possesses the same parameters as the performance space. The floor is taped-out with markings that indicate the precise positions of walls, doors, furniture and other spatial elements. The rehearsal is all about the insertion of humans/ characters into the space. When we do so, the space approaches its real potential. As I allude to above, space develops via an interaction with life. Living humans, even theatrical characters, adapt, reform and transform the space. So, life defines the space. And the life is gestated in the rehearsal process, wherein a key dialogue between space and life ensues and morphs into a dream realized. Therefore, space is a parent in the birthing of a dream realized.

There is a point when the performers, the human life I refer to above, exit the rehearsal space and move to the stage, or the "real" space. As we move to this point, we approach, confront, address and encounter the body of space directly. It becomes visible and tangible and its potential is defined. It is something we can see and analyze. One way we do this is in a manner similar to the physicist. Another manner is similar to that of the Geographer. A discussion of that manner follows.

4

Geography

Part of seeing and describing space is the consideration of space's layout and shape. In Chapter 3, we are pseudo-physicists, regarding the dimensional body, the outsides, insides and the potential for energy and life. As pseudo-geographers we regard the charting, the placements and the overall forms of space. We use concepts from geography that help us break down a space's direction, its progressions and its discernable regions. This helps us map a space's potential.

Imagine if you will a designer crafting a scrapbook record of her spatial creation, or a space she is studying. Allegorically speaking, this scrapbook is a kind of "atlas." This is an exercise of great value, as it will help her further see and describe that which she must know. The atlas is comprised of her sketches, her research and eventually her aforementioned design documents. She will include segments on various spatial components, breaking the space down into describable and logical portions. Each portion has its own significance and must be considered with a serious gaze. Each leaf of the atlas could focus on one of these portions, a specific characteristic or factor. Each leaf contributes to the whole. In the far lower right corner of the atlas' frontispiece is reiterated the central spirit of design and the core essence of composition, "*E Pluribus Unum.*" This seemingly favorite theme of mine is a reminder that from many considerations comes one design. The following are some of subjects you would see in the designer's atlas, the geographical considerations of space—all contributors to the "whole" understanding.

Periphery

The periphery is the container of space, the surround. It is whatever encloses or holds the action and life of the space. Many peripheries are possible. There can be walls, shrouds, decorative backings (in the theatre we have painted or projected backdrops), blackness, whiteness, color-ness, the sky (in theatre we use a fabric drop called the cyclorama to give us a sense of sky), a sea or a nebulous mist. Some theatre designs may include a dark void, achieved with black velour curtains and no peripheral lighting. This allows the foreground objects to stand out and be appreciated as individually detailed sculptures. Another design may include a glowing sheet of color in the background that might create an interesting silhouette of the objects in the foreground, giving the whole space a creepy identity. The surround may also be more conceptual. On a production of Harnick and Bock's *She Loves*

Me, a musical about tender romance in a European perfume shop, my design employs a painted collage of larger-than-life flowers on a surrounding arch over the central playing area. This kind of container exudes a sensibility and mood for the piece. I believe that every show should have its appropriate container, like the gift-wrap on the present we pass to the audience.

The surround can also be a frame of reference, a reliable and ever-present representation that can help the audience, or the tenant group, remind itself of the world they are in, the world we've created. For example, this can be a permanent decorative border around an ever-changing internal space. Or it may be a leading portal that draws us in, like an enlarged picture frame or window frame. This is a frequent characteristic of retail spaces. In the theatre, it might be as simple as a consistent backdrop, in front of which are placed various structures and furniture elements that specify the locales from scene to scene. The consistency of the backdrop gives a theme to the changing picture, a stable home base for the shifting action. The container might even be the ground on which we walk, a floor that is uniform and reliable as the literal grounding for the event. I frequently design a multi-scene show with a permanent deck, like a hardwood planked floor that could be the logical base for an interior scene, a credible base for a scene on a veranda and even a plausible base for a scene out in a field as the linear floorboards become the furrows of a crop.

Periphery influences and impacts the nature of space in many ways. It dwarfs, traps, compresses, allows, liberates, dignifies, reduces, heightens, contradicts, echoes, embraces, enwraps, forbids, threatens, etc. For instance, a space that houses a tale about the power of fate over a prideful dweller who is in denial might include a domineering sun that is unre-

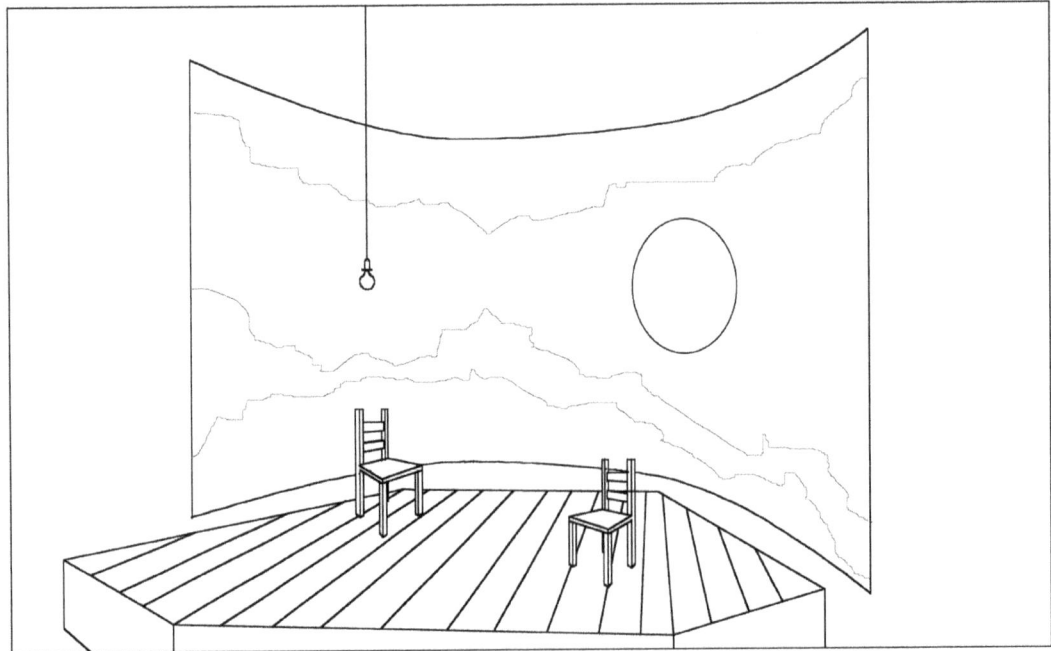

A wrapping backdrop and simple platform can become the surround for a scenic space. Props such as chairs and other elements can be placed in the surround for specific scenes.

lenting in its tyrannical taunts. This could be a decorative or metaphorical representation. The sun might be analogous to the omnipotence of fate, despite the expectations of the dweller. This is an example of a peripheral object functioning as an agent of pressure on the life of the tenant/character within. The periphery can also have influence by virtue of its makeup as well.

The surround can be opaque and solid or transparent and perforated. The level of opacity and resulting level of enclosure, can deliver a sense of oppression vs. liberation as well as protection vs. exposure. This impacts vulnerability. In a stage design, the space could include six columns in a circle around a large expanse of floor. The audience can see through and the actors can move through the columns like trees in a forest. The monumental distinction of the column arrangement, set against the open air, can give a sense of grandeur and consecration to that which it contains. And seeing through the columns allows a sense of attainability in the viewer/participant. It is not a forbidding wall. It seems to be a part of the environment and part of the life of the viewer/participant.

Periphery also dictates means of access and traffic patterns and as such functions like a governing participant in the spatial culture. The container of the space can be the mother figure, the protector or womb of the spatial action. It can also be the father, the head, the lawgiver and guide of the spatial action. By the same reasoning, it can be the lover, the teacher and the fool as well. Often it is the friend or enemy of spatial action. This all depends on the choices of the designer. Does she want the interpersonal relationship between periphery and central action to be amicable or contentious, benevolent or vicious? The method of crafting such relationships involves strategic placement and structuring of access points and paths of movement, because, in a living space, motion governs.

The periphery holds the dynamics of the event together. The event may be as energetic as an inspired child, running with abandon and frolic to all extents and interests. The container of the show gives the space its home, its identity. This keeps the action in a place where we can expect, recognize and rely on it. Like the driven child's playpen, it acts as a safe haven, or a prison. Without it, you have transient action. Periphery is the keeper of action.

The periphery is an impactive box, an identifying permanence. It is usually reliable. Within the periphery, is the real substance of space, all those things that engage the participants. There are many ways to consider the components of that substance. We will continue to use concepts from geography to do so.

Axis

Axis refers to the viewer's angle of engagement with

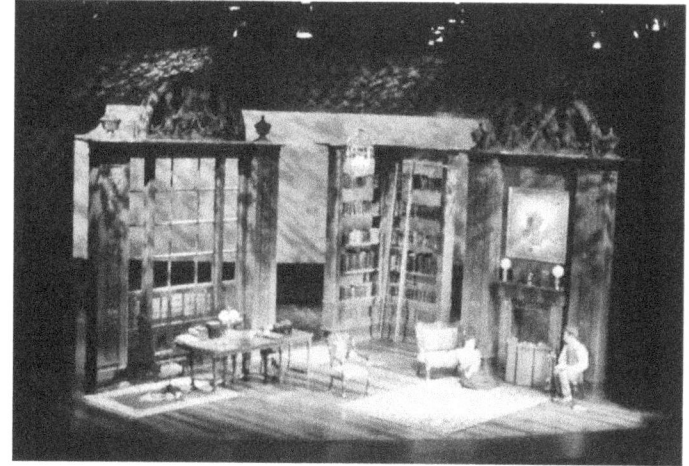

A perforated set emphasizes the periphery. A design for *Candida* by George Bernard Shaw. Design by the author.

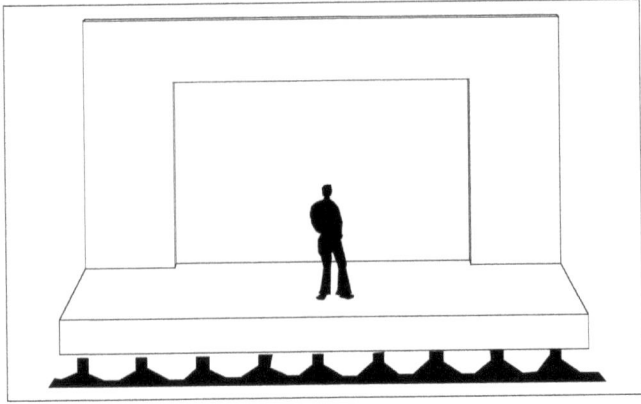

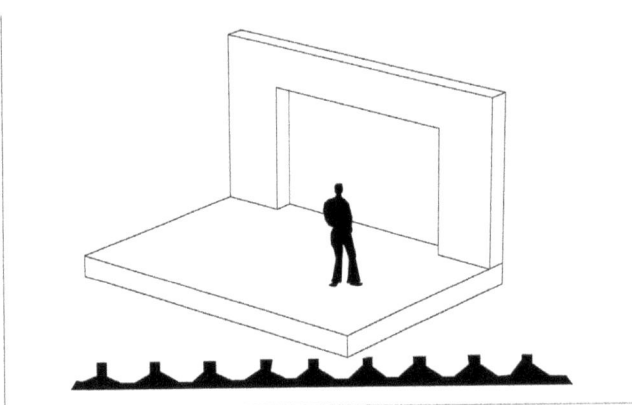

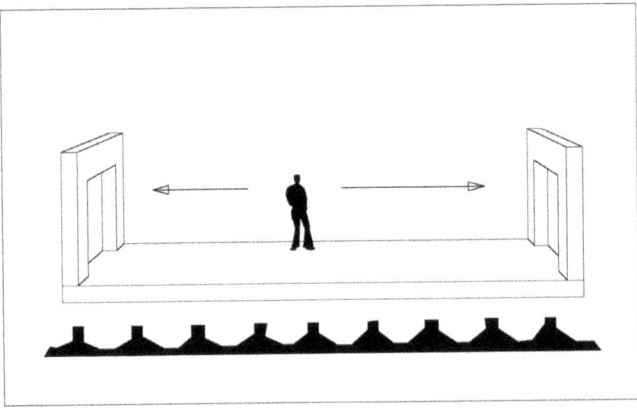

Top: A stage space with an axis perpendicular to the first row of audience seats. This has a formality and presentational quality. *Middle:* A stage space with a central axis at an angle unrelated to the audience give a sense of drama, dynamics and sometimes tension. *Above:* A stage space with a central axis that runs parallel to the first row of audience seats gives a sense of linearity, direction and potential for movement.

space. In the theatre, it is the defining centerline that relates the audience's vantage point to the core of the spatial design. The centerline can run perpendicular to the first row of audience seats (and the proscenium arch). It can also run at an obtuse angle, unrelated to the arrangement of house and stage. It can even run laterally and parallel to the audience seating rows. The axis is also the linear fulcrum on which the space can be balanced. Regardless of orientation, a composition of spatial elements should have a sense of balance, perhaps asymmetrical balance. Finding the fulcrum point and extending it in a line that follows the logical split between the balancing halves establishes the axis. With all this, the axis defines the orientation of space.

The orientation and the ensuing type of balance influence the emotional and psychological expression of space. Emotional and psychological expression can affect the perception of the viewer/participant. Manipulating the axis means manipulating the audience's perception of reality. (This is an example of designer empowerment again. If you haven't noticed by now, I am fond of empowering the designer. I even dare to use a "creator-of-worlds" job descriptor in the last chapter. Perhaps this suggests arrogance and overconfidence. I maintain that my real agenda is to reinforce the importance of the worlds around us to our lives. And I use theatre design as a vehicle in my presentation. Because space impacts our lives as much as it does, I believe that designers should be aware not only of their power, but also their obligation.) The following are examples of ways different axes influence perception.

The axis that lies perpendicular to the audience rows (and the proscenium arch) suggests formality and decorum. The relationship of viewer to space is refined and straightforward. It does not try to skew the union. It is a gentleman's handshake, face-to-face and proper. The audience sees the face of the space with no hedging. There is a sense of respect between the two entities, and so this arrangement suggests civility and in turn, suggests reason. The civil mind can reason logically and does not get overwhelmed by carnal desires and emotional passions. Therefore a straight-on, face-to-face relationship is "safe." But as it suggests these honorable qualities, it also suggests pretension. There is usually a grandiose presence to this arrangement and a pomposity follows. The kind of plays that are produced in this axial arrangement are comedies of manners, where dandy characters pretend magnificently to be something they are not, and grand operas with airs of higher-than-life self-fulfillment. There is a sense of equilibrium to this attitude. The space is confident, gallant and presents itself with a showy fashion, full-on and frontal.

When the axis takes an unrelated angle, an attitude that aligns with none of the prominent features of the stage and house, it suggests a world in tension and unrest, or a world in transition that might be shifting toward or away from equilibrium. This axial arrangement can also suggest a sense of quirky humor or informality in that it disregards the cultural norm and even lampoons it. It is daring because it toys with our comfort and offers an alternative way into the world. The types of plays that reside in this arrangement include dramas with a sharp social, political or emotional edge. These tend to be serious affairs, but can also be smart, irreverent and witty comedies.

One of my many uses of an angled axis, a set design for Chekhov's *The Cherry Orchard*, tries to capture the social transition from the old czarist order in 19th Century Russia to the coming revolution, a time of unrest and dramatic change well suited to an angular design. The stage uses a raked platform (sloping up as it goes back along the axis). The axis is set at an angle pointing from upstage left down to downstage right. This axis is the centerline of the raked platform. And that platform has myriad fragmentary architectural elements attaching to it as it progresses from scene to scene (two interiors and an exterior). The platform is the unifying element for all of the scenes. I remember the director coming into the theatre as the set was first being erected and saying "its all wrong, the set is pointing off to one half of the house and not down directly to the center of the house...." Naturally, the early scenic model clearly shows this angularity, so it should have been predictable. But this kind of oversight happens sometimes. The director and I are now happy with the design. The angled axis doesn't impede the actors' positioning and visibility, as they can still face straight downstage. But it does offer a great sense of tension and drama, heightening the audience's perception.

Occasionally, an axis can run parallel to the audience rows and the proscenium arch. This kind of stage set is a lateral construction with a very horizontal appearance. This version aligns the action with the perspective of the viewer. They perceive an evenness and a side-to-side directionality. It suggests linearity, a narrative aesthetic and perhaps a road on which one travels. Another occasional situation is one where you have multiple axes in a single design. This is usually a busy design, but it can still have unity. It suggests

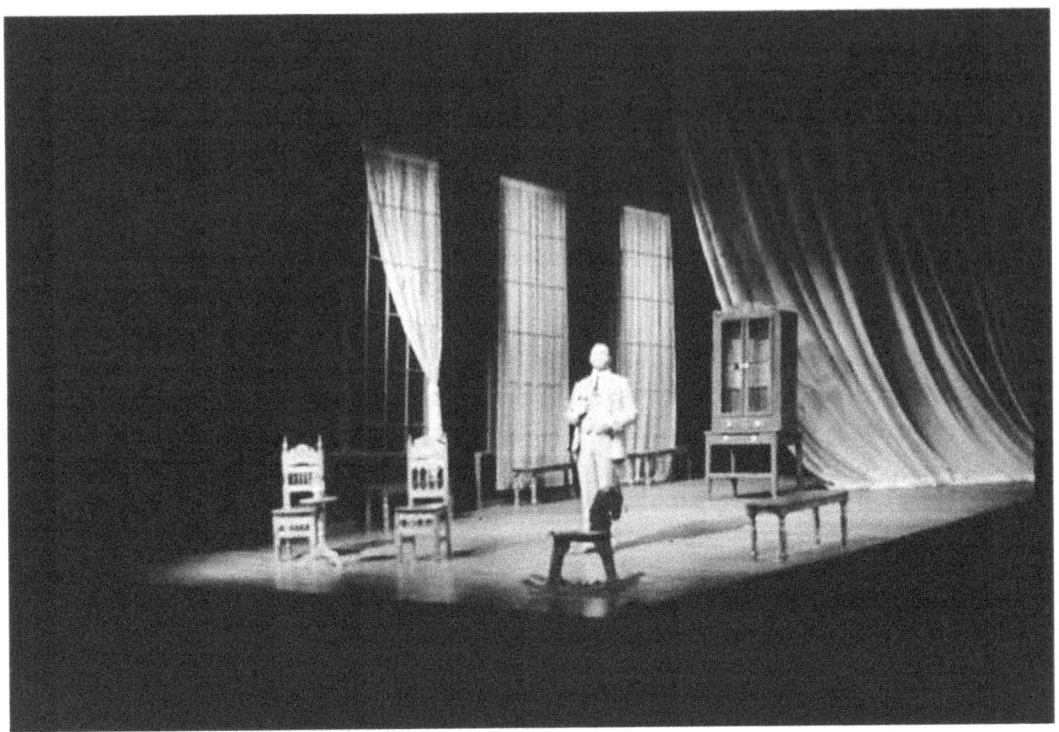

An angled axis design for *The Cherry Orchard* by Anton Chekhov. Design by the author.

confrontation and conflict, a world of oppositions. This is especially true with two countering angled axes. It also suggests alternatives and choice. By this I mean that it compels intrigue and curiosity about "the other way." On another level, it's easy to imagine how a multi-axial arrangement can boost the compositional interest of the spatial look. It can have a visual value too.

Axial arrangements are obviously important choices for a theatre designer. They occur early in the process, and much of the design detail lies on top of the chosen axes. My allies in other design veins must consider these axes with an eye toward their impact of their user. These axial choices can lock a user into the perceptual state that they will carry with them through the time of their use.

Area

Area refers to the magnitude of the regions in space, or the relative sizes of forms. Too often, designers must juggle issues of proportion when they select sizes. This is due to the givens of the format in which they are working. In the theatre, the format is the stage and house. The stage is the canvas, with its boundaries concrete. The threshold between stage and house is the formatting aperture, also with concrete and fixed dimensions. Sometimes the canvas or aperture is too small or too large for the objectives of the design. Part of the craft of design is the effective manipulation of space to make the areas seem appropriate in their context. It's a practice of necessary deceit.

You can appear to shrink a spatial area by scaling down, uniformly, all of the internal components. A set with a cityscape, complete with solid buildings, a street, and all the dressings, yet assigned to a postage-stamp stage, can be made passable by rendering the architectures in a ¾ reduction of size. What would normally be a twenty-foot building façade becomes a fifteen-foot stage structure, and so on. It still looks plausible, yet fits the format. On the other hand, you may be formulating a tender and intimate set with only a bed and a table on an opera-house stage. The easiest solution is to hand the problem over to the lighting designer, asking him to create "isolated lighting," putting focus on the space where the bed and table reside and leaving the expansive real estate around it in darkness. Frankly, this works. So I won't take this any further. I applaud good lighting.

My global advice to designers is this: Area is often a given. Embrace its gifts despite its drawbacks. Accept, adapt and create. Like a culture adapts to its given locality, its habitat and its environment, so must the designer. But be mindful of proportion, especially the proportion of spatial areas to the human figure. At times you will fortify the figure and at times emasculate him. It all depends on the text and the context. Once you have the sizing established, you can indulge yourself in the positioning of that figure in space.

Level

If you are a hiker, hunter or backcountry-cyclist, you probably are aware of the topographic map. This graphic document indicates the rise and fall of terrain. It helps you find your bearings and calculates the best course of travel. It's all about level, how high or low you go in space. Topography addresses the vertical positioning in space relative to a constant that is at "sea-level." Design considers topography in a sense as well. And for us the constant is called "ground-level," the level of the permanent stage floor in the theatre. As an aspect of spatial geography, level refers to the use of height, altitude, buoyancy, platforming, etc. to raise certain sections or uses of space. This is the elevation of space.

Elevation allows you to stretch upward. It allows spatial qualities that cannot be met if you reduce the design to a flat floor. These include hierarchy, the positioning of characters based on social or cultural rank. This can establish a dynamic of power and weakness, of dominion and servitude. Levels, like stairs, can get you somewhere. You climb to reach a destination. In this sense, level is a transporter and when employed in space, suggests a quest. Elevation allows you to compose dramatic stage pictures as it aids visibility and clarity of comprehension. If some characters and design elements are elevated over others, all of the details come better into view. The composition is better appreciated. Sightlines improve.

There is also a mystique to elevated, or vertical space. If you go up, you go against gravity. Anti-gravity is anti-nature (since gravity is a fundamental law of nature). This presents a mystery in the design. If a character or object levitates, it must have a force behind it that exists outside our routine awareness. The mystery of this expands our awareness, because we look closer. Vertical space, above the normal living plane, is regarded by many as the domain of the spirit. Use of such space evokes a mystic spirituality. It allows you to break the bond to earth. Figures aloft, relating to one another in the vertical realms can broadcast a visual statement of mystifying transcendence. A conversation on high can don an ethereal charisma. This is because it projects an apparent significance, higher than that of its earthbound counterpart. A similar dialogue on a diagonal between a higher figure and a lower one implies tension between the characters.

Shakespeare's plays at the Globe theatre in London use level quite well. The Globe has a feature in its architecture where a portion of the stage structure, above the stage proper, is a kind of balcony called the "inner-above." Scenes with a good deal of internalized intensity, like Hamlet struggling with the workings of his own mind, and scenes that have a spiritual nature, such as a fairy enchanting a courtier, are often assigned to this lofty zone by their staging authority.

The utilization of overhead space, where we climb up to varied levels, often completes the design and helps to fulfill the potential of space. It allows for the potential of human relationships to develop. Level expands the dynamism of space and the dynamism of the life within it. Every artist and designer will find a different meaning of spatial elevation. They will draft their own topographic language and chart a gallery of symbolic identities for the varying grades. This is a creative candy store. Level, like other aspects of the layout of space, is a vital concern but is, even more, a powerful opportunity.

Point of View

Usually, we are aware of our vantage point when we look upon an interesting subject or event. It is our secured domain. We arrive at it for different reasons, depending on the situation we are in. It may be a place we've earned, a status point. It may be a place that we choose because it makes us feel safe and secluded. It may be a place that friends have invited us to share, so we may see from their point. The place where we stand is selected by and for us, but it is our position either way. For the moment, we own it and all that we see is dependent on it. I always find myself looking down and around when I position myself at a play production, a concert or at a site of a sudden event of great importance. This way I remind myself of my domain, my coordinates and how my place measures up to the rest of the viewers. In geography, the appraisal of a land area is inextricable from its point of view, the standing place of the appraiser. The place where we stand (or sit in the theatre) is the vantage point from which we perceive space. It is our point of view and our point of engagement.

The engagement of which I speak is our visual connection with space. Like many other aspects of spatial encounter, the point of engagement and the manner of engagement influence perception. I will discuss several examples of this influence below. One way that point of view influences us, in the theatre and in certain architectural scenarios, is by its use of a frame of reference such as a portal. A portal acts as an aperture through which you may see into a space. It shapes the space, gives it distinction and possibly prominence. The frame decides what you are allowed to see. It steers your vision and as a result, influences your understanding. The positioning of points of view in relationship to the position of that we see also impacts our encounters. Looking from a certain angle means seeing a certain way. Some of the vision is crisp and sharp and some of it is hidden. This means that point of view governs aesthetic distance. Aesthetic distance is the psychological detachment between a viewer and a work of art. Our perceptual position can increase or decrease this level of detachment. We identify and pass judgment simply by our angle of visual engagement. A rundown of various, common types of point of view seen in the theatre follows.

Looking Straight in at Eye Level

Here, the audience is at the same height as the eye-level of the performer. The audience and the stage space relate reality-to-reality, head-on. This puts the audience on an even playing field with the performance. We connect to it without awe or arrogance and with familiarity and affinity. The players are neither revered nor sneered. We all see eye-to-eye. With this point of view, we interpret what we see in the manner of a painter. We see the contours and negative vs. positive space. We gauge the relative sizes of the details and can break the space down into coordinating segments. As analytical as this seems, this point of view is akin to the interpretation of an artist. In it is an appreciative regard for beauty and truth taken at face value. This point of view fosters lateral perception. Above all, we appreciate breadth.

Looking Up

In this scheme, the audience is seated below the stage level and looks up at the performers and their space. The upper regions of the space are more visible than the lower. The floor is virtually invisible. By nature, the performance is exalted here. It is seen as greater than the sum of its parts. Or, the performance is distinguished, seen as special with a noble cause. Another possibility is that the performance becomes an entertainment, by virtue of its separation. Because it is distant, the performance cannot achieve intimate interaction with us. Rather it becomes the joker, the juggler and the jester for our whims. In regards to spatial composition, height is exposed here. We look up and see up. We focus on that which is above the stage. If there is too much attention paid to the details above, the performers are dwarfed. By darkening the value of these higher elements, or minimizing their level of intricacy, we can reduce the dwarfing effect. This point of view fosters elevational perception and a child's interpretation. We regard height and verticality and presume meanings for these qualities. We gaze up at them like children viewing adults, seeing power in them and granting them trust.

Looking Down

In the previous scenario, the floor plan is diminished to a point of near imperceptibility. In this one, it is king. The ground, the floor, the layout of traffic patterns and the relationships of entries, exits and seating elements all become tantamount. This point of view fosters medial perception. We appreciate depth over breadth. Because we can see the interplay of spatial parts that exist at the feet of the performers, we start to notice an accent on the value of dimensionality. The background is separated from the foreground, pulling the performer forward into a better light. For this reason, looking down fosters sculptural interpretation. We read the space like a sculptor, finding dimensional nuances and knowing how things come and go, not just how they shape up.

Looking Way Down (from a Perch Well Above)

In rare circumstances, the audience can be raised to an extremely high position above the stage and look down at the action in the manner of a medical school's surgical viewing room. This point of view generates a "laboratory rat" effect. You have an absolute and sometimes exaggerated engagement with the traffic lanes and the layout. A maze design is ideal in this situation. Like following the rat as he negotiates a maze, the audience has the ability to see ahead, to predict the outcomes and assess the potential of the future. We literally see the plan. This situation fosters a seer's interpretation and linear perception.

Changing Points of View

It is not unreasonable that your stance might change during a theatre event. Sometimes you enact the change, by moving along as you are guided. Sometimes, the action moves about you, forcing your point of view to change while the target moves. This occurs most prominently in environmental staging, especially in the works of American designer Eugene Lee (b. 1939). In this kind of staging, the action surrounds you and you adjust to look. It flows or revolves before you and diverts your bearing. Changing points of view put you into the action because you interact with the changing space. This happens when your focus isn't fixed and you must work to engage. I believe that when theatre makes you work, it improves your experience. This dynamic condition fosters kinetic perception and a dancer's interpretation. It's all in motion and can spin around.

Looking Through

Whether it be a decorative portal or one that plays with your field of view, looking through a layer or layers to see a subject puts that subject in a stylistic context and stamps it with the level of reality you experience. A cartoony looking scenic frame establishes a cartoony style and you don't take its subject too seriously. By contrast, looking through several melancholy panels of elegant lace can place a brooding sense of remembrance and longing upon the actors standing in their midst. Looking through fosters a photographer's interpretation and telescopic perception.

Ultimately, point of view is about framing the viewer's focus in a fashion that is appropriate to the subject. The place where you stand and the way you look, will dictate what you see. And what we see becomes what we know.

Zones

I suspect that many of you have read the great, albeit brooding, American classic *The Glass Menagerie* by Tennessee Williams. It is still a staple of high school literature classes. Williams' autobiographical testimony of his dysfunctional family life in Saint Louis challenges the best stage designers because it is a memory play. You cannot simply design it realistically; you must give it a layer of "haze" and abbreviate it selectively. Williams tells us this in his stage directions. The other challenge is to construct a floor plan that reinforces the dysfunction of the three main characters. Amanda, the mother, is a frustrated bastion of an old southern order, with genteel manners and dreams of gentleman callers. Laura is the crippled and frail daughter, domineered by Amanda. Tom, the son, the narrator and the one who remembers the action in the play, is a desperate romantic who spends much of the play in an act of flight, literally standing out on the family's fire escape. Tom represents the new order of the industrious twentieth century, American dreams, both good and bad. So, naturally, Amanda and Tom are in constant conflict. Laura is trapped between them clinging to her precious, yet fragile sentiments, signified by a collection of tiny glass animals.

For this play to work, you must assign zones of the stage to the characters. They usually dwell in their own zones, Tom on the escape and Amanda in the kitchen. But occasionally they drift into the other's territory, causing tension. It's like the geography of war. Zones are domains in space, segmented divisions of the floor plan area. They are human-based realms, defined by the range of influence of the "owner" of the zone, such as Tom or Amanda. Zones can allow privacy and personal escape such as with restaurant booths or bathrooms. Zones can also welcome company by being compelling, warm and open, such as a stylish lobby in a high-end hotel. Designers delineate these zones via a marking mechanism. This could include a change of level, a color border, lines on the floor, dividing walls (complex or suggestive) and even through light.

The impetus for zonal design stems from an understanding of the characters in the play and knowing how a given character might "own" a zone or locale in the space. We see this all the time in architecture. There are designated bedrooms and closets, office cubicles and the aforementioned eating booths. Zones, like cells of a hive, are one of the primary structuring rubrics in spatial design. As a theatre designer reads characters in order to effectively assign zones, so must an architect read his tenant culture to establish the proper living realms.

Access

Geographers are certainly interested in access: access to harbors, access to population areas from freeways, access for freight trains to centers of business, etc. In spatial design, the architect, landscaper, theatre designer and interior designer all construct their compositions around these vital points of entry and exit. I will follow suit with my discussion, dividing it into subcategories of Entrance and Exit.

The Entrance

The entrance is the method for introducing people to the space. The quality of the entrance introduces the experience. My design for Caryl Churchill's episodic play *Mad Forest* is an environmental affair. The action flows around, behind and through the audience. This is a play about the fall of communist dictatorship in Romania during the end of the cold war. It follows the lives of two families and through a sequence of many short scenes gives the audience a visceral sense of what the revolution was like. The environmental approach is an obvious choice. It puts the audience inside of the revolution. They feel the cultural shift. This design includes a "Checkpoint Charlie" entry gate at the front of the black box playing space. Guards meet the attendees at the gate and usher them at gunpoint to their assigned seats. The attendees are issued simple pillows to sit on and the guards, with force, direct them to sit in an assigned area, away from their friends and family, in orderly rows on the floor. The intent is to demonstrate the controlled lifestyle of Romanian citizens before the revolution. This is a case where the entrance really serves the experience. It sets up the entire event. And first impressions carry weight.

Access takes many forms. And the form of access impacts the behavior in the space. A grand entrance yields confidence among the inhabitants. You can envision a prince and princess entering a ballroom via a grand staircase to a roar of applause. A troublesome entrance yields a reactive response (one of accomplishment or frustration) among its inhabitants. Here you might envision a physical comic stumbling through an entry turnstile and getting spun around and flipped over. The frustration he exhibits is hilarious because the comic's reactive response is so familiar to us. Many of us have been through that kind of troublesome entry when traveling to unfamiliar places.

The Exit

Certainly, an entrance and exit can be one and the same. The way it is used by the culture within the space is significant. An exit may be an egress, an escape or a departure. An egress is an intentional design that promotes the orderly movements of the culture. This includes fire exits and aisles on an aircraft. An escape is the way out, a possibility to get away from some oppressive force within. It implies that there is such oppression. This could be an open window, a hole in the wall, a rocky face with just the right footings, etc. A departure means a socially supported leaving, such as a "bon voyage," and often involves a grand exit, like a gangway up to a ship. It carries a "statement" with it. All of these kinds of exits are on the menu of choices for the designer and are selected based on the course of the action they serve.

Gradation

Gradation refers to progressions in space. Geographers study topographic progression, rises and falls in elevation. They also study progressions in climatic mapping, where isobars delineate progressive changes in the typical weather patterns for a region. In space, we design progressions to promote a feeling or a sensibility. Our progressions usually involve slope and scale.

The presence of slope and scale promotes musicality and lyricality in space. There can be a raked floor or an ascending grade. There can be an ombre blending of one hue/tone to another in a sky. There can be a progression of dark to light in a room. There can be a progression of narrow to wide in a corridor. I can go on. All of these gradations can convey a sense of motion and a sense of ranging emotion in a space, like certain melodies and verse. Visual progressions imply intolerance for the static. They seem to call out for movement and flow. This allows the space another level of dynamic range.

Gradation serves space in another way. It can influence visibility and therefore impact perception. For instance, slopes, rakes and grades help expose individuals at a higher level over the lower ones, making a crowd more appreciable. Like other aspects of design, this improves sightlines and encourages depth perception. Darkness at the top of a wall, progressing smoothly to lightness below, pulls the audience's focus down to the human level, reducing the impression of excessive height. This assists the viewer with comprehension because the viewer isn't caught up in the overhead details and isn't distracted by an abrupt shift from dark to light. While remaining subconsciously aware of the entire wall, the viewer focuses on those things that matter, down below and among the people.

Frankly, a flat floor and a flatly painted wall on a stage are tedious to the eye. We crave range. Our audiences sit for about two and a half hours in their cramped seats trying to get their money's worth out of a show. It is our duty, as theatre artists, to make every effort to tell the story effectively and to guide the viewer to the message being sent by the story. In doing so, it is our extended duty to provide enough dynamic range in the visual production to maintain the interest of that audience member. Gradation is a proven ingredient, developed over centuries that can be mixed into a visual tonic for aiding those who aren't naturally predisposed to theatrical immersion.

Cartography

When maps are charted, the cartographers employ visual contrast to distinguish the landmasses from the sea. They may simply make the sea blue and the continents brown or green. Or they may make each a different shade of the same hue. But, no matter the technique, the intention is what is significant here. There must be a clear distinction between these areas because they each possess key attributes, one being made of earth and one being made of water. In design, we have a similar distinction to make. We deal with the relationship of positive and negative space. The positive is comprised of the spatial forms in the foreground whereas the negative is the spatial field. In a sense, these represent our continents and sea.

You might have seen the optical illusion images that deal with positive and negative space. Sometimes it is hard to discern what is "real," the positive form or the resulting shape of the negative space. One of the graphic images that demonstrates this is the vase-faces drawing. If you look carefully at it, you will find yourself at times perceiving a vase, and at times perceiving two faces, in profile, looking at one another. This shows the interplay of positive and negative perceptions going on in your brain. Think of it as design tectonics.

Designers are interested in how our forms are shaped and how those shapes relate to one another. Forms can have "contour-meanings," like the shapes of states on a U.S. map. We might decide to utilize those contours in a symbolic way in a design. For instance, a series of angular, cross-like shapes might be arranged to create an eerie kind of tree, one that might have a dark, religious connotation. Forms can shift and redefine the space as continental drift redefines our planet. We might toy with shapes like jigsaw puzzle pieces, creating a montage of churning forms. This is especially effective when you have multiple rolling platforms on a bare stage repositioning with one another like line dancers in a nightclub. The relative density of positive versus negative spaces is also a consideration. Densely populated positive shapes can say one thing, perhaps a suggestion of a busy urban world. Sparseness can say another, perhaps suggesting the austerity of loneliness. We must choose wisely to find the appropriate relative density for the mood of the event. It's a judgment call.

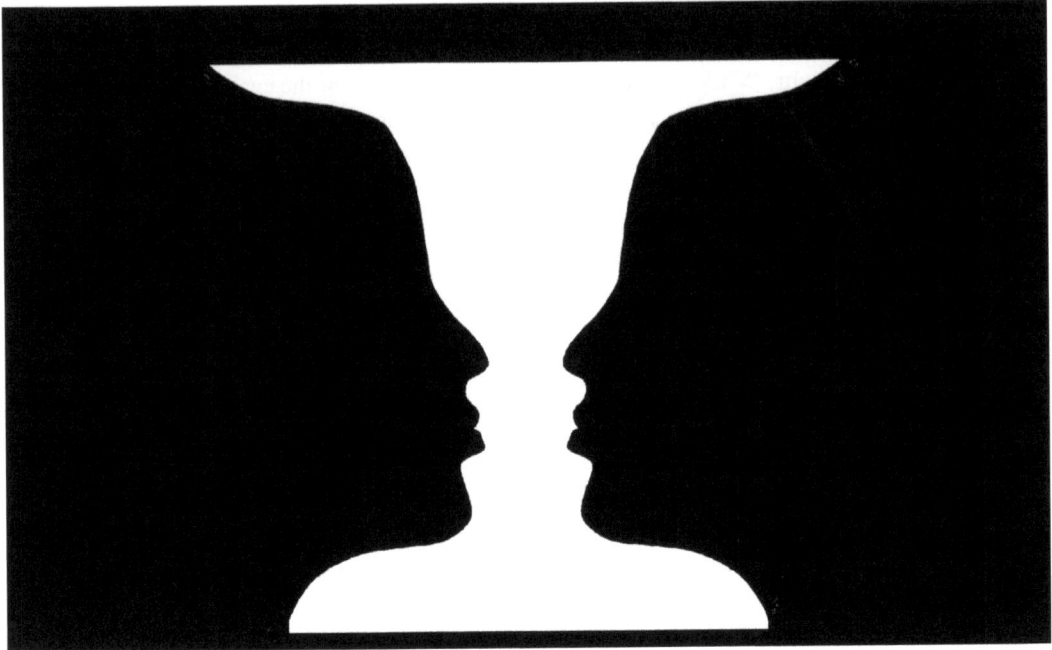

The "Vase-Faces" optical illusion. Are you looking at a vase (the negative space) or two faces looking at one another (the positive space)? The interplay of positive and negative is key in a design.

The abstract shapes of spatial components plays a huge role in conveying a mood, a level of realism and a meaning (maybe even a moral statement) to the proceedings. So, the study of shapes is a key part of our design geography. It is also a key part of geometry, the discipline I address next.

5
Geometry

If you say that a person has character, you say that the person has interesting features that set him apart, usually in a virtuous way. If you say that he *is* a character, then you are saying that his behavior is consistently idiosyncratic. His behavior has interesting (and sometimes annoying) features that become his norm. A "character actor" plays a type of idiosyncratic role many times over. He is known to reliably reprise that role. That role has an array of interesting and recognizable features that sets it apart. Essentially, character refers to qualities that distinguish someone in some way. These qualities are known as characteristics or the traits that give someone definition. People have character, are characters and may play characters.

Space has character as well. Strange as it may seem, the *measure* of spatial worlds reveals character. With space, its easy to consider the properties and relationships of spatial points, lines, angles, curves, surfaces and solids. And we use those considerations to refer to the character of space. The character of space is the composition of visual qualities that distinguish its overall feeling, impression and identity. These qualities can be broken down and described via geometric observation. This is a routine form of observation for theatre designers. The use of geometry is as familiar to a designer as an old friend. We find ourselves returning to it at all stages of our process. Either we use it to calculate angles of incidence and reflection, or to resolve the drafting of a seven-pointed star, etc. But we also read by its illumination.

The following is a series of geometrical qualities that frequently occur in spatial design. I will address how these qualities set the space apart and give it character.

Verticality—The West

If we think about the West, we conjure an image of the "onward and upward" ideal, of progress and production. "The sky's the limit!" "Go west, young man!" "If you don't have one, make one!" etc. You will note that the three preceding statements all end with exclamation points. The West is all about enthusiasm for invention and adventure. At least, that is how it wishes to be known. The West has character. The West IS character.

The West I speak of could be the American West or the Western Hemisphere. They have common ideals. And these ideals often manifest in vertical spatial designs. This follows logic. The Western God is on high. The West built gothic cathedrals that point to the sky, guiding the eyes of the faithful to their divinity above. These cathedrals have their cusped arches, their flying buttresses and their steeply pitched roofs forcing the eye up. In the West, the faithful raise their hands and pray His blessings come down upon them. When they die, they hope their soul rises up to heaven, etc. In the same way, the Western vision for the future is an ascent of progress. It was the first global realm to build great skyscrapers that also point to the sky. Commerce and industry embrace a vertical ideal. You climb the corporate ladder, raise your revenues and watch your stock go up. Even great institutions of government and education, have vertical pillars that point to a humanist ideal, that there are no limits to how high a mind may reach or how high a society may evolve. Consider the Greeks (both the classic age of antiquity and college fraternities); consider architectural structures in Washington D.C. (the Washington monument's obelisk comes to mind); consider the libraries of Ivy League schools (pilasters abound), etc. You might be put on an ivory tower.

Verticality implies a high cultural regard for power and strength. And the West depends on power and strength as salvation. Culturally, the West reveres those heroes who rise up and conquer, find power and strength as they race up the stairs to rescue the endangered. Heroes are put on a pedestal. A sports hero is at the top of the leader board. Spatial design in the West follows suit. Look for the vertical lines. In Neoclassicism, busts of the great ones are placed in niches between strong vertical wall dividers. Verticals frame us today as well. Just look around Manhattan.

Verticality itself is made with a progressive process. It is built on strata, like geology. It is layered up over time by an idea system that refuses to accept a top, yet continues to reach for one. Our cultural structures are often stratified vertical systems, like hierarchies and class divisions based on scales of wealth. This implies that we should reach as high as we can, if we can. And this ideal is not lost in science. Rockets shoot for the moon. We believe we can trek even higher. We craft devices, vehicles and computing systems that may stretch us up to the galaxies, "to boldly go where no one has gone before."

Verticality in design can represent dreams of the ascent. It can also represent perceptions of reliability and confidence. Vertical elements that possess this character include trees (especially sequoias and the like), towers, columns and spires. These elements can be key features in a space. And these elements can reflect a tenant character that is equally powerful, strong, reliable and confident, like a god, a ruler/leader (including tyrants), a governing body, a guiding force, ... or a healthy phallus...

And that leads me to an example of verticality in one of my designs. There is a musical version of Aristophanes' politically and sexually charged comedy, *Lysistrata*. It is titled *Go Lysistrata!* (note the exclamation point again), an adaptation by Cecilia Pang and Billy Wolff from 1994. The musical, like the play, pits the genders against one another. A war is going on and the men are off to battle. The lonely women, back in Thebes, want them home. In order to sway the men to end the fighting, they begin to extort them by refusing sex, and the comedy rolls on with a twist here and there. The lampooning of sexual tension abounds, as does the self-aggrandizing potency of a show set in the Greek golden age.

My design is rich with vertical forms, especially phallic columns rising up all over the place. At a key moment, when the women triumph, the capitals of the two most erect columns burst open and spew two enormous inflatable balloons that blow up into two enormous, naked breasts. This design suggests that triumph earns you the desirable position at the cap of the highest pole, like the thunderbird on the totem. And you hope and dream to get even higher. To be perfectly honest, the West, by its very character, can be a bit phallic. And verticality in design exudes this healthy spirit.

But geometry shows us that the lines can also run on the perpendicular, as the globe turns...

Horizontality—The East

If the West looks up, then the East looks out. While the West might aspire to a salvation above and fear a descent to that which lies below, the East might seek a path of moderation and meditation in the space in between. This is not an opinion where I intend to take sides. I am western. I climb mountains for the fun of it. I admire and am inspired by the passion of the ascent. I appreciate the climb and relish the summit when I reach it. I am quite vertical myself. So, I do not advocate that the East, with its moderate path and centered spirit, is somehow advanced or "better" than the West nor vice versa. All directions have merit. Frankly, there is plenty of the East in the West, including attitudes about religion, meditation, design and the landscape. But I still find a distinction between the two and enjoy that diversity when I observe the world generally and when I observe design specifically. For me, there is an equation between the East and Horizontality.

The heritage of eastern ideals often manifests in horizontal spatial designs, or more importantly, in designs that value breadth and expanse. The character of horizontal design accepts the vastness of what is given at the earthly level and is much less a quest for the sky. We can see this in the design conventions of Kabuki theatre in Japan. Like much of traditional Japanese architecture, Kabuki design is famously horizontal. The stage is wide and the surface of the stage is low. Movement, gesture and posing at the stage level comprise the fundamental nature of its performance style. While certain stage effects might occasionally lift a character into the air or up from below the stage, the core essence of Kabuki is the magic and mystery of that which is immediately in front of you, including illusions and spiritual moments. Perhaps the most important component of the Kabuki stage is a horizontal ramp called the hanamichi that leads from the back of the house, along the side of the audience, to the stage. Grand entrances on the hanamichi do not rely on a grand staircase. They flow along the expanded horizon.

So, horizontality looks outward rather than upward. It reconsiders the land on which we reside. The earth is sufficient. Horizons, like the skies above us, are dreams. But these dreams exist on a human plane. They compel us to move in our own domain, to confront ourselves at eye level, and to embrace ourselves in the same way. Horizontality expresses a vastness that can be at the same time intimidating and invigorating.

There is rarely as powerful a design encounter with horizontality than when working on John Steinbeck's epic novel-turned-play, *The Grapes of Wrath*. The Joad family leaves their homestead in Oklahoma for a horizon they do not know. They move on a kernel of hope, a touch of faith and a family-based resolve. But, for the most part, they embark because they have no choice. Their homeland is dead, a victim of a sweeping dust storm. They eventually make it to California, the perfect destination for a horizontal quest. They come over an arid ridge to see the awe of a fruited valley, only to later encounter issues of labor and socialism, etc. My design for this play is all about the land, the expanse, those nightmares, dreams and the rickety accidentals along the line. There is the open stage floor, the family truck moving all about it and the sweeping nature of time and change. Draperies sweep across the stage laterally, scenery enters and exits the same way, exactly like clouds (of dust, water vapor and the American dream) passing across the sky. Ironically, *Grapes* is not an Eastern tale. But, like I said, there is plenty of the east in the west. It's often found on the horizon.

Verticality is stable, like the pillars of community, etc. Horizontality is even more so. That is due to its comfort with itself. To illustrate by contrast, horizontality suggests a curiosity coupled with self-regard and verticality suggests an aggressive quest coupled with the manner of honor. One wears its skin, the other a uniform.

So the globe turns as the lines intersect. And as the globe turns, so the day passes into night…

Angularity—The Day

One of the most remarkable conveniences in human life is the regularity of day and night. It's a biological fact that we must sleep. And, unless you live near a polar region, the rotation of the earth allows a regulated up time and down time, light to see our task and dark to rest our eyes and go to slumber. I often wonder if we were to be transported to a planet of lengthier rotation, would our sleep patterns change? I believe that science has surely tested this, and the results are likely that our sleep patterns would change. What is important here is that day and night serve differing purposes and generate corresponding characters of life during those times. Most of the purposes for day and night relate to survival. Interestingly, the corresponding characteristics of life in the day and night find expression in the use of the visual lines seen in spatial design.

Angular lines in spatial design often represent concerns of the daytime:

- Of industry, where machines, mechanics and motors have harsh lines and aggressive operations and charts and graphs of productivity use jagged lines and arrows;
- Of modern progress, where we aim to incline on a clean and diagonal trajectory toward a better way of life;
- Of boldness and cutting-through, getting heard and getting seen by carrying ourselves with striking, and dashing lines in clothing and behavior;
- Of stark reality, with no mysteries, no places to hide, the reality of duty and action signified by directional lines that lead us on our way;
- Of the dissonance and din of the busy world, visualized on sound-sensing instruments as quick crosshatches and peaks and jabs;
- Of interruptions to simple life and the daring avoidance of parallels and confirmative lines, instead opting for diagonal adventure;
- Of violations of comfort, like waking and darting out of bed;
- And more benevolently, of the spirit of invention which commands that you try angular and unconventional approaches.

Angularity confronts religion as well. It dares to do so, feeling unthreatened under the safety of daylight (metaphorically speaking). There are fewer fears of divine repercussion when you have the sun to protect you. After all, "monsters" only come out at night. Like daylight, angularity is a great revealer of form. And so, it is a great revealer of truth. If it reveals truths that can be readily verified, it provides a bold challenge to certain religions and their mystery of faith. This is because it avoids any truth that cannot be defined by a rectilinear construct, such as the immeasurable truth of deep and personal belief. Angularity plays loudly to the crowd, hawking its most evocative and enticing polygonal forms to the masses. It doesn't promote its wares to the internal person nearly so much.

On a simpler level, angular designs tend to be modern, progressive and edgy. This gives them a striking presence that captures attention, like a loud car horn on a city street. And this projects a masculine and energetic ("in your face") aspect of human life. It is one that evokes

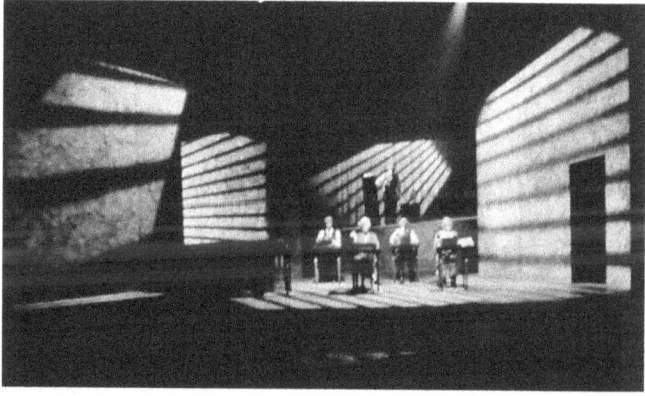

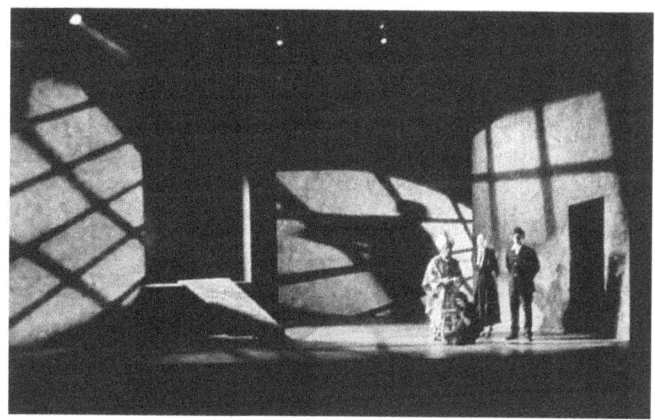

Top: An angular set gives a sense of tension, confrontation and the toils of the day. A design for Scene 1 in *Machinal* by Sophie Treadwell. Design by the author. *Above:* Another scene in *Machinal.*

the importance of technology to the progressive and edgy modern world. It's all very "twentieth century," as it avoids sensitivity and celebrates machines. A design that can exemplify this is my work on Sophie Treadwell's early feminist drama, *Machinal.*

In *Machinal*, the protagonist, a sensitive woman, lives out the structure of a normal mid-century American life, as daughter, wife and would-be mother to antagonists that constantly distract her internal nature like a loud and constantly running machine. It's a fable on the dangers of technology, and on a masculine cultural order that doesn't nurture with tenderness and warmth. I feel that the play's mood is actually a bit exaggerated by its grim imagery. But it is a strong and alarming work. My design is a unit set, unchanging in its basic form for the many episodic scenes. It is a stark and angular box set, devoid of nuance, personality and detail. The walls are bare, just grey textured forms like the saddest prison cell. On the walls are projected gaunt shapes that signify aspects of the various locales, like window blinds in an office and black and white shadows of fire escapes for the apartment scene. It is blatant as the daytime, no hidden mysteries and nothing to ponder.

The character of life in the play is captured in the character of the lines in the space. I can recall architectural and other designed spaces that reflect the same image, such as in the Bauhaus style (from an angular time in Europe) and the housing projects of the 1960's. These kinds of designs stun you with their sharpness. They don't want you to sleep. They keep you in the day.

Curvilinearity—The Night

There is more to the night than sleep, a lot more. And there is more to sleep than rest. Many odd maneuverings spin around and through us, like reckless moths, during the night. When the sun goes down, a secret part of us emerges, the part that cannot speak so boldly that it may be heard in the noisy day. The stars cannot cut through the day's blinding light, but they are there behind the glowing blue. Much the same are the twinkling lights of our essential cores, our subconscious impulses, hidden behind the shells of our diurnal toil, swirling and spiraling in curvy lines unseen until the dowsing of the sun releases them into the night.

Designers mimic this nocturnal choreography. Curvilinear spatial designs often represent concerns of the night, including sexuality and sensuality. Curvaceous design elements can serve as the sexuality of space, being the seducer and provider of erotic visual pleasures. Curves also lend sensuality to space, an approachable and tender willingness to touch and be touched. If you look at the flow of certain art nouveau border designs, you can appreciate this allure. If you look upon gentle rolls of scrollwork on an elegant William Morris print, you can feel its sensuous character. These kinds of curves tend to be made of French curves, S-curves and spirals, like softly undulating waves.

But I won't belabor this geometric eroticism. Instead, I'll delve into the "letters of the night." Curvilinearity emanates a lyrical quality. It has a beckoning nature and like the siren, calls you in. Its attraction is a spellbinding lure of swirls and rhythmic gestures that try to snare you and pull you close. When it has you it can offer you the embrace of its poetry and lilting verse. The lines enwrap you with bending arcs, rendered in a sweet calligraphy. The patterns of words and rhymes skip along like the procession of sine waves. Curvilinearity also suggests romance and romanticism, the act and the art. Like a romantic, the character of curves is lost in its own loops. Like the paintings and music of the romantic age, it is more reflective of nature than structure, of night more than day, of love more than aggression, of dreams more than consciousness.

In fact, curves do well suggesting the realm of dreams (and nightmares), free flowing nocturnal encounters with the subconscious, unbound by the affairs of the day. Dreams don't stand still. They move along without a rigid path, straying here, there and everywhere. While there may be a narrative in a dream, it takes turns and detours that we cannot predict. The subconscious writes its own personal myths and these tales are steered by impulse rather than logic. Impulse drives off the road. So do curvy lines.

Like seduction, Curvilinearity lures with enchantment. It evokes the magic of the night. At night, there are forbidden mysteries in the shadows, glimpsed only by the glow cast by the curving wisps of the fleeting fairy's flight-trails. You might dare to spy them and ponder what they mean. The night allows you to do so and Curvilinearity supplies you with ample subject matter. As you sit and soak it all in, you might feel the enchantment of the moment, a dusting of inspiration cast by a corkscrew spiral of elementals moving in your midst. You follow them and enter a world that your imagination could never generate. This Curvilinearity releases your tensity and for a moment dances you outside the mortal coil.

Enchantment might be read as an act of generosity, giving and grace. And these are certainly direct contributions of Curvilinearity as well. Curves add a graceful flow to a visual design, as well as elegance and sophistication. In this way, it presents the feminine side of things. And it's all very "nineteenth century." While straight lines have a fixed nature and are set in their ways, curves have an interest in exploration, and encourage you to discover yourself and them too, a venture you might try in the privacy of night.

On a completely different turn, curves have another familiar quality. They can be comedic. Curves pose no threat. While angles often imply danger (the sharp points and edges) and possible tragedy (such as falling upon the pointy edge), curves have soft edges and allow you to suspend your worries and laugh. They relax you. Comedic curves have a far bolder character than those of seduction, lyricality, enchantment and grace. They bounce and roll with the silliness of life and reduce the serious stance of stoic stares. Curves usually don't get caught in the trappings of a quest and they don't have the same determined will

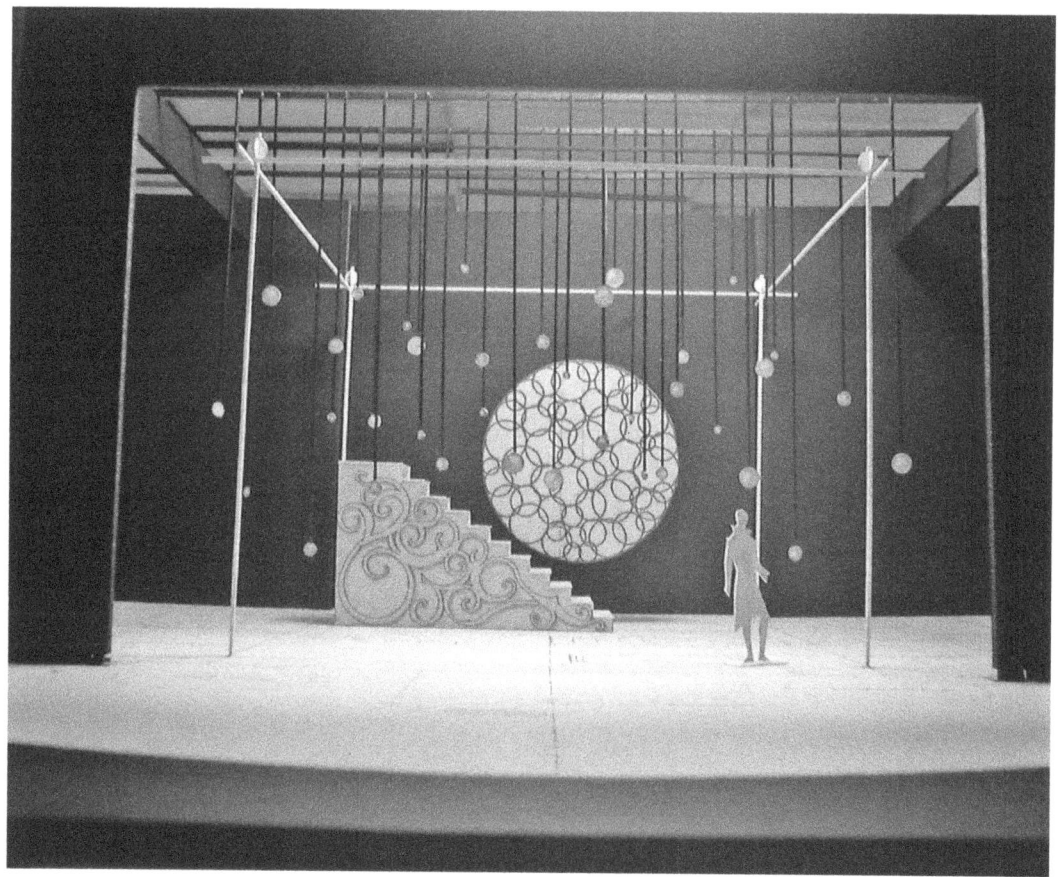

Design for *A Midsummer Night's Dream* by Shakespeare. A design with curvilinear elements and a curving progression from scene to scene.

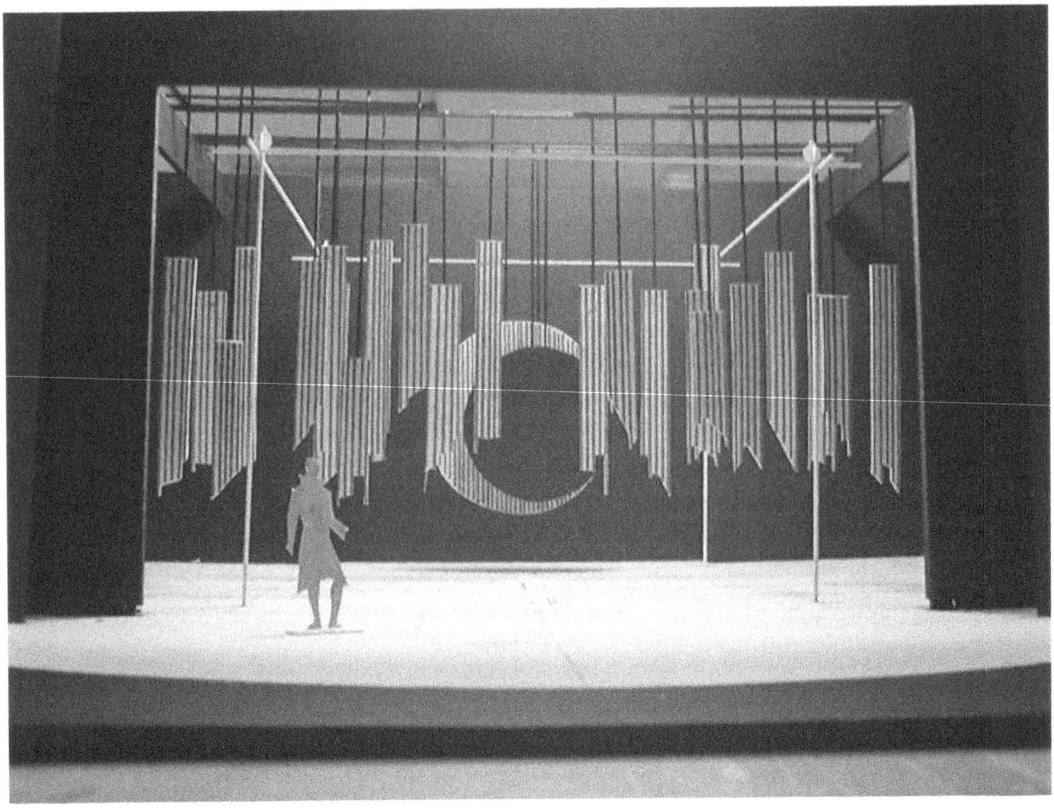

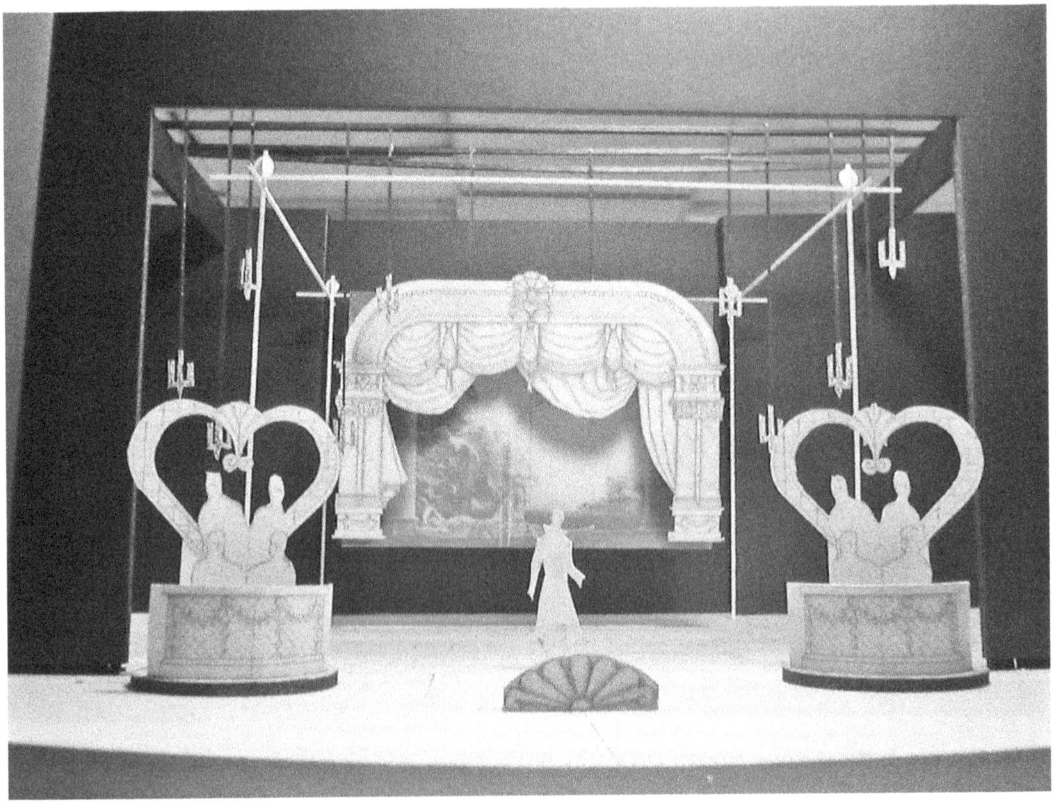

to confront tragedy as straight, angular and intersecting lines. But is comedy a nighttime thing? Does it follow my line of reasoning? I believe we laugh more at night, because we are released from the duties of the day. You get the work done and then go out to a show, all for the entertainment.

In summary, curves resonate with circles and orbs like companions to the moon. They often diffuse the hard definitions of things you see in the day, being more of the night. And curves deviate from the ruling line and so allow a whimsy and freedom and encourage an exploration that goes about the space like a dream. A play that calls in all these notions of Curvilinearity quite well is Shakespeare's *A Midsummer Night's Dream*.

My design for an ambitious production of this fantastic play takes the notion to heart that dreams have no logic in the way they move and transform through their course. The subconscious mind does not defer to the unities of time, place and action. Each scene is a different picture, with different scenic elements, constantly changing, flowing in a liquid fashion from look to look, locale to locale as we progress. The only constant, a peripheral framing device, is an open cube defined by pieces of steel pipe. The cube, ironically, is an angular container for the show. It represents the frame of real life, the life of the court and the life of mortality. But into it flows the dream. Spiraling, swirling, curving and rotating flow the many pieces of architecture, symbols and imagery dancing through the context of the cube as the scenes shift. This is an expensive and time-consuming effort, a pragmatist's nightmare. But this is how you mount a dream. No scenic elements repeat. And they all move in a curvilinear path. In fact, most of them are curvilinear forms. The result is a sensation among the audience saying: "What was that?" "What did I just experience?" It's like waking from a dream. It's like rising in the night. Curvilinearity, in motion and in shape, delivers this spatial character, the character of the night.

Most curves, surprisingly, are drawn with instruments, such as compasses, ellipse tools, French curves and others. The instruments smooth the curves. And they are constructed with focal loci, cubic-spline points, Bezier points, arcs and spring points, etc. I wont bore you with a deep discussion of that kind of intense geometry, but know that the romance of the nocturne, as discussed above, is born of careful crafting. On the other hand, a designer might rather doodle. I discuss that next.

Free Forms

The designer may opt to freehand the design. And he may want to create his own "free" forms instead of relying on established forms. While Euclidean geometric forms and natural forms already exist, and find repeated use as stock characters in design, free forms are new inventions in space. Designers create them from scratch by doodling them as they work. These new inventions are wanderings from cultural expectation. They go where inspiration takes them. These may include some bastardized morphing of a polygon, or a jaggedly scribble, etc. The only requirement is that the ends of the contour lines meet and close the form.

Opposite, top: Another scene in ***Midsummer***: The moon eclipses while other elements float in curvy patterns in the space. ***Bottom:*** Another scene showing more curvilinear elements reinforcing the mood of love and romance.

In essence, free forms exemplify the spirit of human creativity. There is virtually no limit to free formation. Some of the creations may be plain ugly, but they are original and that's the spirit. These forms are often grouped together and the composition of many free forms makes an interesting, and possibly meaningful collage. Sometimes free forms attempt to generate a new language that might communicate the message of a culture, like freshly minted hieroglyphs. This is true in spatial design. Its seen in the armadillo-like constructions of architect Frank Gehry (b. Canada 1929) and in the surreal stage compositions of British designer Ralph Koltai (b. Berlin 1924), who frequently scatters cracked and torn shards of metal and plaster about the space. The work of both of these designers tells a fresh story about our cultural character, if you make the effort to read it. It displays how exciting the invention of the unexpected and the deconstruction of the expected can be.

Expectations are cultural structures. The creative human makes free forms to reject such structures, and to construct new ones. He tries to communicate with an alternative language, hoping that the alternative language is more effective than the expected one. Another approach might be to take the expected norm and pull it apart, chop it up, deconstruct it and reform the pieces into a new form that is comprised of the original elements put in a new order. This forces us to reconsider what is at the core of our reality. It's an unexpected composition of expected facets. The composition moves us to turn our heads, with an eyebrow raised, to glance at what might be the real nature of our structure.

Free forms possess a mixed identity. These abstract forms are human-made. Thus, they are free from mathematical generation or natural development, and are not easily recognizable. They are inventions, not generations or evolutions. And so, they have a distinction of being umbilically connected to the whims of their creator and his own unique cultural aesthetics. But they do not follow all the standards that humanity sets up. This is because they deviate from expectation and do their own thing. Yet, often, they speak effectively, possess a form of logic and add a real character to the design, be it stylish or clunky. They are characters of complex makeup and an independent spirit. The character they represent in design is that of independence and it is distinctive and intriguing for this reason.

I contrast these with another non–Euclidean formation, that which is formed by nature, the fractal.

Fractal Forms

Not very long ago, science conceived a new type of geometry, that of the fractal. Observing and modeling fractals involves complex equations and extensive computations. It is less important for a designer to comprehend the mathematics involved in these, although much is accessible online and in books. It is more important to know how they interface with design and the character of space. Fractals, as a concept, have a substantial value to designers. And since about the 1980's, artists have used digitally produced fractal imagery in graphic art. These psychedelic looking images offer an interesting, and fresh visual catalog for creative fields. And they do materialize a staggering idea: that infinity might extend in both directions of time *and* space.

Fractals signify forever. They are progressions of irregular or fragmented shapes that can be repeatedly subdivided into parts, each of which is a smaller copy of the whole. So, a big cactus-like shape projected in front of you on a screen can be zoomed in upon to reveal that it is itself a composition of many smaller, exactly duplicate, cacti shapes and each of those is really made of many more littler cacti shapes and so on. This takes a powerful microscope.

Real fractal shapes are much more complex and abstract in appearance than cacti. But they are observed extensively in nature, so they can be quite familiar. The web-like scrawl of capillaries in a human nose reappears in the sinews of a leaf and bigger yet in a satellite image of a river delta.

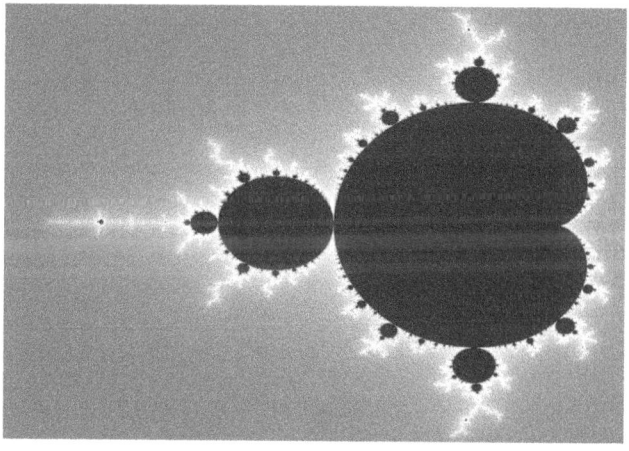

A fractal is essentially an abstract shape that when magnified is made of many smaller versions of the same, larger shape.

The mind can easily begin to contemplate the notion that maybe the universe itself, as we know it, might be a macrocosm of many microcosms, and then sub-microcosms, as galaxies reduce to solar systems and solar systems reduce to atoms and beyond. The universe might be the atom of a much larger cosmos. After all, the objects I mention all appear as small orbs rotating around a central nucleus. In other words, fractals are spatial generations that increase and decrease in size exponentially onto forever. This suggests that "all is one" and each is a miniature of a larger version of itself, extending eternally in both directions of the size scale.

Cosmologists would dress me down for suggesting this, as there are vast quantities of detail to consider that I do not present. But, the artist and designer take interest in this suggestion. It has charisma and intrigue, though it is hardly original or new. I can imagine that many people under the influence of certain chemicals get eyes like saucers as they land on this "epiphany," but don't discount it for that.

If we meditate on fractals a while we start to realize that they echo something primordial, ancient, profoundly simple, lucid and telling. And to some degree they provide a psychedelic observation of reality, meaning a reality that is envisioned with an altered, heightened and maybe clarified perception. They tell us that we are all made of the same stuff. Anytime you can detect a resonance of cosmic commonality extending through generations of existence, you will see creativity emerge. Creativity is inspired when the muse discloses a universal secret, especially one that inherently has stunning visuality. Fractals do. We should put them to work.

Fractals, at a glance, appear to be free forms. But they are very deceptive. They are in fact, rigidly structured. They possess order disguised as chaos. And this means that nature wears a veil of apparent randomness that we perceive as such. Yet we are deceived, because within the wanderings lies an interconnectedness that relates all matter together. Fractals might be defined as "magical repetition." And the notion of defining all substance by breaking it down to simplistic formations is alluring to the designer and artist, including those working in spatial design.

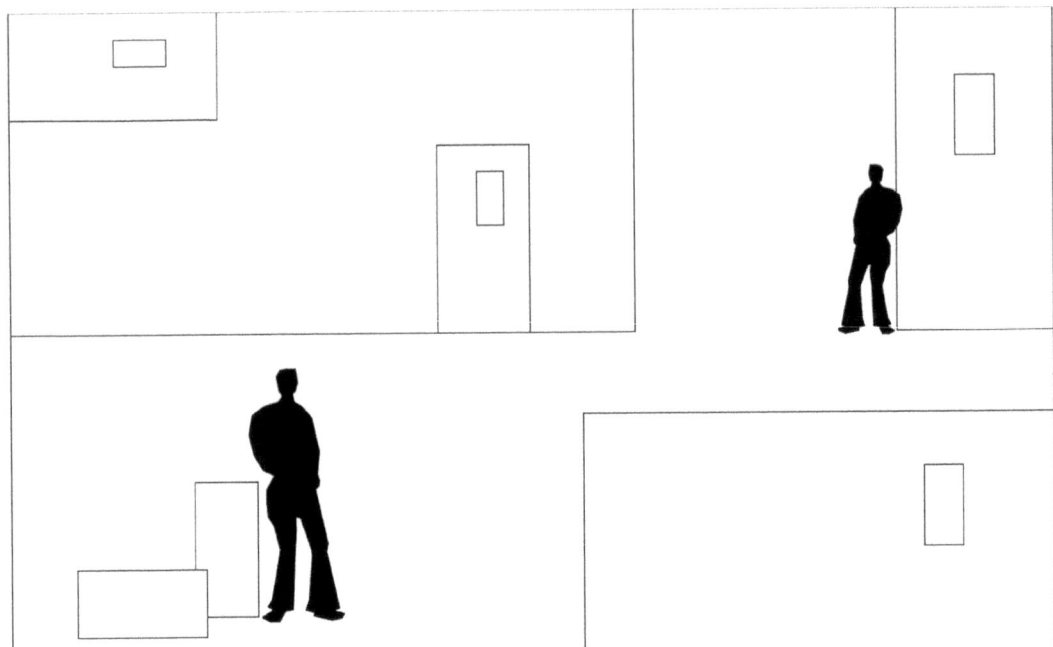

A design influenced by fractals. Here, a simple street scene uses generations of the same rectangular form. The repetition of form can give the space unity.

In spatial design, regenerating common shapes in varying proportions, and repeating these generations throughout the space can mimic fractals. You can envision a proscenium that is dimensionally a golden rectangle, framing a wall on a set that is a smaller golden rectangle. And the wall may have tiny windows that are smaller such rectangles and in them panes that are smaller rectangles still, and so on. This concept can be used with many if not all base shapes. The shapes themselves may not, in this case, be organic in nature. But the conceptual idea behind the design is inspired by fractal geometry, and that is the geometry of nature. So, an inorganic design can still refer to nature.

By the way, the actual shapes you use in regenerative designs might not matter at all, or even be necessary. The regenerative theme might be a construction of common ideas rather than shapes. You might restate a common idea, like the idea of diffused shadow play for instance, throughout the components of space in regenerative expressions that give the space a sense of unity and lend character to its look. You don't even use shapes per se. Unity and character are your main goals. And the use of fractals is more a philosophy than mimicry.

No matter how fractals are employed, they present a dignity of character in the design. Anytime you employ geometric concepts that present the possibilities of infinity, the space will vibrate with a depth and density of character. It dons the characteristics of an elder statesman or a sage. And in it is a reverberation of something ancient and something relieving to the spirit, speaking that a single essence manifests everywhere and connects all things. The space becomes a knowing character.

6

Aesthetics

In the previous chapter, I discuss character. The geometry of space reveals the character of space, its distinctive traits that give it interest. Character is something that is presented outwardly and noticed from a detached observation, like taking a measurement. Personality, on the other hand is a totality of all aspects of one's being. And personality, to be truly seen, must involve an interactive engagement with the subject.

The engagement is not rudimentary. It is an engagement at select moments, meaningful moments, and transcendent moments, when the personality comes through and is shared. Those who practice the discipline of aesthetics seek to enter the world of their subjects, works of art and beauty, by finding these kinds of moments. And so I refer to the personality of space by using concepts from the study of aesthetics.

Designers consider moments in space, when the space communicates and shares its personality. When it engages in a dialogue with its inhabitants, we, as designers or students of space, try to participate, or at least listen. This goes deeper than an analysis of the material reality of space. This addresses the key moments of engagement between humans and space, in a sense, person to person, assuming we can personify a space. I believe we personify them all the time. There are "he" and "she" spaces, "fighter" and "lover" spaces, etc. If you look at them that way, you will see them that way.

Some of these moments are described below, as a student of aesthetics might describe an interaction with art. I also describe the means of expression that the personality of space employs in a theatre situation, its manner of communication for these moments. I must emphasize that the key feature of each moment is the relationship between the space and its inhabitants, its culture and the observers.

Environment

This is the moment when space becomes place.

"Place" is defined as a portion of general space where someone can BE, implying a living area, and a live area. This transcendent moment happens when the environment of a space is devised to a point where it assumes a recognizable identity as a *living place* or a place of existence. This is a moment when the space functions and evolves with its culture and reflects the personality of its culture. You encounter it when you become aware, immediately upon entry that this is a place where certain kinds of things happen, and then they do happen. You "feel" the place and you become affected by its environmental qualities. You see the face of the place's personality. The look on that face is suddenly everywhere around you. It may grimace or smile and when it does it reaches your emotions and triggers a response. The grimace or smile projects the place's environmental condition, and the condition of the culture. A personality is usually an outgrowth of an underlying condition. This is true of humans and spaces.

This all works if the space contributes an environment for its culture. The environment may nurture its inhabitant culture, or contradict it in an ironic manner. But it should somehow operate with the action of its culture. In life, the action of culture means the primary movements that extend from its primary motivations, urges or mere survival. In the theatre, action is the life of the plot, the goings-on that are triggered by tension between a protagonist vs. an antagonist or other dramatic instigators in the play's story. The spatial environment in a stage production must coincide and reinforce the action of the play. By doing so, the personality of the space is presented as a projection of the overall cultural personality therein. The culture of a play is made of its characters, their story and the audience that experiences the story. The personality of the space indicates the mode of operation of the event. It tells us how it is going about its business and how its environmental traits make that work. We get that information as we sense the environment of the place.

An example of this kind of transcendent moment is in my stage design for a production of Bertolt Brecht's *Mother Courage and Her Children*. This is a political play about war and indicts those who profit from war. It is set against a bleak Europe, ravaged by the winds of war. This image of Europe exists in great irony around the energies of the entrepreneurial main character. The spatial design takes on the personality of its landscape and draws the audience into its midst, as it is an environmental design. The lead character sells her wares as she rolls a cart through the audience on a narrow winding path that resembles a muddy European country road. The winds of war, and the textured face of this bleak and exhausted environmental personality are reinforced by a multitude of torn shards of brown paper caught on ropes dangling in the space like bugs on a cobweb. And the torn and wrinkled paper, with highly textured relief, spans the walls all around the audience as well. This textural environment, like the bleakness of Europe, does not project a lively personality although the main character does. The contrast is dynamic. And the contrast helps to amplify that which the environment projects. The audience recognizes the messy and ravaged milieu and expects the impact it delivers.

Immersion

This is the moment when one places oneself in space.

Aestheticists might call this the point when the viewer becomes "one" with the art. It's not a matter of simple entry. It's a matter of yielding the shell of the self, removing the filters that shield one from the full impact and suspending disbelief. This is a moment when you allow the experience of the space to commence around you. And you absorb the experience. You sense it and feel it. The spatial world becomes tangible, its personality engages with your own through the conduit of feeling, toward a deepening visceral encounter. This kind of encounter grows and intensifies, if you allow it. It becomes a pair's dance of two personalities, the world and the inhabitant, sometimes consensual and sometimes adversarial. The variant is how the space makes you feel and what it compels you to do.

The "feeling of the space" is an important moment because it is baptismal. When you emerge, you are transformed. It is your initiation into a spatial culture and a marking of your identity with the world around you. It's an initiation and temporary purification from the pollutants of external space. It draws you in and you begin the dance. Designers can craft this immersion. They can funnel you into a ritual seat, through proper entryways, along linear guidelines and by magnifying key focal points. They can enhance the experience by reinforcing the atmosphere, conjuring moods and by erecting a machine to facilitate the tangibility of the spatial features. The designer can play with your feelings by texturing a wall a certain way, allowing light to enter and reflect upon you to a certain degree of diffusion, slanting a floor or a wall slightly to affect your balance, etc. Once done, the space gives you an impression and you accept the feeling, and act on it as your nature suggests. You dance impulsively, instinctively. And soon you become aware of the personality given off by the tangibility of the space and your own personality arises to face it eye-to-eye and hand-to-hand. This is an act of willingness. You buy the ticket and trust the designer to place you in the most effective spot. Then you play along.

In the theatre, immersion is often invited and ushered by the actor. After all, the actor is a part of the space. He becomes part of the spatial experience. He impacts your feelings; not only by the lines he recites and the character he creates, but also by his aesthetic presence. This includes his movement, voice, gesture and costume. I call it the environment of acting. It's about the air of influence radiating from him, effused by some delivery system we know but cannot always directly identify. The actor himself refines this source, because he must encounter the "feeling of the space" on his own as he prepares. He arrives early before the show and warms up in the space; He walks the space before applying makeup. He immerses into the space through his fight calls, movement exercises and finally by donning his garb. Once he is initiated himself, he can help initiate you into his culture, the culture of the space, in a moment of transcendent sharing and engagement, a moment vitally linked to considerations of the design process.

Intrusion

This is the moment when a human body or object enters and affects the space.

A human body in action has a sphere of influence. Think of it as the extent of one's ability to reach others around the space and the space itself. This reaching can include physical, emotional, psychological and even spiritual contact. It is not only the circumference created by the extent of the limbs. It is also the orb of mind and soul. The sphere of influence is the body's own impactive space. The human body defines its own space within the overall space. And the two react to one another and redefine one another. This is all a part of that dance I describe above in the section on immersion. There is action and reaction. It's like when you drop a marble into a glass of water. The water is displaced and it splashes out. There is an intrusion, a splash and a ripple effect. It's much the same when personalities collide. Or when one personality must intrude on another to affect change. The intrusion triggers a life action, much like the life action and reaction between parent and child.

A significant object, like a tree, can be inserted into a space. In the theatre, a designer could insert a tree into the middle of a room, an interesting non sequitur (I've seen it done). When inserted, it becomes an obstacle. Any obstacle in space governs traffic. And traffic patterns govern the motion, and eventually the resolutions, impulses and choices of the tenants in the space. So, the object impacts the quality of the life in the space. The tree can disturb, disrupt and change the lives of the people who dwell in the room. This is due to the way the intruding tree activates motion. And motion governs the group. It might also stir emotion. And emotion governs the self. When these moments of activation and stirring occur, personalities emerge and inflate. And then they influence each other, often in powerful ways.

In the theatre, a highly charged character can enter a playing space and immediately impact the mood and course of action. The other characters may cower from or confront him and all subsequent action might revolve around the intruder. The setting may begin as peaceful and be thrust upon by the intruder like a dart piercing a balloon. We see it in tragedy, comedy and realistic drama all the time. As I mention above, an object like the tree can have a similar impact. And at the moment when it intrudes, all conversations, thinking, motivations and actions by those in the room might circulate around an obsession over the entering object. It's all quite effective and useful to a designer or director.

Interaction

This is the moment when relations between individuals are manipulated by the personality of space.

The space's "personality" is defined in part by its shape and how its component physical parts are arranged. In other words, its physical design can generate its doings, its ways and its impact, or the actions of its "personality." The way the space is made can facilitate or hinder relationships of those within the space. And this is a huge influencer on the life of the space, be it real or theatrical. Relationships build action. They are the prime catalysts of a social group.

The following are some kinds of relationships that space can manipulate.

Love

Love is fostered by two kinds of spatial construction. On one hand you can create an environment that allows free and private interaction, a space that has no inhibitors and no competition, a place of cozy and safe liberties. I keep thinking of the film *The Blue Lagoon*. On the other hand, and maybe more effectively, a space for love can be a sanctuary from danger, an escape that fosters an "us against the world" mentality. This could be a simple room with a few pillows walled off from an obvious threat, such as war, outside. When two people are forced together in the midst of conflict, they often bond and face the challenges together. This bond can build into love. To hinder love you must not allow the tenants in the space to find a common cause. This means that you must provide many potent distractions and ways to avoid the discovery of common interests.

Aggression

A space that facilitates aggression is one that clearly defines two adversarial domains. It sets up camps and a border to encourage conflict. If you wanted to hinder aggression, you would create secret, alternative ways for people to connect. You would build bridges where reason might overcome the primal urge to attack.

Power

Power is control. You must give the one seeking power a control point, a perch or a governing center. To hold power you must be able to see your constituency, so the space must expose the lesser group. To hinder power you remove the clear division and confuse the layout of the space. Confusion breeds chaos and chaos is the opposite of control. Confound the tenants and you diminish power.

Desire

A space for desire is one that holds the desired thing/person beyond arm's reach. It separates and idealizes the dream.

Fear

Fear means not knowing what is truly present, and an uncertainty of outcome. A space for fear has a lack of clarity and a sense of mystery in the shadows and behind the doors.

Competition

A space for competition requires a deliberate staging for the engagement. All of the gear is provided along with a fair playing field. The space is set to give the opponents their devices and a spectator's stand for viewing.

Companionship

Companions need a familiar setting with the things they've collected together present and reliable. You provide for the old traditional conversations, routine activities and account for the reason the companions need one another.

Communication/Contact

Obviously, you want to build lines and mechanisms for connection here. You allow for secret communication with private nooks, and social discourse with a forum-like arrangement. There may be tunnels of access, walls with windows, a clever series of calling towers for specific voices to relay the message of the group. These can go on.

Designers, be they architects, interior designers or theatre artists, must employ this powerful option at their disposal. You can plan a deliberate manipulation of relationships and the course of life in the space by giving the physical space a certain personality. The space for love will have a personality that appreciates the bonding that occurs when individuals have a common cause and will nurture and provide for the fertilization of that relationship, in a mothering way. A space for aggression will have a bloodthirsty personality seeking the catharsis of watching a duel. The space for power will crave order in its personality. It will abhor chaos. And so on...

Recognition

This is the moment when we reach an affinity with the designed space.

There comes a time when we enter (or observe) the space and it shows its face to us, its outward personality. And when we relate with it, we see a bit of ourselves in it. When we move to commune with it, it reflects us. It's like the child finding and embracing its mother, knowing her by instinctive recognition, because she comes from the same bloodline. All this affirms a notion that space is a parent of its culture. We emerge from it; we see ourselves, good and bad, in it. It guides and controls our lives. Our process of recognition involves encountering substances in the space that are indicative of its personality. The substances are recognizable because they may have roots in our collective unconscious. There may be ancient threads in the colors, shapes and textures of the spatial surface that were born long ago and are carried in our genes. Or, there may be things that simply resonate with our own individual personalities, like a "funky" wall mural that reflects a quirky and fun-loving quality in the tenant. This affinity is the result of a kind of communication between the personality of the space and us.

I can identify a design moment that demonstrates this in my set for the musical *Cabaret*. We know the great moment in the movie version when the camera pans from the stage of the Kit Kat Klub, with the MC singing and glaring at us, to a distorted mirror in the space. In the mirror's image appear several figures, heretofore unseen, wearing Nazi regalia. It's a moment of blatant reflection, showing a culture lost in the confused decadence of the Weimar republic moving toward a darker and more sinister side of themselves, one that would emerge with great power in the years to come.

My own take on a staged version of this musical includes a setting that begins the show as a dense collage of suspended artifacts from a rich past, including cabinets, pianos, fireplaces, candelabra, swags of lush curtains, jewelry, etc. But, in the manner of "pop art," they are painted in ridiculous and vibrant colors such as hot red, chartreuse, magenta, orange and turquoise. This is an expressionistic take on the decadence and discord in the culture. As the show progresses, these elements slowly disappear, one by one, working down to bare and skeletal remains, like life leaving the face of the world.

At the very end, the lights black out and then come up quickly again to reveal an enormous swastika flag that has been quickly lowered into the space. It shows what has replaced the face of the past. The space reflects the fate of the inhabitants. And they, and the audience watching, reach a moment of affinity and understanding. The moment grips us, because it is us.

Both moments from *Cabaret* demonstrate how space communicates with us in some fashion. Communication, especially the kind we easily recognize, is another vital objective of the design process. Designers should try to set up that dialogue. And the means by which a created work communicates is a prime concern of Aestheticists. The following sections cover five means by which designed spaces communicate with us: *details, material, symbols/ imagery, mood and motion.*

Details

Details, including decoration and ornament, convey spatial personality. Details are those things that embellish a spatial composition when they are applied to the base structure, or frame, of the composition. Like a costume, they give the space identity, character, individuality and complete its makeup. They help define its "person." There may be decorative details that "finish" the space, giving it polish or a veneer. Some details will give a space a historical identity by realistically depicting the look of a past world. And in some cases, details may be abstract and graphically altered in a distinctive manner, meaning that they are *stylized*.

In art and design, stylization is the *way* you depart from realism. It is the way you distort reality to an effect. Visual details may be stylized in the manner of an art movement, such as impressionism, expressionism or surrealism. But be careful. The use of these shouldn't be flippant. It takes a serious investigation into the genesis, evolution and context of these historic movements to appreciate their real substance and value. You don't just hang the melted clock on the tree and call it surreal. If you stylize in a manner you hope echoes Dalí's work, you must look into the things that lead Dalí to that clock. You may also model the visual style after a musical genre including jazz (loose, wandering and improvisational), heavy metal (massive, leaden and angular) or hip hop (palpable, aggressive and rhythmic), etc. Details can also be distorted to depict a mood or mindset such as melancholy, dreaming, a nightmare, etc. In these cases, the style doesn't try to imitate another art, but tries to match a sensation that exists in another mind, a mind that is not experiencing the immediate reality. Stylization, on the whole, is intended to present a distorted version of reality in hopes of heightening the meaning it communicates. This means that details should have meaning and should "say" something. The style choice works best when it stays consistent throughout the entirety of the composition.

Be it stylized or real, a designed space may have ornamentation. This ornamentation may be, and in most cases should be, thematic. There may be visual motifs and recurring patterns of ornament. These themes can give a space unity. And variations within the themes give the space diversity. A balance of unity and diversity means the space has a coherent expression of its personality. And, importantly, the ornamental details should reflect the collective personality of the culture and the story of the culture. In the theatre, spatial details should reflect the personality of the language in the play's text or the personalities of the characters speaking the text.

There are many examples of this. The detailing could be fussy and shallow like the characters and language in Oscar Wilde's *The Importance of Being Earnest.* Algernon, Jack and Lady Bracknell are all dandy characters and the witticisms they expound are filled with Victorian manners and satirical relevance. But the ornament adorning them and their speech is completely on the surface. It is a silly play with clever barbs all dressed up in ribbons, bows and fluff, like pretty, preening peacocks all prancing about in their gilded cage. It's a symbol of the audacity of arrogance and appearance. The setting for this play should be equally fussy and surface-laden with excessive detail, absent of soul beneath. On the other hand, the detailing for a different play could be very sparse and austere. Take the language of Harold Pinter's plays. They are famous for the pauses in between the spoken words. The physical spaces for nearly all his plays should be equally sparse, with only momentary visual blips on the spatial radar. One could deliberately design against these plays, making their spaces thick with all the details the language lacks and that could be equally effective, if consistently rendered. It's a choice, but the choice should be thoroughly realized.

You may have heard that God and/or the devil are in the details. Mies Van der Rohe may be responsible for coining all that. Such idioms make sense in many ways. It might be amusing to hear a befuddled client asking a non-traditional church builder where God is in his steeple-less design. The builder might reply as you predict with the cast-off line. And an accountant, who examines the deepest webs of a business ledger, might knowingly agree on the opposing expression. I have some additional thoughts.

Is God in the details? If God is the central and core source of life energy in the universe, His presence emerges in all things. The same concept can be applied to space. There is a central spirit in each successful design, perhaps its central purpose or its meaning. This is the "god" of the design, if you will. And this central spirit emerges in sublime ways. It is in the details. It is in the mass of details together and hidden in the minutiae as well. Kaufmann and Hart's *You Can't Take It with You* is a whimsical tale of an eccentric group of individuals living together in a New York house. They seem to have found happiness in this sanctuary doing whatever pleases them, ignoring the realities of the busy and often stifling world around them. In this house, they have accumulated a treasure trove of artifacts from all their little adventures. The message is that you can't take material wealth with you when you pass, so why not enjoy it and spend it while you are here. Basically, enjoy living. My design for this play follows tradition. It is a world of dressing and detail. What emerges is the collective spirit of these free individuals. Each item in this busy set has a story, a life and a positive energy behind it. It is an appendage of one of the bliss-following characters. The mass of all of the detail is a sculpture of ornament that expresses life. Living means engaging with those things that are of your spirit. When those details are engaged, they start to become luminous and when collected they become a cornucopia of effervescence.

Is the devil in the details? If the devil is the entity that pulls your attention away from positive energy (or the central spirit of the design or the show), a designer can put that devil to work. She could choose to intentionally distract you by charging the "devil" with drawing you off course. There could be twists and turns in the layout that are counter-intuitive and unexpected. They might force you to stray and follow other distractions. This might not necessarily be a bad thing. They might broaden your scope by taking you to a multiplicity of experiences rather than one central and focused communion. And the details of the space would embody that deceit. It could be a world that is confusing by design. Or it may be by mistake. A designer might errantly inject an excess of details that clouds the focus. This is common among enthusiastic designers who cannot stop adding things, thinking that more is more. It is also possible to insert improper choices that do not fit or conform to the central spirit. Their qualities clash with the unity of the space and again distract those who experience it.

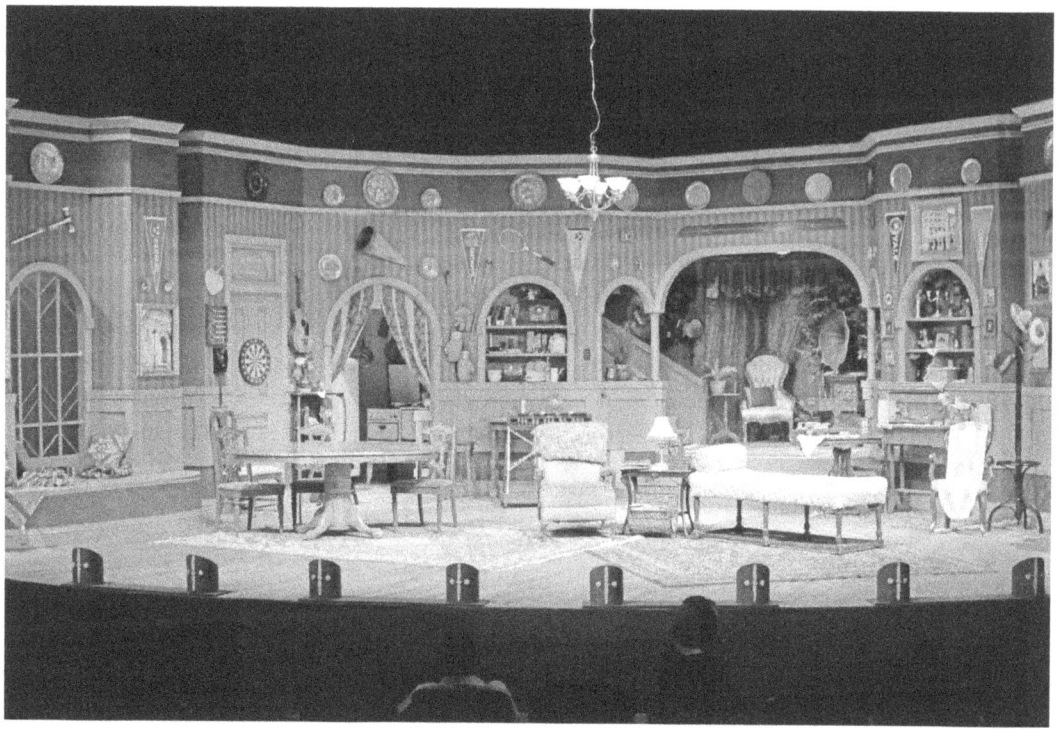

Details on a set help to tell the story. A very busy design for *You Can't Take It with You* by Kaufman and Hart. Design by the author.

Material

The physical elements in a space are made of materials. That is obvious. But the type of materials, or the illusion of these materials, can be a prime consideration in the world of the space. There may be one predominant material used such as wood, metal, stone, paint, fabric, etc. The predominant material may even be a replica, created through faux finishing, molding processes and other tricks of illusion. Either way, the material, or its convincing facsimile, should reflect an aspect of the space's culture. Aestheticists might look at sculpture and regard it material makeup as a key aspect of its expression. Bronze and marble might reflect the established culture of its origin, confident and bold. Sticks and burlap in a primitive sculpture might reflect a rustic culture with tenuous self-impressions and an air of impermanence. I will suggest that spatial materials do two important things. They echo what I call the "*song*" of the space's culture. The song is an expression that comes from deep within, usually truthful and essential. And they reflect the *poetry* of the culture, the thing the culture tells us about itself through imagery and suggestion.

Regarding song, this is well exemplified in Opera design. In opera, the designer designs the music more than the words. Libretti are crucial, of course. But the reason patrons attend opera is to enjoy the singing, the orchestra and the overall spectacle. Rarely are they there to seek the morals of the plots. That might sound a little jaded, but you can research it easily. Surveys identify the voices, instruments and visual imagery as tantamount to the sustained popularity of this musical, not literary, form. An opera like Verdi's *Falstaff* has music that is very brassy. The trumpets and trombones really cut through. And the lead character has the same brashness, so a successful design for *Falstaff* might employ brassy or other golden, metallic materials. Bizet's *Carmen* has attributes of both strength/solidity mixed with fragility. You can appreciate that coupling in the way the Spanish rhythms marry with bittersweet melodies. The perfect materials for this are a mix of stuccoed stone and rose petals — societal rigidity mixed with the delicacy of personal passion.

Poetry has a veneer, its discernable texture and feel. Its wrap exudes the nature of its substance, stemming from the words and images within. The materials used in a space should reflect that sensory quality, the coat of cultural truth. I can identify some examples from poetic theatre. John Steinbeck's great play (based on his own novella) *Of Mice and Men* is an American love story about two wandering men who look out for each other and find sanctuary in their modest dreams. The culture of the story is an adolescent western America, going through a depression, yet grasping at distant desires. The heart of this culture, the growing America, is wood. A design for *Of Mice and Men* will have rustic wood floors, planked walls and robust trees. It's about wood, a material susceptible to rot yet possessing a dignity and a rough and ready character, not unlike the men in the play.

A spatial design for a play might also employ ghostly materials. In my design for *The Laramie Project* by Moises Kaufman, which covers the true tragic death of Matthew Shepard, I use real, found materials from the actual death site in Wyoming. The backdrop is painted with a textural mix of stones, grasses and earth from the actual site and latex paint. The

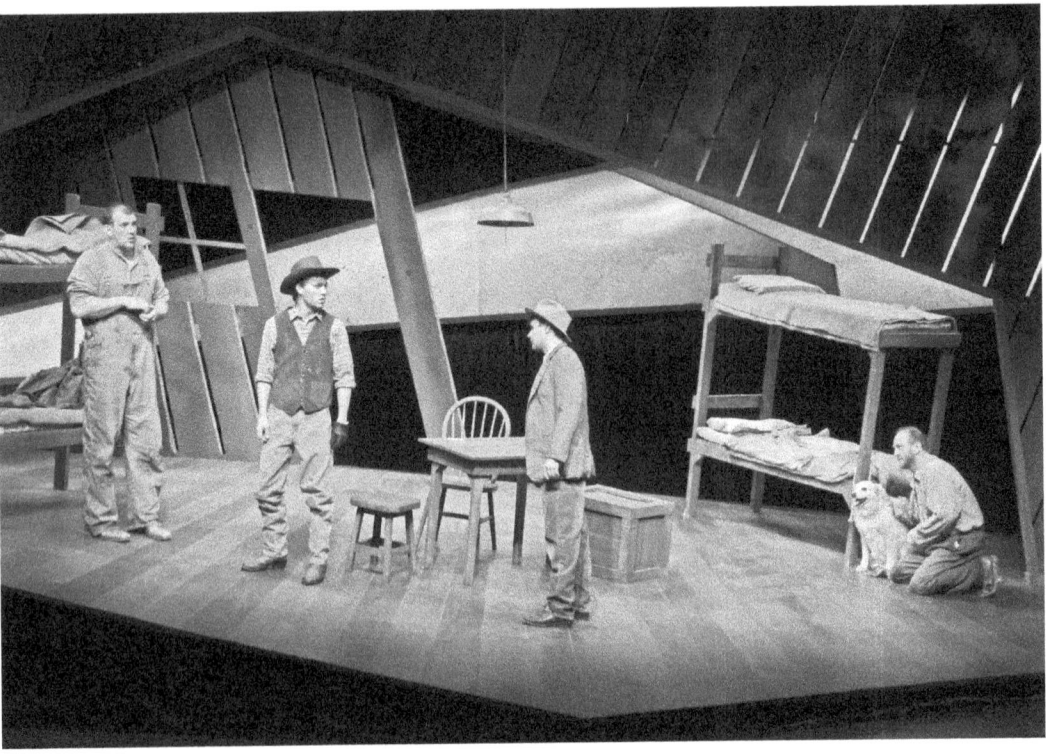

A set made of rough-hewn, earthy wood for *Of Mice and Men* by John Steinbeck. Design by the author.

6. Aesthetics

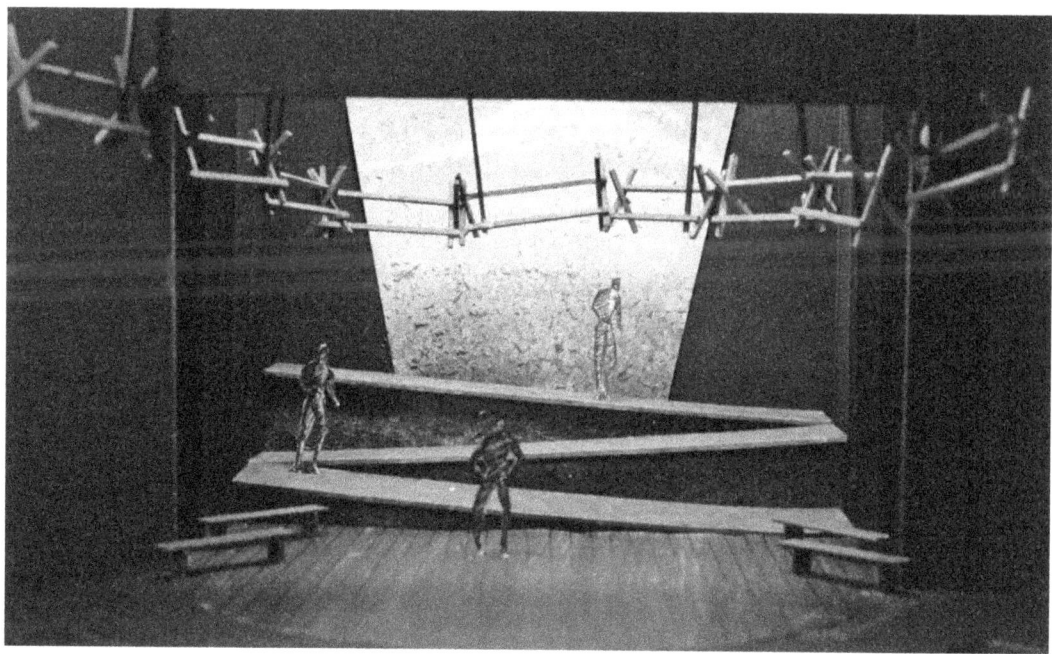

A set made of found textural materials for *The Laramie Project* by Moises Kaufmann. Design by the author.

value for this is more in the heart than in the actual visual results. But the backdrop does reflect, in a subtle and personal way, some extraordinary latent poetry.

A play like Peter Weiss's *Marat/Sade*, set in an asylum in France, presents a culture at odds with itself bearing a nod to nobility and a historic power. My design for this play is made of broken shards of stone, suggesting that a powerful culture exists, but its broken quality puts it into question. In all, materials give a space's personality its impressing cloak and the cloak projects the heart of the spatial culture's songs and poems, the cultural truth.

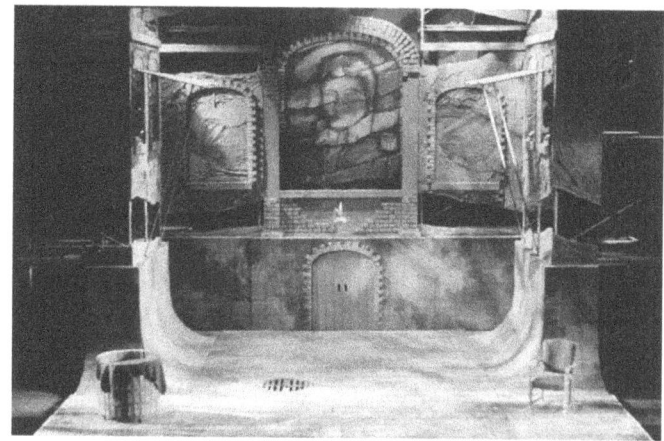

A set made of stony slabs for *Marat/Sade* by Peter Weiss. Design by the author.

Symbols and Imagery

This is the invented language of space, its semiotics. And it represents the "speech" of the personality of space because it regards how something is said or signified in a spatial design. In most cases, these are visual statements. And these statements are made using some form of representative figure that compares to or stands in the place of a real object or idea. There are a variety of types:

Metaphors

These are comparative examples that equate a figure in a design with a real object. In a spatial design, a large red sphere floating in the plenum above a traffic area could be a metaphor for the life energy, not to mention the sun itself. A large, tattered flag hanging at the back of a stage might suggest the decay of an empire for a historical play. These are spatial and visual metaphors.

Allegories

These refer to story aspects in a design that that represent a deeper idea. A space could have a massive bas relief wall with carvings of stylized animals each wearing different cherished object around their necks: a fox with a bone, a tiger with a sword, an elephant with a book and bird with a glowing orb. The collective carving could represent the ascending ages of humanity. The fox could be the spirited newbie with all value placed on simple survival. The tiger is the warring and imperialist stage with weapons held in high esteem. The elephant depicts a maturing wisdom, focused on learning and reason. And the bird is a transcendent creature that is approaching enlightenment and can soar above the bondage of gravity. The progression of the ages is the allegorical storyline.

Analogies

Analogies are comparisons used to clarify meaning. For instance, you may wish to convey a sense of the runaway nature of technological progress in a design. You might say that progress in this day and age is an operation of uncontrollable kinetics. To create an analogy for this you might somehow create an enormous pinball machine with a ball that wont quit shooting around, knocking over people and natural objects inside the playing field as it racks up numbers that seem to have no end. The pinball machine is a designed analogy.

Emblems

Essentially, these are visual badges that represent human objects or ideas. You might hang a religious emblem such as the holy cross, the star of David or the star and crescent in a space and it would represent an identity of faith. In much the same way you can hang an oversize wilting leaf above the open stage for a play about melancholy loners who lament their passing youth. The leaf becomes an emblem of loneliness and aging, and an emblem of the characters themselves.

Mythic Icons

An icon is basically a symbol that is universally accepted and immediately recognized in the culture as representative of something greater/deeper. Chairman Mao's portrait in a 1960's Chinese square is obviously an icon for the politics and priorities of that society. The looming profile of a dark nuclear plant's cooling tower in the background of a staged concert in the 1980's might be an icon for the environmental concerns expressed at the concert. These are some examples of visual icons that I admit are a bit cliché, but they illustrate my point.

Signs

Signs are active and immediate conveyers of information. The information itself may not be readily apparent, so the sign becomes useful. While most signs are common, some are original or obscure. A designer can lead people directionally with signs. Or he can tell them where they are and what to think. Signs can also indicate that something has or will happen and these are often the most intriguing. Bertolt Brecht calls for lettered signs to hang on the sets for his plays that tell the location of the scene. Signs that employ symbols such as arrows or warning graphics can also be used and these tend to be a little more imaginative. A sign can also be a star in the sky or a cloud looming on the horizon, harbingers of coming events.

Relatable Images

Images involve the poetic echoing of something. They require some familiarity with the context of the images and/or interpretation. These are less obvious than the others I mention above, because they require a bit more imagination or back-story. Images can be any visually interesting occurrence in a space. They should have some relevant meaning to the culture, but could be very subtle. They might echo the mood of the group in some way. For instance, a lone red balloon floating across a grey sky might be simply curious to most who see it. To the imaginative and/or informed viewer, it becomes an echo of the wanderings of the childlike soul, something you recall from your own past and appreciate with the balloon's flight. There needs to be an understanding in the viewer of the superimposition of red on grey and enough savvy for him to make the connection.

A symbol in a space usually carries a message. The message, in some cases, might be coded or disguised so its secret is decipherable only those in the tenant culture. It might be covert, avoiding disclosure to power authorities who could lay ramifications on the tenants for exchanging the message, possibly one that is subversive. A theatrical example of this can be seen in the Cold-war work of Czech Scenographer Josef Svoboda (1920–2002), especially work with the" Laterna Magika," a multimedia and non-verbal theatre in Prague. It doesn't take a detective to deduce how a non-verbal theatre resembles the silence of an abiding mass in a socialist realm. In front of the silence is strong and well-rooted visual imagery. Much of Svoboda's work employs imagery that latently critiques his own political authorities. These authorities are too busy and driven to bother with interpretations. The symbols may be deeply cultural, understood by the masses like folklore, laid out in camouflage by a designer who is a poet of space.

On the other hand, it is not unusual to have symbolic messages being expressed via blatant signage, held up for the viewer rather than residing in the intricacies of the place's context. The designer chooses the most effective means to convey the point. No matter how extroverted or introverted, a space's signage and imagery can be the speaking voice of the personality of space.

Mood

Mood is the emotional condition of the space and is conveyed as a part of the personality package of a space. A space may vent its mood by various tangible expressers.

Coloration

There are no guidelines as to what colors signify what moods. That would contradict the nature of creativity. Palettes are devised by trial and error and there is usually a consensus among the creative team as to what works and what doesn't. Generally, colors that have warmth remind us of the warm sun and our own life's blood, so warm colors are used to convey vitality and the intensities of life. Blues and violets resemble the skin upon death and so they evoke a sad feeling or dreariness and cold. Greens are the colors of decay and wilderness, so they can be read as macabre or discomforting.

But, these generalizations can be limiting. It's best to play around with colors until something hits your eyes and generates an appropriate feeling. The notion here is that color can be felt. Color is emotional. It is also tied to our memory. A color can easily remind you of a place you've visited and if you enjoyed that place, the color gives you a pleasant mood. Colors also can *represent* certain places, objects or ideas. An aqua blue reminds us of the sea, an orange of fire and violet of revered social positions. The designer should consider cultural associations and definitions of color as well as use gut instinct.

Lighting

Light is the only thing you can see. The rest is shadow. Light is reflected from whatever source illuminates the space. Most of what we see is reflected light. Reflected light can be sharp and focused or soft and undefined. This is known as the quality of the light. The quality of the light and the relationship between light and shadow is what contributes to the mood of a space. There are different degrees of reflection: *local light* which is the flat field of light that hits the majority of the surfaces in the space, *highlight* which strikes things that protrude out from the base surface and *flash highlights* that glint select points of detail when the surface is particularly shiny. Reflection can be direct, where the surface is glossy like a mirror and the reflected beam is identical to the originating beam. Reflection can also spread out and soften if the surface is matte. Generally, direct reflection with sharp shadow edges is more dramatic and mysterious than diffused qualities.

Texture

Texture is the tactile modifier of form. It is degreed as well. Deep relief, like on a cave wall laden with rocks and sinewy roots gives an impression of beastliness and a grizzly nature. This creates a mood of potential danger. Sometimes deep relief gives a sense of coziness as with high pile carpets and furry fabrics. Slimy, undulating textures give a grotesque feel and a queasy feeling. Smooth surfaces appear clean and sophisticated and give you a prideful or pleasant mood. The choices aren't difficult, but should be considered carefully when devising the emotional makeup of a space.

Think of whether the world is earthy or refined. That is the continuum of texture. Worlds where there is a great deal of contact with a steady civilization are generally glossier and smoother than those where there is instability. Gloss surfaces require upkeep and therefore require a stable economy and a servant class. If unattended, surfaces will decay and revert back to roughness and relief, the textures of nature. Civilized humanity must struggle to hold back the process of degradation. And that requires the time and resources to do the work.

Atmosphere

Gradation, lighting and texture can collectively create a moody atmosphere. Certain grey colors painted on a surface with considerable tooth, and struck with just the right kind of cool light, will give a convincing illusion of mist in a space. The diffusion of light alone can give a peculiar atmospheric impression. Light passing through a sheer will create a vaporous glow and that can in turn impact mood. In the theatre, we have special effects to heighten all this. We use chemical foggers to create an illusion of clouds or plumes of smoke. Dry ice machines create a low-lying carpet of white fog at the floor that is very spooky and ghostly under the right light. We also have hazers that create an aerosol effect so that beams of light become visible and create a mood of grandiosity. As you can guess, the mixing of color, light, texture and atmosphere all blend toward creating the right mood.

Historically, an architectural or living space evoked the mood of its time. So, a mood can be culturally based. It can take the feeling of the culture or an individual from the culture. In theatre, the spatial mood might evoke the mood of the central character. A great example of this is from Charles Dickens' *A Christmas Carol*.

I have a design for the stage version of this Victorian classic in rotation at a renowned Shakespeare festival. The show focuses mainly on the mind and soul of Scrooge. The entire space is made with an incarnation or outgrowth of his four-post bed. This set piece transforms into a table for feasting, a closet for spirits and a platform for levels. Scrooge's mood is that of a frustrated spirit, grumbling and humbugging his way around his miserly existence while the world around him plods through legitimately tough times. The colors are cool. Even the wood tones are grayed out, more taupe than brown. The greenery in the ivy wreaths is verging on a dusty olive or sage. The lighting is icy-blue throughout. Only at the appearances of the first two spirits do we see a glimmer approaching warmth. The lighting is modeled after some book illustrations that were rendered in the same frigid palette and the textures are all rough, as if they've been left unattended to dust and weathering. There is a consistency of gloom across the space and it directly reflects the bleak winter of Scrooge's soul. When Scrooge finds his redemption, the space again takes on an injection of gold, a moment of hope like a warm morning sun to melt the frost. This warming effect is achieved by the introduction of bits of reflective, gold fabric in the clothes during the last scene, a slight intensification of the light, a relaxing of the near ever-present haze in the space and the smiles on the actor's faces as they recite: "God bless us everyone...."

Like Scrooge's early ways, it is typical for a person with a certain mood to want others to share that mood. He may want to inoculate them, or drag them down. Like a person or character shares his mood, a space may functionally share its mood the same way, to visitors and audience.

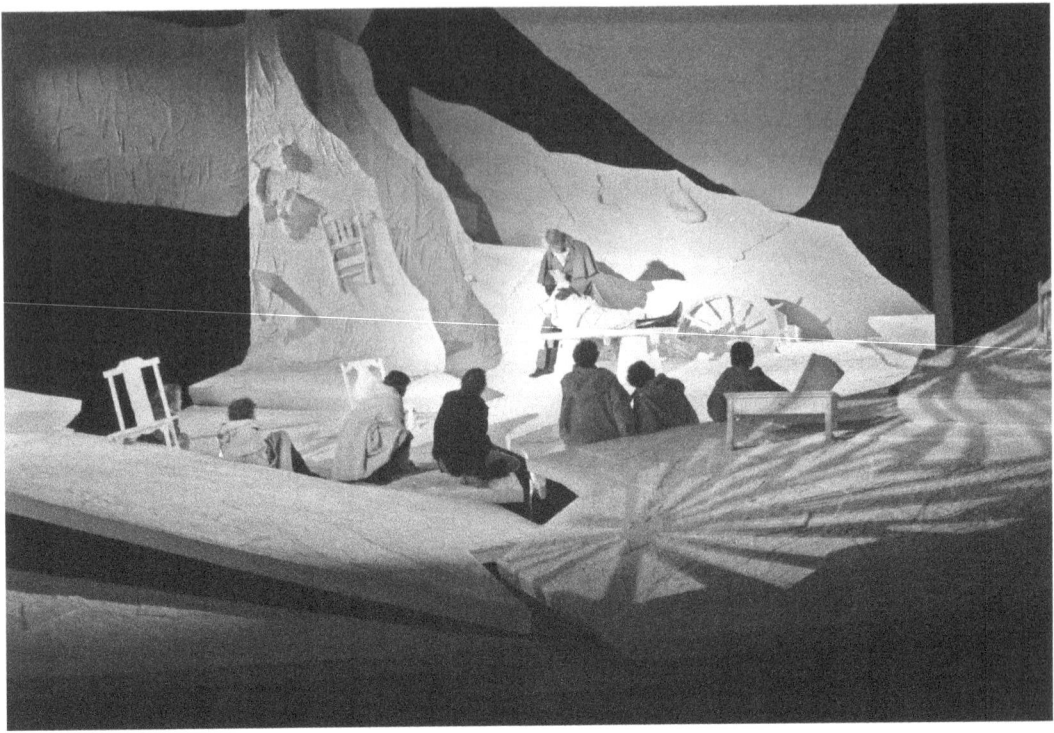

Mood is expressed by space. The sharp edges, uneven floor and odd shapes in this production of *Frankenstein* create a mood of discomfort and uncertainty. Design by the author.

Motion

As I state a number of times in this book, theatre design is a design of occurrences. We do not only design static spaces; we also consider how it all moves. We are more like orchestrators of music than sculptors. I believe that all spaces are in fact dynamic and the manner of their motion contributes to their personalities. Motion refers to the morphing and shifting of space through its use and the space's transformation over the time of its use. A space's use usually follows a linear progression like a story. This motion may be perfectly literal or obliquely figurative. In a theatre space, the characters and the dynamics of the story's telling create the type of motion. A few examples of types of spatial motion seen in the theatre (and could also exist in architecture or other forms of spatial planning) follow.

As a story is told, the narrative and the scenic elements in the space may flow, like liquid, as time goes on. The characters in this case could literally move in swirling patterns with no rigidity of direction like the foam on waves. The whole show could follow suit with the blocking of actors. The reciting of lines and the commencing of action would happen here and there with no specific destination. This is an interesting and disorienting kind of motion. The motion of a show could also be an arc, a journey out and back. It could rise and build in intensity as the show begins and then release at a climax and return back down as the show wraps up. Staging, lighting and physical movement by the actors would play along with this crescendo/decrescendo. The motion may also be a process of unfolding, a disclosure. This would be like the progressive solving of a mystery. The space would open up, as would revelations of truth in the text. It could also be a reveal or conceal, a rotation or a spiral, an expansion or a contraction, many things. It can be a hybrid of these and others.

Motion governs. With it, you have the working event. The event relies on it and is bound to its ways. The motion of the characters, the plot, the music and words can be identified, sometimes by a simple gesture caught by an observant eye. Its something you, as a designer, grab on to, and design to. When I design, I watch the actors in rehearsal moving about. I also watch the director's gestures as she speaks to me about the design. She might swirl her hands round and round like the director on my production of John Gay's *The Beggar's Opera*. As I watch, I see the actors in rehearsal do the same. Watching this led me to conclude that *The Beggars Opera* is clearly a show that needs a circular floor plan. My design is an oval arrangement of varying platforms that allow a circular trek. The show also needs to go up and down. It's all like a carousel, up-down-and-round-and-round. The design has ladders and scaffolds that reach into the flies and a spiral stairs that descends into the pit. This all stems from watching casual gestures and movements in early discussions and in rehearsal.

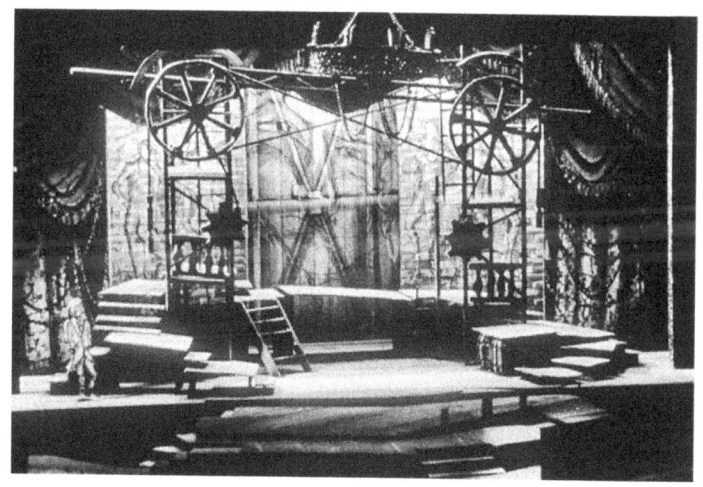

A design that calls for circular movements. Model for *The Beggar's Opera* by John Gay. Design by the author.

The point is to observe, watch and find nourishments in the orchards you might not expect to be fruitful. Nothing is insignificant or mundane in the creative process. That is both maddening and liberating. Motion is maybe the most important part of the aesthetics of space. It represents the dynamics of the personality of the space and it represents evolution. The space may recreate itself and rejuvenate itself as it goes along. This makes for a very organic kind of motion. And this motion could have a *musical* quality. That leads me to the next chapter.

7

Music

The spirit moves you. There is no other art form that can summon the spirit quite like music. And you can tell exactly how that spirit moves by watching dancers in a nightclub. I believe that, in a way, a designed space has a spirit, an inner nature that is the most truthful rendition of its self. I also believe that space has musical qualities. And to follow my logic, I believe that the spirit of a space can be sensed and expressed in its "musicality."

Concepts of music theory and composition are effective ways to refer to the spirit of space. We can discuss a space's visual and structural attributes as being rhythmic, harmonious, and melodic, etc. And in turn, that discussion will reveal a bit about the spirit of the space. The connection is a bit mysterious, but it bears out. The personality and character discussed in the previous chapters are surface features. The spirit is deep and requires a powerful device to stir its manifestation. Music is such a device. This chapter will cover the musicality of space and introduce some thoughts about space's spirit. I will go deeper into spirituality in the second section of the book. In the manner of the last few chapters, I will break down the concept of spatial spirit by following a series of specific subjects germane to the study of music.

Rhythm

Even though it's a hard word to spell, it's a very good place to start. Rhythm is basic and primitive. It doesn't require much thought. I realize that percussion aficionados and ethnomusicologists will bring up the multi-layered patterns in African tribal drumming and the odd time signatures of East European folk music. I get it. But, ultimately, even those seemingly multifarious forms of rhythm make you move. They don't make you contemplate or calculate (unless you are a drummer). Rhythm is the part of music that makes you dance. It mimics the heartbeat and the motive forces of life. It can also lock in to the heartbeats of many members of a group, collectively creating polyrhythms and eventually creating choreography.

Rhythm refers to patterns that repeat, often with interesting variations like syncopation. It is intricate in its scoring, created with layers of notation riffing off a steady metronomic clock-beat. It refers also to tempo or pacing. It's the timing mechanism of music. It's the motor.

And it's the dance of space. Spatial details can have visual patterns. These can be arranged to suggest an implied musical motion, with or without *real* motion. By this, I mean that you can have a series of visual objects that are grouped into small repeating ensembles: three lines, then three more, then three more, etc. Its like striped wallpaper, with a three-line repeating motif. The wallpaper lines create a little visual waltz, going: one-to-three, one-two-three, etc. The wallpaper doesn't move as it's pasted to a wall, yet it *moves*. In essence, spatial details can dance and they can compel the tenants to dance, with their eyes or their bodies. The dance can be bright and energetic or ponderous and lethargic — allegro or largo.

No matter the speed, *the spirit loves to dance*. Frequently, visual composition will use patterning and the density of the patterns establishes the rate of the rhythm. Lots of frequently repeating objects in a space, like the striated lines of window blinds, radiators and floorboards gives the spatial rhythm a quick staccato pace. It makes you want to get busy and shuffle along. A few long, graceful swags of luxurious fabric draping from side to side gives you a slow swing rhythm, one that might lull you to sleep. This gives the designer another unique power and another responsibility. He must think earnestly about what kind of dance the spirit of the space commands or desires. What is the goal and how can you arrange the details to serve that interest? Is it "three/four" gallantry or is it a "four/four" march? Does it have "swing eighths" or Latin triplets? The message here and in this entire chapter is to encourage visual designers to compose the music of their space. And beginning with the rhythm is a viable choice. But if you prefer western traditions, such as with the music of J.S. Bach, you will want to start with the chords.

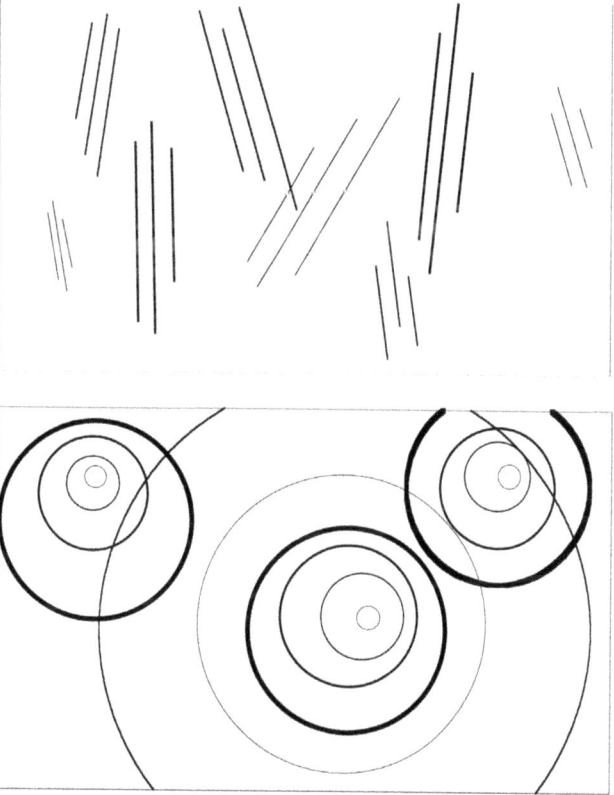

Top: Rhythm in a visual design. Here, simple repetitions of three line sets give the design a spatial rhythm, almost a dance. Note the variation of size, angle and line weight. *Above:* Another example of rhythm using a ripple motif. This suggests a different kind of spatial dance.

Harmony

Harmony is the foundation of music. It is the chord progression on which one builds composition. Chords, in case you don't know, are groupings of related notes (usually three or four notes) that are played concurrently. The notes usually resonate with one another and make sense to our ears. The chords in music change from one to another in a rhythmic sequence called the chord progression. These can be highly complex like in modern jazz or quite simple like in the blues. Usually the chord sequence repeats with subtle variations. The grouping of the notes is called harmony and on top of harmony you build the rest of the song.

Harmony is essentially the strata beneath, the layers that relate to one another and support what is residing on top. Music is usually written on a staff that way. The chords are below, the rest on top. It is the flowing undercurrent, the vibrating ground. We learn from our cultural life which chords make sense to us as being harmonious. There really cannot be a wrong chord. It may sound dissonant to our ears, but it cannot be morally judged. It simply has to make sense to its creator and she can hope it will make sense to her audience. New music, with experimental harmony, is good as long as it advances culture.

In space, harmony is the relationship of visual parts and how they resonate with one another. It's how they radiate off the central core and metaphorically "vibrate." This gives the spatial inhabitants a base on which they can sing their song. And the song identifies them with the spirit of the space. *The spirit hums.*

An example might be a series of similarly shaped mounds of dirt in a space. One is tall and wide in the center. It appears in the shape of a kidney bean when you see it from above. Two others, close in shape but different in size, are near the central, core mound. Between them are little ditches of running water that flow between the curves of the mounds and resemble the wavy sense of the shapes. It's all like a curvy radiation of related lines swirling in S-curves around and through one another. This space could be a sort of miniature golf range, a park attraction, or a landscape design. The repeating lines relate and visually "vibrate" together. They are in harmony. The movement of people in this space and the rest its design elements key off of this harmony. One of the basic elements of music that resides on top of harmony is the melody.

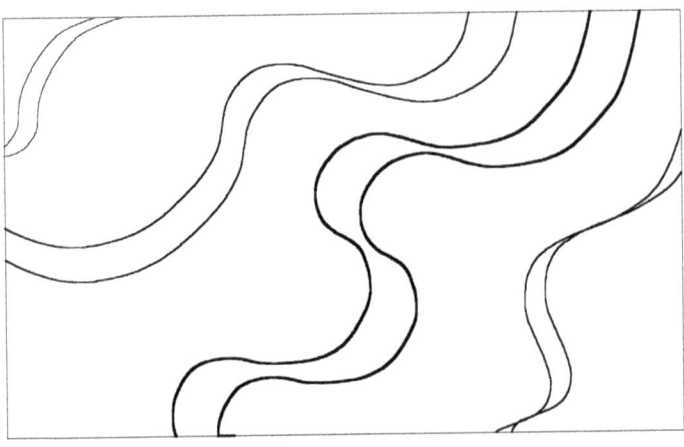

Harmonious design elements. The ribbons in this design are not duplicate forms, but they relate to one another creating a harmonic unity via the benefit of some variation.

Melody

The melody is the linear journey of music. It is the tune, the thing we most recognize. It is also the carriage of the words and the song the voice sings. We hum it. We identify the composition by it. It is really *the* thing in music. When you think of the Ninth, you can hear the lead line of *Ode to Joy*. When you think of *Appalachian Spring,* you can hear the strain of that old Shaker hymn *Simple Gifts* coming down like an ecstatic rainstorm. The melody comes to you first like the lead actor in a play. It reaches you because it is well supported underneath by harmony and rhythm. The greatest melodies refer back to their foundations like the lead actor depends on his chorus. But they ultimately take the spotlight, step out front and capture us. This is because melody functions as a guide for the soul. Our spirit takes its hand and we go as it goes and if it is effective we get to a place that can drain our eyes and raise our follicles and convince us that everything suddenly makes sense. That result requires a journey. Melody is the way.

There is also a journey in space. It is much like melody. It is the journey the eye takes as it looks at the features of a space. We call this visual journey the "eye path." The eye path is a kind of imaginary line that is created by a clever compositional arrangement in the space. It depends on a fairly savvy and conscious designer who deliberately strives to make it. As we the audience watch, experience or participate in a space, we follow the eye path through like our spirits follow melody. The path can be made of a series of subtle visual gestures such as a broomstick slanting up from the floor meeting three circular picture frames on a wall in a vertical row. They take your eye up to a crown molding that extends horizontally across to the other side where a tall plant stands and leads the eye down to a chair on the floor. On the chair sits an important figure. The figure is the landing spot, usually the focal point of the space. The eye path takes us to this focal point like the melody leads to the fermata.

When the fermata sounds, we might contemplate the journey and reach some epiphany. When we land on the visual focal point, we know we have found what we need to see.

Now, it is possible to have numerous focal points in a composition. The melody of a space can take us to visit them one by one, like a pageant along a riverside. These can be thematic "points" that repeat in a rhythmic way. Your eye may travel to a window then on to a bust of Beethoven, then up to a grand chandelier and back down to the figure in the chair. This is also like finding a tavern on every corner as you stumble down a series of city streets at midnight. Usually one of the focal points takes the lead and governs the rest in this scenario. Be they many or one, focal points represent the purpose, destination or objective of spatial melody. And those points are what the spirit of the space intends for you to see, the revelations. For you, the composition of space provides a journey and *the spirit knows the tune.*

Voice

The voice is the source of poetry in music. It provides the most human expression of all of the instruments. When the voice sings, the sound comes propelled from the gut, pushed up by the diaphragm muscle and thrust with air from the lungs. It goes through the vocal chords causing vibrations that are acoustically projected by the mouth to the masses. Greatly skilled singers can reach the back rows of the largest houses, touching the audience's ears. Those ears vibrate to the same tune sung. And the vibrations trigger neurotransmitters in the audience member that tell the brain what is happening and from this comes musical comprehension, appreciation, emotional reaction and possibly the spirit moving. In the midst of all this activity is the actual music, sung by a voice in solo, or by a small ensemble of nicely relating vocal timbres, or by a full chorus all banked together on risers like the pipes on a grand organ in the proudest chancel. With voice, the poetry of music is brought by human figures to our souls.

The poetry of space is brought to our souls by a voice as well. Poetry is the language of the spirit. It reveals without explaining. And the spirit requires a voice to transmit that poetry. In music it is the singer as I discuss above. In a play it is the actor. Obviously, in the theatre, the actors provide voices. These are really the voices of the text and of the author. And in due course, they are the voices of the dramatic event. But here, I refer to something else. I refer to the voice of space, a medium that lies between the spirit of the space and the person encountering the space. The voice of space is form.

Form is essentially the fundamental shape and structure of the space, as conceived by and realized with the oversight of the designer. All of the design elements serve form; they color and texture it; they stylize it and give it personality and mood. They even give it meaning or identity. But the form itself, the basic physical entity, is what delivers the poetry in earnest. A space that is a long, narrowing and darkening corridor sings the poetry of despair and diminishing hope. A space that has great internal height and stairs that lead up without a clear top recites the poetry of aspiration and anticipation. A space that is tight, claustrophobic and symmetrically rigid chants the poetry of conformity and containment. As you pass through the space, you encounter its form. And in that encounter, you "read" the poetry of the space with your imagination, your emotions and other internal feelings. It figuratively tells you about your place in life without forcing analysis. As an old Beat poet once said: you read literature but "you feel poetry." In a space, you "feel" form. I don't mean feeling as in tactile touch, but feeling — like with jazz — as "getting it" on the inside. Your inside.

The poetry of space can be voiced in the manner of music. It can come as a solo, ensemble or chorus. As a "solo," the form is simple and unified, having one voice, one single expression that says it all. The space could be a single room, a hallway, a tower, a lawn, a grove of trees, a garden, a road, a corner or a lake. In cases such as these, the poetry echoes through the space with clarity and draws focus. It is succinct. You "get it" immediately. It doesn't rely on overtones or ambiance or other attempts toward density and layering. This is a pure voice for the spirit. It can be very effective at storytelling and summary statements. It is not so good at dialogue, exchanging differing views and "power in numbers." That is where we get into multiple voicing.

As an "ensemble," the voices converse. There can be call and response. There can be echoing. Counterpoint. Descant. And there can be "spatial music"— voices coming from various parcels — demonstrating the dimensions of the spirit. Spatially, this is where you have a more complex form. It can be one with varying tiers, chambers, levels, apertures, windows, doors and relief. Voices can emanate from high and low, corner to corner, from numerous places in the space you encounter as you pass through. You sense them; you see them; you even hear them in the reverberation of your own steps. The voices, spaced apart like nightingales in different trees, beckon you in one direction, then the next. You want to ponder the nooks and crannies and if you will, you'll find in them dimensional poetry, multiple expressions of a common message, and a world worth exploring deeper. The spatial ensemble encourages you to join in and sing along.

The largest ensemble is the chorus. It fills the space with a collective voice, a fullness that heightens the experience. It can mimic angelic rapture or the cacophony of demons. Both extremes are possible, and anything in-between. The chorus demands something akin to a tabernacle or the expanse of the internal mind. Because it fills space, it needs space. And when it gets space, it lets go. The spatial form for a chorus is usually large, but is always rich with potential. It has many possibilities. There can be great height with great incumbent formations that give it splendor such as vaults and columns. There can be breadth with many possible ways to go laterally, like radiating wings setting in all directions. It could be an open vessel with enough spatial perches for people to go that it offers a near infinite array of destinations. These kinds of forms allow more than exploration and dialectic exchanges. They allow resonance. They lend power to the poetry. They conduct a chorus of many voices, each voice being a facet of the form, and hold it in unison to make the spatial experience bold.

I will add that the acoustics, illumination and atmosphere of the space can reinforce the voice. All these together foster the delivery of poetry. Poetry encourages imagination. And imagination seeks the spirit. Following suit, the spirit seeks a voice. And when it finds one, *the spirit sings* to us. So, the voice connects us to the spirit, meaning the voice is shamanistic. And if the voice of space is form, the form is shamanistic as well. All of this talk is well and good, but at some point you need to think practically. The spirit needs to get to work and put something together. Here is how that goes...

Orchestration

If voice refers to form, then orchestration refers to function. Function is the "doing" of space. Orchestration, in music, involves "doing" as well. It involves putting the parts together in an orderly fashion. This requires great imagination and the ability to hear the sounds in your head. The parts that are put together include rhythm, harmony, melody, voice and the collective pitches, ranges, tones and timbres of the instruments in the ensemble. The orchestration is the way the music is arranged. It's the charging of tasks, the assigning of roles, putting the tune together with a job for every instrument. And the art for this is in the choices made by the arranger. Orchestration takes the basics and makes them come alive, with a diversity of sounds and a unity of purpose toward a logical and beautiful whole. Hopefully, you recall how similar this is to my early definitions of visual composition and design.

Spatial orchestration refers to spatial dynamics. A space has a diversity of components or parts. These include the surround, access, paths of movement, details and interactive objects. As with music, the parts of space are like instruments that perform together, each serving a purpose. By performing their duties, the parts promote activity in the space like action in a drama. If orchestrated successfully, the result can be a logical/beautiful whole. And this "whole" is not static. It functions. It becomes an *event*, an occurrence that is the dynamic life of the space.

The spatial event is the spirit alive. And in the spatial event, the spirit bears a function, a role it plays out. As part of its functioning, *the spirit plays* a symphony that transforms the spatial experience into that perfect thing, everything all together as one, serving its purpose. An example of this is a well-designed retail establishment. This kind of space performs for its clientele with the intent to lure. It does so by dazzling the eye with dramatically lit attractions and crafty channels of access to the allure. In the channeling, you encounter some of these attractions along the way. It becomes a process. There is a multi-movement opus being played in the layout. It has a beginning, middle and end. The various displays and staging areas are the sections of the orchestra. The main attraction, or the focal point of the store's visual displays, is like the solo instrument that calls our attention.

We enter the store and the baton comes down. There is an intro, a sensing of what the store's identity is, usually at the front window or one of the first displays we see. Then we patrons move to the varying focal attractions, like audience members following soloists in a music piece. At times, we look around and take the whole place in. It's like hearing the full orchestra sound. We gather a few things and try them on for size. And that is like the orchestration weaving through themes and variations. As we shop, our pace changes like the tempo changes from an allegro to a largo in a romantic concerto. When we head to the point of purchase, the finale builds. By our farewells with packages in hand, the coda plays out and the piece resolves to its end. A space can be a concert. The designer thinks of this.

The designer thinks of the spirit of the space and does so by considering the musicality of the space. If she tries, she can listen and hear a space's song. And if she is especially creative, she can compose the songs of new spaces as she forms their visual and structural essences. Part of that composition is a reflection on *the culture* of the space and that is the primary subject of Chapter 8.

* * *

The Orchestration of Light

Stage Lighting is truly orchestrated. Every lighting design for the stage employs a vast array of varied lighting fixtures. There are spotlights, floodlights, automated/intelligent fixtures, "wash" luminaires and variable focus fixtures. These fixtures are known in the trade as lighting instruments. And each instrument is separately controlled by a complex electronic system. So, each instrument can have a role and can have a distinct duty, a part to play. During a show, these instruments change intensity, color and direction as the control operator plays them like a Wurlitzer theatre organ, triggering a myriad of single purpose commands. And she plays the chart as it is composed by the stage lighting designer during the technical rehearsals.

The lighting script is the score. It has the notation, the timing, the actions and the dynamics clearly indicated. The stage manager is the conductor and the piece plays out as the actors play their roles, in concert with one another. The lighting moves with the movements of the show. It coincides with the text and action and flows with the dynamic changes and dramatic punctuation. The colors and textures of the light are like the tones and timbres of the musical ensemble.

8
History

When a social scientist observes culture, he usually follows a precise methodology. These methodologies vary among observers and follow the trends of the field at the time. But, it is safe to say that the consideration of cultural origins, especially when the observation involves the field of archeology, will likely play an integral role in his study. This is because it structures interpretation and understanding. It provides context. In many cases, the concrete history and development of a culture is documented or documentable. In some cases it lies in abstract form, awaiting an observer's reading. It is my assertion that either way, history serves three purposes in the consideration of culture. It reveals, justifies and illuminates. It is read the same way in the field of design, especially stage design where designers must employ some degree of historical overview to inform their work.

In the hands of a designer, history is a tool. In the eyes of a designer, it is a lens. As such, history reveals the roots of culture. A stage designer might approach a production that is set in archaic Scotland by visually researching extant stone constructions from a time just prior to the setting. The shaping of the stones, their proximity to the quarries and the level of care invested in their placement tell the story of the social climate at the time of their making. Rough-hewn stones collected at nearby quarries laid in haste suggest a culture rooted in desperation, a world under threat from some natural or hostile force that has made its presence known. This informs the designer. The world he creates must be constructed on a base of historical fear, instability and reactionary aggression. His world may end up with sharp-edged forms, random angularity, opposing diagonal lines and a sense of sloppy impermanence, a world not supported by ample pylons but by anxious paranoia.

History also justifies the present. A costume designer might be working on a show that is set in a recent decade, such as the 1970's. She may wonder why she is using so much polyester and such wide neckties. Why is there so much drabness on the women and so much vibrancy on the men (with disco-styled leisure suits, etc.)? What is the justification for all this? A brief look at cultural history can inform and validate her choices. The 1970's are interpreted as a time of emasculation among some men. This stems from a slow evolution away from traditional male roles, such as hunting and gathering and hand-to-hand warfare. This evolution seems to reach a critical point as the middle of the twentieth century arrives.

Technology is advancing; leisure time becomes accessible to commoners; and concepts of the value of peace and the empowerment of women is gaining acceptance. The advance of technology and the increase of leisure time contribute to increased cultural valuing of expedient and inexpensive production of goods. The economy in the 1970s is also weak, contributing to the value of cheap production. Hence, we see polyester. Polyester is generally a bit reflective. It looks showy. Wide neckties and vibrant color are also showy. They help to "sell" the male image like a peacock's plumage, replacing demonstrations of strength now undervalued by women, in realms such as the workplace, discotheques and on urban streets. This "sale" is directed at potential mates and follows the notion among males that vain displays of dazzling color/texture might attract females who are unimpressed by blatant masculinity. Pure physique and demonstrative aggression are insufficient in a culture that reduces its reverence for war and power. So the costumer is primping and preening the actors in her stead with garish frocks. An understanding of the course of history justifies her creating the rather ugly garb.

If history reveals the roots of culture and justifies the present conditions, it follows by illuminating the future. For a designer, it functions as a headlight or a beacon. A stage lighting designer may be working on a production of a play about the future of an industrial culture that has over the years experienced an inflating reliance on a definitive morality. His research may begin by charting the trajectory of the moral code in that culture's past.

A lighting designer is interested in the emotional qualities of the visual. And it follows logic that he interprets emotional range as running parallel to the scale of contrast between light and shadow. He will scrutinize the level of contrast and also the character, color and angles of the light in the periods he researches. He will look at period paintings, photos and atmospheric history for evidence of all this. And to guess, or imagine, what kind of light and visual emotion might exist in the culture's future, he will track its course through time so far. He might see a trend of decreasing shadows as encroaching moral rules rob the world of romance and privacy, two aspects of life that require shadows. Light may be turning more even and flat and less dimensional and chromatic as the culture is pressured to moral conformity. He might assess that human individuality diminishes when lit by a light that floods to all corners. So he will proceed to create that kind of unyielding light in his show. The designer sees a culture's destiny by the light of its train.

Designers look back to see forward. And they use historical research for accuracy in their creations, if accuracy is important. I'd say that if the cultural milieu being portrayed is important to tell the story, then it deserves an accurate rendition. Educated observers will notice and can be distracted if the expressed history in a design is a wild guess or a poorly interpreted doodle. It should have some grounding in the realities of a genuine past and the designer should fully comprehend that reality. History can also be used for effect. Designers might insert or reference bits of history simply to magnify a point. For instance, a projection designer might be working on a "timeless" reading of a grand opera. There might be an aria that calls for an arresting stage picture that evokes radiant, internal beauty. The designer might recall that Gothic cathedral architects used rose windows that could be aligned with the sunrise in the spring, glowing intensely and casting a reddish radiance upon parishioners at Easter Mass. He might insert an abstracted image of the rosette during said aria.

Designers become historians as they work, all for the purpose of making an environment appropriate to the culture of their concern and to serve that culture's story. The device of history allows observation of the culture of space. In a descriptive manner I derive from meteorology, spatial design assesses cultural development, evaluates current conditions and constructs a forecast as it commences its process. The following addresses these three phases as they relate to space.

Development

Meteorologists record the way weather systems develop. A storm may originate in a low-pressure system out at sea or by the jet stream sweeping through the plains. This is reported with satellite imagery. They broadcast the current conditions every ten minutes in fetching graphics on their media outlets to a public demanding such immediate coverage. And then they dutifully forecast what they expect for the coming days, so we may prepare our activities and apparel. Designers regard the culture of space in a similar fashion.

A space has origins. The origins make up its cultural backstory. These are the cultural roots that form and feed the space. They are not necessarily seen on the surface. When designers look at space, be it a space they study or a space they create, they often begin by considering the base form of the culture that did, will or does reside in the space. This involves an encounter with history. The designers ask: What laid the groundwork? What was the core of the spatial past? A deep dig can and should ensue. Research into cultural development can and should proceed. In order to embrace space, you need to dig down to those roots and explore them. By doing so, the surface will become clearer. For instance, you might be creating a space that depicts Napoleonic France. Research into paintings from the period is the obvious first step. But, *the meaning* of the details in the space will be clearer, and better designed, if you look backward to see how the monarchy transitioned through the eighteenth century into the conditions under Napoleon. You read the developmental narrative of the culture's process.

In research, designers creating period spaces do more than seek evidence of details. It's not enough to know the silhouette of the period's gowns or the scale of the crown moldings in the period décor. Good designers will seek the reasoning behind the details. They will read back to the cultural and societal structure, the originating framework. They will interpret the rituals that built the behavior that the spatial details reflect, follow and foster. This research will involve looking at visual images from the past. But these images cannot be read without contextual referencing. The past is not a series of static pictures, isolated in time. It is a flow of passing moments in a linear evolution, with modifications and influences coming at it from many sources before, after and all around. History is read like a time-lapse reel of weather developing across the globe. It moves like flowing liquid, changing with the ripples, waves and tides it encounters. In researching space, you must see the whole flow, including the influences coming from the margins.

Conditions

How's the weather? If asked, you would go to the window or check the media outlets that report current conditions. You can look right in front of you. It's there. Living weather. Spatial designers read the culture of their spaces the same way. They check the current conditions and design accordingly. They may look into a space and see. It's there in front of them. Living culture. For the culture, there is living design. Design for the present considers current trends and the zeitgeist. The zeitgeist, or "spirit of the time," born from the dusty corridors of the past and emerging in the now, whispers or shouts the story of the culture to all who can hear. Designers must harness that zeitgeist and tap into its message.

The present is a vital concern because it is "life" defined. In reality, you could argue that the present is all there is. The past exists only in memory and the future only in dreams. What counts is the living, not the dead or unborn, but "the snap of a finger" or your immediate conscious moment. This all gets very "Zen." In other words, what matters is what is immediately in front of you. Now. These are the current conditions. And the current conditions of culture manifest in the current conditions of space. Designed space, in its present condition, is in a constant, dynamic engagement with the cycling of cultural time. It is crafted by the knife of change and its form anticipates the next stage of change. Architecture, by example, responds to the leading edge of life, then turns to propel its culture forward, like an oscillating wave. And since it's all in constant motion, you could also argue that there is no real present, but a liquid redefinition in constant metaphysical flow.

But I'll leave the grander musings to the philosophers. My main concern is with space. And one thing I know is that the better designers of space tune in to their current conditions and design to the current song they hear. An architect may acknowledge a zeitgeist in the culture around her that sings a song of conservation and environmental stewardship. She then designs a space made of responsible materials with a layout that efficiently conserves energy. Even a designer creating a period space will instill an edge of the current time. There is no exact replica. A Victorian homage will likely have a glint of some bold, current color somewhere in it. Designs about yesterday usually have a touch of today. The better designers can use that to their advantage. And the best designers of space begin to project their creations into the culture's tomorrow. A space may hold up its latest banner of identity for a while. But it is never at rest. In a flash of a moment it will move along. The best designs guide it.

Space echoes the sounds of its cultural past. But it also houses a reverberation of tones coming from the world just outside the door. The conditions outside cannot be held away. The weather seeps in. And the designer knows.

Forecast

"The weatherman says there'll be rain...." That's a line from a fairly well known play. It's also a line muttered by older gentlemen on the bench outside a nursing home near my house. I've heard them say it. Again and again. The forecast is their expectation. It's a topic of concern. Will the two gents be able to stay outside, chat and watch the squirrels? Or will they need to retreat to the common room for a round of coffee? How accurate is the weather report? By bedtime, they will know. The weather experts cannot steer the rain to the men. They can only predict it. A designer can predict as well. He can guess where the culture may turn, and design in anticipation. But the designer can also attempt to and sometimes will succeed in actually steering the turn. That might happen if he is a leading edge visionary. Based on this, it would be great to hear the old men say: "The designer says there'll be yellow...."

A cultural forecast is made of expectations and anticipations of where things might go. It is based on what is trending now and the trajectory of what has been. In a sense, the present cannot help but to begin to write the story of tomorrow. And designers should begin to write the story of where their space may go. They should perpetuate it. A good space has staying power, or implied staying power. It can be relied on to have a life. And by the merits of its own design, it should suggest its own future in its present. It should lean forward. This includes the theatre space, with a creeping specter or glow of promise, on the horizon ("I can see the wave of the future through the crack in the dam"). Essentially, the space should hold a kernel of the inhabiting culture's future in its confines, somewhere and somehow.

As a design leans forward, the manner or style of the design can and should be a leaning as well. Such manners and styles lead toward advances in the art form. A fresh theatre design can spark a trend or a new way of thinking about the artistic approach. From revolutionary designs can come new forms of theatre such as *Spatial Theatre*, where a linear narrative is no longer the core of the experience. The experience itself, engaged at all vectors of a performance realm, is the thing. Or you can have *Media Theatre*, featuring electronic interaction with the audience, all live and self-propelling with the latest tools and devices. There can be artistic ventures into cyber-space and mind-space, even new rejuvenations of ancient ways — going "back to the future." In architecture, you might see new trends and advancements of old trends. You might see progress in "aesthetic sustainability" or "sustainable aesthetics," etc. Who knows? The idea is to design toward something. And that something is the designer's own cultural forecast. It is his personal outlook on where the "sun and rain" will appear. He becomes a bit of a seer.

Ultimately, spatial design involves a "whole" consideration of time. It looks at time like a wave rolling forward. It's a cyclic wave. It comes full round and then rolls again. You refer to the past; you comprehend the present; and you project the future. All the while you roll along with it as it pushes and pulls you the same way you push and pull it. There is no separation. It refers, comprehends and projects you as you do it and the whole story flows along and along and along with no real beginning and no real end, like the globe turning round, and the weather reinventing itself continuously along the way.

* * *

Completing the Circle

The Progression of Dramatic Space Through History
(How Performance Locations Evolved — a Cyclic Chronology)

The following is a much-abbreviated chronology of the general development of Western theatre spaces. It demonstrates how Dramatic space cycled back to its original shape from one of our oldest known predecessors to very recent forms.

Prehistoric Theatre: This is ritual theatre. The space is a circle of standing or dancing cultural participants. There is a story at the center of the circle. It could be a myth. It could be a tale. At the center is a shaman. It is a full circle with a central focal point, the shaman who is the thread between heaven and the people. The shaman is not a performer but a facilitator of ritual.

Archaic Greeks: The first performer comes into the circle. He might reenact a story of a hunt or something. For the first time we see mimicry. The space is still a circle.

Early Civilized Greeks: The early famed performer, Thespis, performs in a circle of community people. There is visual evidence that shows him standing and performing on a cart for a circle of watchers. This is the first time we see a performer elevated above the audience, held at a separate plane of existence. In a sense, this is the first time we see "aesthetic distance" in a dramatic space.

Early Classic Greeks: There is evidence that scaffolds are constructed in a circle for audience members to sit. Later, the seating is built into a hillside. For the first time we see a concern for audience comfort and a clear division between audience space and performance space. The space is still a circle.

Classic Greeks: A building is erected at one end (tangent) of the circle. The building breaks the circle. The building is a changing house for actors to prepare, await their entry, change costume and to retrieve masks and props. The building is also a vessel for scenery. The building becomes known as the skene. This is the dawn of spectacle in the theatre, the first use of scenery and the first time the circle is broken. It is interesting that the circle is broken by spectacle. Grand outdoor theatres with lavish and permanent skenes are built into hillsides like at Epidauros. The audience area is now a horseshoe-shaped configuration

Late Greeks and Romans: Theatres are built as stand-alone structures. The audience area is reduced to a half circle and the skene is greatly enlarged and has become a lavishly decorated stage. Spectacle really begins to dominate dramatic storytelling. There is a clear and rigid architectural dividing line between audience and performers.

The Renaissance: The audience is seated indoors and separate, facing the stage directly. Very little of a rounded audience area remains. There is an extreme dividing line between audience space and spectacle space. There is a "picture frame" in-between. The audience looks through the picture frame in awe of a "living painting" onstage. This arrangement aligns with the celebration of human ingenuity and invention. It's now about looking at and watching instead of participating. The craving for spectacle ushered in a theatre about detachment and ushered out ritualistic and communal aspects.

Nineteenth Century: The Proscenium Theatre is firmly established. The audience sits in parallel rows all looking directly at a framed and elevated stage, often a long distance away. It is about looking into life. Plays are about reality (naturalism and realism comes into the fold). This aligns with the advent of modern science. Theatre is like probing into life, capturing life like a photographer (the proscenium arch is like the aperture of a camera). Theatre is now protected voyeurism.

Early Twentieth Century: Swiss designer Adolphe Appia proposes that theatre is more about the story and less about spectacle. He advocates for dimensional space, the performer heightened and given form. Scenery diminishes and yields its space to the dynamic performance. There are lots of levels and reinforcing lighting. This aligns with the dawn of film. Film takes over spectacle while theatre starts to get back to the heart of the storytelling. The proscenium is still the dominant architectural style because so many plays have been written with that structure in mind.

By the 1960's: There are new advances in theatre architecture. Authors address Appia's notions. Theatre is experimenting with expressionistic and non-realistic plays, Playwrights write plays that do not depend on a proscenium format. This opens doors for the architects. Theatre-in-the-round and other intimate performance spaces develop. Found spaces and informal spaces begin to appear.

By the 1980's: Environmental Theatre, with the audience and performers deliberately intermingled with no spatial division, is established by American designer Eugene Lee and

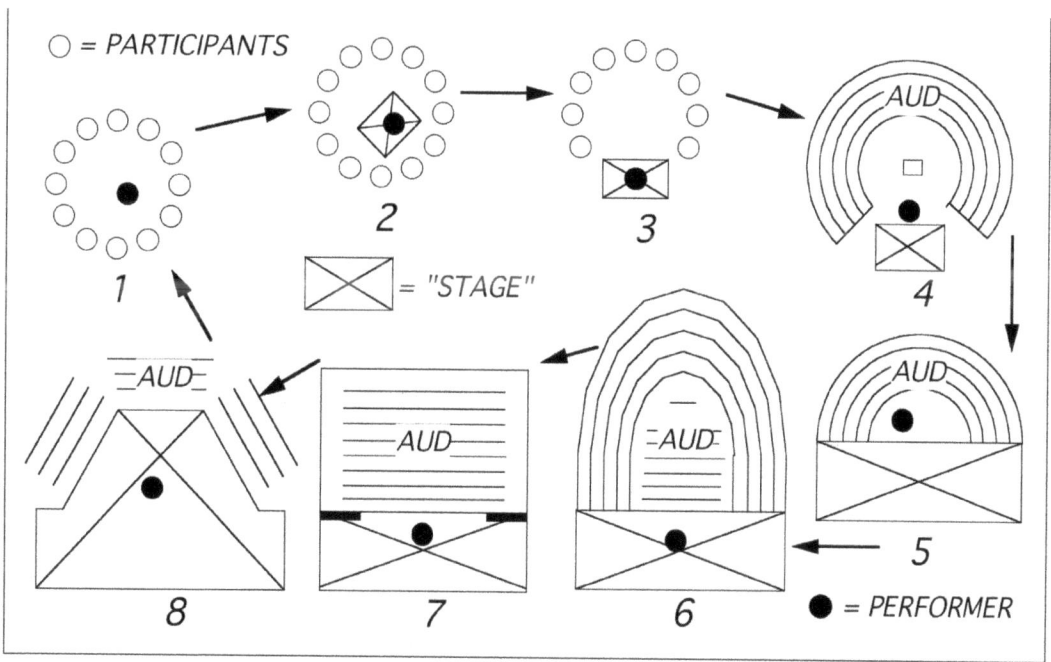

The Dramatic Space Historical Cycle. Over many centuries, dramatic spaces have undergone a cyclic evolution: (1) The basic form of prehistoric ritual theatre. (2) The Archaic Greeks — a performer stood on a cart, the earliest aesthetic distance. (3) Later the performer moved to a scaffold stage on the circumference, breaking the circle for the first time. (4) The classic Greek age with the familiar amphitheatre built into a hillside. (5) The Late Greeks and Romans shifted the audience into a half-round arrangement with connected stage and house. (6) By the Renaissance, the stage became large and detached. (7) By the nineteenth century, the stage is separated from the audience by a proscenium arch; the dramatic space is a rectangle. (8) In the twentieth century, Sir Tyrone Guthrie built his famous thrust theatre, extending the performer back out into the audience. 1. Again, in the mid twentieth century, a return to the circle via "theatre-in-the-round" and the "black-box" space.

others. The proscenium still exists on Broadway and in London, but that is due more to tradition than trends. Exciting regional theatres, with alternative seating arrangements like the thrust stage and arena seating are flourishing. It's more about the experience.

The Present: The circle returns and closes. We return to a need for ritual because television, the web, film and commercial entertainment "own" spectacle but cannot provide ritual. Spectacle is plentiful all around us. Live catharsis is rare. There is more and more fiscally poor and artistically strong theatre around. New theatres are village theatres. With communal theatre, you go back to confronting the self in a very real, tangible and earthy way.

All said, this is the life cycle of dramatic space. And at each moment in the cycle, we see a different kind of connection of the dramatic space to the humans who use it. Chapter 9 continues the discussion about such connections.

9

The Connective Thread

In the previous chapters, I share a way of looking at and describing space. Whether consciously or by some kind of instinct, many designers and artists approach their work this way. As I hope you have observed, it seems like a complex exercise. There are many angles and varied considerations in the mix. No doubt, I have left a few out. The nice thing is that as we gain experience, we learn to consider many of the things I discuss simultaneously, and at times subconsciously. We can study and build spaces without a checklist. It can be a concurrent and "whole" making, where as you consider form, you also are considering detail, meaning, structure, etc. I call this "the composition of process." When you achieve this as a designer, the design process moves along naturally and you create without the anxiety of crosschecking your thoughts.

The design process is a step-by-step progression that starts with an initial idea and gradually refines it into a finished and well-honed product. In the ideal situation, it becomes easy and at times you feel driven. It fuses into a single evolution, a single journey toward a single goal. As an athlete might say, you are in a "zone." For me, these are usually the best projects because they are centered in my creative focus. At other times you may find the process scattering and are unsure which track to follow. At these times, you may need to resort to stepping back and evaluating things methodically. Going through some of the categories in Part One might be a good start.

Ultimately, it's about a way of seeing. I encourage people to pay attention to the meaning of things you see in everyday life and if you are a creative person, to "make" with a productive consideration of the aspects in your work that connect to humanity. As I say above, this consideration gets smoother and more intuitive as you do it. The main objective is to find the connection points, the tissue that marries substance to soul. One way is to find the "story" that is being or should be told. With space, the story can be historic, poetic, mythic and at times cryptic.

If you are studying a space, evaluating it for some reason, you won't really know it until you can read its central story, the human story behind it. If you are creating a new space, you need to find the story that you need to tell. It's often written in a code and can only be unlocked when you bring two distinct keys to the endeavor. One key is via the hand of research and appreciable "looking." The other is in the hand of your own creative energy, talent and background. On one side you have informed understanding, and on the other you have individual intuition. The two hands together manifest the story. Your designs become the storytelling incarnate.

In theatre this is obvious. We are in the business of telling stories in a live performance. The playwright lays the foundation of the story before us. We bring it to life. I think it's important to note that the play's script is seldom the whole story. It takes the actors, artists and audience who bring their "selves" to the project to help unlock and decode the story with their experiences, energies and efforts. We, as creative thinkers and doers, are required to see, in many ways, the sinew that binds life to world. For this book and I, it is about observing the connective thread that ties humanity and space. The reason I find this important is that space is an indicator of cultural realities. Culture influences design and design moves culture. Space tells that story.

Connective threads are observed in two ways with space. They are observed in the *bold, universal strokes* and in the *subtle nuances*.

The Bold Strokes

A space can make a bold gesture. It can possess a grand sweep. This is common in creative architecture, monument design and in stage performances of high style, such as with opera and epic plays. Such a bold stroke can be easily discerned. It is usually the dominating form in the space, such as a curving wall that enwraps the world or a monolithic cliff-like structure that rises into the sky. Everything in the space resonates with its statement. It sings the song of its collective culture. It may radiate from the core life within it or may be carved by the winds that shape the life. Either way, it is a concise expression of the culture. As scholars and makers of space, we need to consider the bold strokes and respond accordingly. This means that we need to imagine how humanity in the space develops, what the governing force in the space is, and how is it expressed. And if we are observing a space that expresses with a bold stroke, we should enter it and soak it all in, let it move us and allow its rapture on us so we may be one with the flow of the people. If we are designing, we should use our imagination and other helpful resources to place ourselves in the culture for which we design. In that place, we can appreciate the energy that drives the culture. Then, we can strike boldly on our own. And that bold visual choice can become the perceptual link between the people and their world.

As a designer, I need to place myself not only in the culture of the play as written, but also in the context of the production concept. It may be that we are setting a play written long ago into our own cultural framework. For that, the bold stroke might emerge from the power of the play *and* the energies driving the world of our setting. My design for Shakespeare's *Richard the Third* is set in a post-apocalyptic, urban future. This is a conceptual choice. It aims to bring recognizable imagery to an audience that is far from Elizabethan England. By doing this, the story is brought to life, making it immediate. The production resonates with an audience not far removed from September 11, 2001. They know the look and feel of turmoil. They can appreciate how chaos and the demolition of previously reliable structures can disrupt our equilibrium. The production concept aims to link the tumultuous nature of King Richard's realm with our current understanding of tumult. The production shows what an urban landscape would look like if the disasters were in surmountable, a world in ruins and abandon.

The set is a bold composition made with shards of previously reliable structures. There

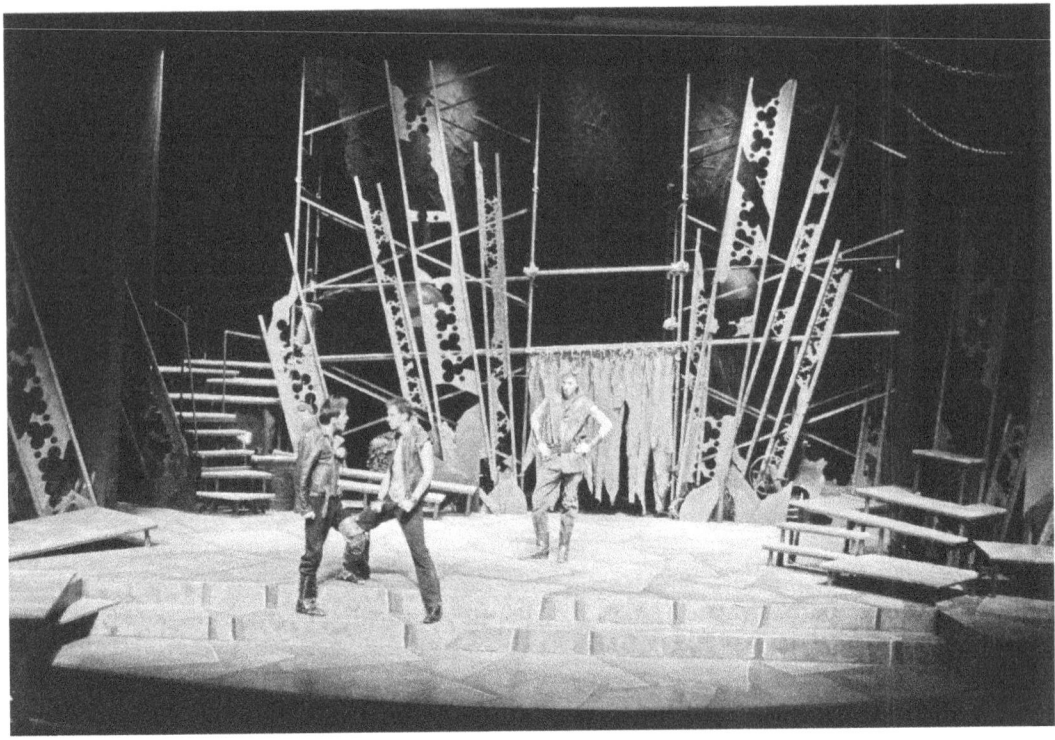

A design for *Richard III* by Shakespeare. Design by the author.

are pieces of trussing, scaffolding, and industrial framework mixed with bits of gothic tracery and buttressing. Skyscrapers and basilicas are crashed to the ground and their remnants stick up like fractured bones on a battlefield. The composite assemblage of these remnants is eerily similar to images of the fallen towers. Yet it doesn't possess the sense of hope and the promise of rebuilding. It is far from salvation. It is rusting through. When you stand back and look at it, you get the impression of an explosion in freeze-frame; all of the remnants make up one collective collage of space in drastic motion. It is a bold stroke that connects the world of the play with the people in it and their audience. It is a connective thread between space and souls.

These kinds of design efforts are routinely successful with plays of great intensity, great language and great characters. I'm always happy to work with Will Shakespeare as his craftwork always inspires me to find a grand statement that might strive to live up to the language.

Subtle Nuances

Not every space speaks so boldly and not every story demands a loud voice. A culture may express itself in softer tones. There can be subtle nuances in a design that do the work. These gentle visual expressions in a space can engage with the inhabitants in a myriad diverse ways. To illustrate this, I'll use a single and subtle device, an object we all can envision, and discuss how that object, a design nuance, might connect with the people in the space where it resides. This is for a hypothetical stage production in a typical theatre space. The object, for the sake of discussion, will be a small, framed portrait sitting on a table in the space of a realistic interior stage setting.

That portrait can impact the people around it — the characters in an imaginary melancholy play — in the following ways. It can *reflect* them, *stimulate* them, *foster* their interests, *connect* them to a larger thing, *lead* them to something or something to them, *carry* something for them, *contradict* notions about them, *question* them or things about them, *steer* them, *echo* their feelings and expressions, *comment* on them, *deepen* the understanding of their lives, *characterize* them, *punctuate* moments of their existence, *accessorize* their lives, and *accompany* them, to name a few. Here's how the little portrait might do these things:

The little portrait is of a handsome young man in black and white. The depth in his eyes is rich enough to be seen from the house. The frame is made of reflective metallic silver and has a delicate relief of scrollwork embossed into it. The people dwelling in the space are a family that is struggling with a loved one's mysterious death. At the same time, they are struggling with confronting their own weaknesses, true natures and the conflict between impulse and decorum. Among other qualities, the face in the portrait has an expression of ambivalence. It's hard to tell if it is smiling or contemplating. It's an enigma, not unlike the *Mona Lisa*.

This lack of emotional commitment *reflects* the struggle between urges and expectations in the family. The handsome face occasionally draws attention and when members of the family glance over to it they see the potential of youth. This *stimulates* some of them to act out, before it is too late. The presence of the portrait encourages a dialogue about the young man's role in the family. Everyone in the group warmly regards him. This *fosters* a bonding among them despite their tendencies to quarrel. In fact, the young man's presence looks somewhat angelic, a benefit of good photographic lighting, reminding one or two of the family of their strength of faith and this *connects* them to a higher power.

The reflective quality of the silver frame *leads* a character closer into the family circle where he recognizes the young man. It *carries* the weight of his guilt because he has certain regrets from his past that he vents out while talking near the portrait. But the frame also is a bit garish and *contradicts* the frugal nature of the family. The juxtaposition of the warmly regarded figure in the frame and the garish frame itself is a bit of a contradiction that *questions* the "real" values in the family. As a result, a discussion on values evolves into an argument; the portrait's features *steer* certain factions to stand aside where they do not see the portrait because it makes them feel uncomfortable as the argument proceeds.

For other factions, the contradictory nature of the frame's appearance *echoes* their internal cries of confusion. There is a certain smirk in the face's expression and that seems to *comment* on the irony of the family's issues. It seems to take a moral stance. As it smirks, it stands isolated in the center of a large table giving it a shrine-like stature. This visually glowing and sparkling image has the effect of *deepening* the magnitude of the scene being played out. The scene begins to look like a cathartic ritual. This *characterizes* the family as an archetypical gathering of representative individuals. The fact that the frame is decorative and an adornment in the center of their gathering, makes it an amulet that *accessorizes* their collective body. It becomes clear, as the play concludes, that this family, likely planning to move from the dwelling they are in, will take the portrait with them as they go. It will *accompany* them because they need it to propel their emotional lives.

There is a story being told here. It is a fairly ordinary family drama with some extraordinary realizations that crop up. The portrait acts as a catalyst for these realizations, a subtle design feature that never has to be directly acknowledged yet connects the people to something much deeper, something once latent in their emotional space that is rising up. The nuance connects people to their space and so tells a meaningful story.

What I've done here is to take a microscope to a minor object and examine how it syncs with culture. When I do this kind of thing, I must ask, rhetorically, if the nuance arrives by some driving force in the present incarnation of the culture. And what, exactly, is that force? Or does it arrive up from a substratum that is the base for this and other living cultures, making it an outgrowth of a much larger power. Either way, it's important to note that there is a force or power behind the subtle nuances manifesting in a space. And surely such a force shapes the bold strokes I discuss above. That force is a vital element in the story of space.

One example of the use of subtle nuances in a realized show comes from my design for the operatic version of Thornton Wilder's great American play *Our Town*. The opera, like the play, avoids the trappings of conventional scenery. It is an empty stage space with a few cosmic gestures like sparkling stars in the air. Nothing much else. In the final act, the heroine, Emily, is dead but returns to her past as a ghost for one fleeting moment. It is her chance to recall the beauty of simple daily life. That moment, which is encapsulated in a scene around a breakfast table on Emily's childhood birthday, should really drive home the notion that life is precious. The audience should emotionally relate to the real beauty in such a simple affair. In our production, the "subtle nuance" for that moment has us frying up some bacon in the orchestra pit and casting an aroma over the audience as the scene plays out. What can remind people of their precious moments at home among family more than the enticing bouquets of a kitchen? Smell is a powerful reminder. The smell of bacon in *Our Town* is the connective thread between the audience and the story of the space.

* * *

On the surface, a space reveals a great deal about itself and its tenants. We can observe that fact when we don the mantles of pseudo-physicists, geographers, musicians and historians, etc., of design. The surface is what we can *see and describe*. But there is a deeper attention that helps us to *know and define*. It involves a less analytical approach than what I address here in Part One. Instead, it is more empirical. It demands that we engage, contemplate, interpret, judge and touch the subject. In other words, we need to immerse ourselves fully in space. I suppose it seems that I'm suggesting we "boldly go where no one has gone before." Whether anyone has gone before does not matter. The boldness lies in the willingness to enter as an individual and discover with a personal reading. We need to go *into* space to *know* space. And that is the subject of Part Two.

Part Two

Knowing

A costume designer I know is conducting a fitting with an actress. The garment, to be used in the climatic last scene, is nearly complete and it is time to decide if it will suit the show. After some fussing with some of the finer details and making some final notes to her draper, the designer looks at the actress with an air of satisfaction, smiles and tells the actress: "This gown will make the final moment *perfect*." The polite and young actress is glad to hear it but can not avoid asking the designer: "How do you know?"

The designer winks at her and replies confidently "I just *know*."

And, that's *OK*.

Sometimes you do "just know." Ask anyone who abides by faith. Ask any expectant mother who envisions the sex of her yet-to-be-born child. Ask the master coach who can read in the eyes of his athlete whether she has completed her drills. Ask the seasoned war general about his sense of enemy movements. They "just know" because they've been through something. They've been through some kind of illuminative journey that exposes certain truths. And as those truths are illuminated, certain sensations occur and mental connections are established. This is experience. And with experience, the participant proceeds with an ability to know.

As I attempt to illustrate in Part One, *Seeing* is analytical. You look. You describe what you see. *Knowing*, on the other hand, is empirical. You step in. You encounter what is there. Through your experience, you can give the subject meaning. By living with it, it takes on meaning. If you can establish it's meaning, you can *define* it. Part Two is about *defining* space.

In Part One, I illustrate what might be described as a kind of "quilt." It is a quilt that, as a whole, represents a process of considering space (and for that matter, considering *design*). Each patch of the quilt is a different component of the consideration. And I label each component with the title of an academic discipline. These are each *ways of looking* at a general reality, a physical body. I'd say it is a fairly comprehensive quilt in that way. These are the ways of looking at space used by a theatre designer. As a whole it is a composition of many glances. But under the quilt lies something much richer. And that is what I approach next.

Part Two asks us to close our eyes. Contemplate instead of look. And it urges us to move toward a firm awareness of that which is beyond our sensory comprehension. This requires what I call a "deep reading" of space, a quest for its mysteries. It's a search for those qualities not immediately evident, yet vital and real. These are qualities that might be spiritual, psychic or interpretive. As a result, they are things we might find a bit ethereal, intangible and therefore troubling. But they are things that are necessary ... necessary to know.

10

The Soul of Space

With an intentional gaze, we can make a concrete observation of space. With good imagination, we can form a fairly clear vision of a space we might design. But our observations and visions will tend to refer to the surface, the tangible topsoil. Might I make a suggestion? I suggest we mine. Mine for a core. I suggest there is a deeper place, a deeper thing to know.

I suggest that space has a soul.

A soul is a thing I define as a deep and true nature, a source of being, a central essence. It doesn't necessarily possess mass or material. It may not don a face. It may not be resolved with equations and formulas. But you know its there. Like the "soul" singer might say, you know soul music when you hear it. It makes you dance or cry. You know the soul of space when you are in there. It's deep. But it radiates throughout. And you can sense it. And, you can read it.

Svoboda's famous design for Durrenmatt's *The Anabaptists* is a timber frame sphere. It is perforated so you can see through it to the characters within. It is essentially a globe, a space reminiscent of our own planet with latitude and longitude lines depicted in arced timbers. You see it and you feel it spinning even though it is rigidly fixed.

The space offers some metaphorical value for the play, but more than that it exudes a distinctive ethereal identity. As you look at it, you sense something on the periphery of your consciousness. It seems primeval like something you have always known, but cannot pinpoint. Resembling a familiar vessel or two cupped hands that hold something or someone, it stokes a feeling of affinity. With elusive and momentary recognition, you sense its significance. Perhaps this is because the sphere ties back to creation, the womb, the earthy origins of culture and thought. It is a distant memory of an importance you *just know* is there. And its presence seems profound and fundamental, connecting to the story of the play *and* to your own story. That is how an encounter with the soul of space may go.

Now, some might find the term "soul" archaic or harboring a distracting religious connotation. I understand. So I'll include a parallel sciential concept. I'll suggest that space also has a psyche. A psyche is a thing I define as a core consciousness, a connection to the universe at large, and, in a way, a kind of mind. This is simultaneously complex and broad. I know. But I've been in this field long enough to believe it can be reduced to its singular importance and understood.

I also suggest that we explore these things (or *thing*, as soul and psyche might be one and the same). Our exploration might include probing the psychology and spirituality of space. We might approach it like an anthropologist as well. Anthropologists immerse themselves into a culture. They become one with the culture, albeit from a necessary margin. By being in the culture, they come to know the psyche and maybe the soul of the culture. More on the Anthropology of Space can be found in Chapter 11.

This kind of exploration or immersion should be contemplative. There should be the allowance for you to incubate the input. It's not a measurement. It's more like osmosis. The value of reaching some understanding of the true nature of space is manifest in how it enhances the design approach. If you are a designer, this applies to your process. By knowing the living natures and potentials for space, you can approach the design with a nobler and wiser intent. You need to define what is at the core of your project's purpose. What is the center of the space's raw existence? Establish that, then design out from there.

Witnessing or experiencing these kinds of elusive natures in the worlds around us emboldens your creative engine. So I suggest pursuing the deeper places mentioned above. To further their understanding, I'll start by discussing the psyche of space in more detail.

The Psyche of Space

The Central Question

The first step I'll take is to confront a central question that never seems to allow escape. It's a nagging query that lies at the root of all civilized institutions, including religion, morality, education and government. Here's the gist of that question:

Does something significant lie underneath the surface of reality as we know it? And is there a core purpose or energy that drives that reality? Some might interpret that kind of question as akin to asking if there is a central power in the universe. Is there a guiding force, with a vision, in the cosmos? And you might find parallel questions in psychology. Is there a deeper essence to the human mind? Is existence a tangle of random action or is it the manifestation of a deeper, unified force residing somehow in the subtissue of our grey matter? And what is the nature/origin of that force?

In my field, that question is modified to ask if there is a deep, unseen and influential "essence" that lies under (or all about) the surface(s) of a space. Is this perhaps an unintended meaning, one that may not have been consciously known by its maker? And, is there a strand that stems from that essence and connects it to its attending culture? Or even to humanity at large? Does the space have a subconscious kind of landscape that connects it to a larger cultural subconscious that lies within the psyches of the tenants? In fewer words, does the space share a similar psyche with its dwellers?

Is a space's essence vital to the existence of that space? Does the space depend on its own central purpose/meaning/core/psyche to exist at all? If so, isn't the space defined by its essence? And are its tenants dependent on that essence to function in the space? If so, doesn't that mean that the core essence is inextricably tied to the cultural inhabitants? And doesn't that, in turn, mean that there may indeed be a kind of collective unconscious that connects space to its people? If so, it's quite a remarkable consideration for a spatial designer. In the theatre, designers try earnestly to establish that deep connection between the play's characters and their onstage physical world. If they are good, they begin there. They lay down the "psyche" first.

To take this all a step further, I wonder if the "psyche" of a space can communicate or express itself in some fashion. Does it possess a hidden voice that exudes sublimely from a deeper realm? Do we need to turn our heads and cock our ears to hear it? And does it use a psychic language that only our own psyches can interpret? Or does it, in fact, speak blatantly, loud and clear and in-your-face? What are the characteristics of the spatial psyche? All such questions are outgrowths from a trunk question regarding the existence of a psyche. Does such a thing exist?

The Answer

Here is the letdown. Here also is the truth: It's impossible to prove this kind of thing. Religion, psychology, philosophy, and the social sciences have all tried to do so admirably. But they have only posed hypotheses and articulated beliefs, not proof. This is because proof is a concept reserved for processes of seeing and documenting tangible evidence. These processes resemble those I discuss in Part One. Law and concrete science depend on proof because extraordinary claims require extraordinary evidence (to paraphrase Carl Sagan in his landmark book *The Demon Haunted World*). But I am not so sure that all manner of knowledge demands documental evidence. In my sectional introduction above, I argue that to *know* does not always command proof, but personal experience. I believe that many artists would concur, as would a bounty of religious devotees.

All I can offer is a prompt to pursue that kind of experience. I nudge the quest to affirm the existence of unseen truths and to come to know them in all one's ventures. Since I am a spatial designer, I urge all other designers to embark on that pursuit deliberately as they pass through existing spaces day to day, and to apply their discoveries in their subsequent creations. And based on their experiences, I encourage them to contemplate the things that arise in the passing. Consider what it all might be saying. If the language perceived in a spatial world seems odd, strive to interpret it. The language will be expressed in spatial moments, chance glimpses and latent qualities that are sensed. Indeed, the soul of space can be read with the senses. There will be messages and meanings and some kinds of understandings that you *just know* are there.

As for the psyche of space, you may find it via brush-ups with the psychological attributes of a space. These attributes emit from a cultural base and manifest momentarily in many ways. It is the responsibility of the visitor to remain open to their manifestation and read them as a psychologist might, or maybe as a curious enthusiast of mysterious behaviors and phenomena. Take an interest and contemplate a meaning based on your own background and instincts. Try and connect the psyche of space to your own psyche and trust where that may lead. It may lead to an affinity and an appreciation of how physical environments join with physical beings via a metaphysical union. Take a moment to listen and to allow the internal voice to emerge. This is what the therapist might do as she conducts an appointment. What follows is a description of what a psychological encounter with space might involve.

The Psychology of Space

A key objective of spatial design is to tap into the deeper substances of spaces and come to know their real value. The value will reflect the spaces' potential. I find this objective activated when I enter an empty theatre space and begin to imagine what kind of dramatic event might blossom in its shell. Part of that imagining involves contemplating the true nature of the stage and house, interpreting how the cultural story connects to the cultural reality. There could be a hard and guarded boundary between audience and performance; or there could be a generous, interactive intimacy, etc. I find that design is about devising the appropriate vessel for that connection. As a result, it has become my exercise to explore existing designed spaces with a probe to unveil such cultural (and personal) connections. In that exercise I become a bit of a spatial psychologist, or in many cases, parapsychologist.

Of course, it is impossible to conduct a real conversation with a space. I cannot ask it the kinds of leading questions you might hear in psychotherapy session. There is no way to uncover deep truths if the hard material of walls and floors cannot actively speak. Instead, I need to open my senses in alternative ways. I need to see the shadows through the dense filigree, hear the nuances behind the din and smell the notes amidst the fervent bouquet. By allowing myself to absorb such multi-dimensional input from my surroundings, I can derive clues and expressions of something fundamental. This requires a walk without too much scrutiny, a mind devoid of distraction. It also requires willingness and curiosity, a desire to find out what thread binds culture and container.

That thread is the relationship. The relationship is the key. The makeup of the space will expose the nature of that relationship and can help tune us into the deeper foundation.

Choices in spatial design and construction methods may reflect the logic, practice and governance of the time when they were made. This can be observed in the history of theatre design. In 1920's Europe, a movement called Constructivism arises. It is evident in other art forms as well. Designs of this movement are characterized by their non-representational quality, pure structure for the sake of providing structure. They could be simple arrangements of steel and wood with barren platforms and skeletal facades that do not depict or even resemble an illusory world. Instead they provide an interesting jungle gym for performers to tell their story. The audience fills in the details with imagination, or more appropriately removes its desire for an aesthetic backdrop and tunes more into the hard messages of the story, taken at face value.

Constructivism itself reflects a critical moment in cultural evolution. It comes at a time of major transition. As the world enters the height of the technological/industrial age, science is boldly treading on grounds that would change religion and philosophy. The world is also between wars and politically unsettled, with no cultural firm-ground, no solid identity. Spirituality is waning. Hard reality, with a bit of off-balance sensory skew is at the center of the artistic community. There seems to be a compulsion to scream or cry out, to push anxiety to the forefront. There is little impulse to look inward or to dream. In fact, there is little chance to sleep; society feels the urge to keep moving, like a machine in the factory.

In a reflective manner, Constructivist theatre sets appear to be haphazardly thrown together. They resemble contraptions, quickly built to carry messengers, but possess no visual "beauty" per se. They get the job done and nothing more. There isn't a hiding place or escape for the inhabitants. And this quality reflects the anxieties of an unsteady world, a world that is in the process of turning toward a new set of values and teeters on a not-yet-established, unreliable base. In the architecture of this time, entrepreneurs are quick to build. But what is built does not hold a place for God. It is an impulsive and an efficient framework, coated with glass and concrete for function's sake, skyscrapers instead of cathedrals. Even the art deco ornamentation is sleek and clean, without lush relief because it stems from a world with little or no relief. In these ways, living spaces reflect the psyche of the time. Walking in or watching an actor walk through Constructivist spaces gives you the sense of the tension, shallow hastiness and lack of equilibrium present in the collective, cultural mind of the time. It reports the status of the collective soul.

Spatial designs may also echo the behavioral roots of the people in them. This can include their wishes, desires, dreams and fears. In fact, it can include all manner of motivational devices, the internal engines that drive action in human beings. In the art world of the late nineteenth century–early twentieth century, this idea is manifest in Romanticism. Romantic artists, poets, composers and writers are famous for their embrace of the nature and inner nature. Unlike Constructivism, Romantic art reverberates with a passion for the exotic and the mysteries of the wild. The "wild" I refer to includes the treacherous caverns of mind and emotions. Romantic art is deep with expression and does not try to restrain from confronting or exposing wishes, desires, dreams and fears of its audience. Spatial designs from this time radiate with the same kind of emotional density. A walk through a lavish arboretum or conservatory filled with thriving flora from distant lands stirs one's imagination. It compels one to dream of the fancies and creatures/characters of worlds beyond. It conjures the subconscious and perhaps inspires lust and longing. Highly emotional music, such as the works of Debussy, has a similar effect.

The reason these effects occur is because the attributes of the created world, or what I call the psyche of the space, has a strong tie to the psyches of the tenants. As I allude to above, the designer's experience with these psyches and/or souls is a kind of psychology/parapsychology. And this psychology/parapsychology is a matter of *encounters*.

As you pass through a space, or observe it with a perspicacious disposition, you may sense a presence of something that commands your attention. The presence may seem oddly indescribable. But it has attributes that reach you and you can relate back to it in some personal fashion. This encounter should make you pause, contemplate and try to find the connection. I believe this is a connection of numerous psyches, old and new, theirs and yours, and vitally important. Such an encounter will eventually express the soul of the space. It's a soul you can know. A list of some possible encounters in this vein follows.

Encounters

Each of the following represents a potential encounter you might have with a space. These are revelatory encounters with spaces that make you feel a certain presence. They tend to be somewhat mysterious, compelling and require contemplation. For each, I will describe:

- The sensation you might feel
- What your contemplation might reveal
- The lesson a designer can take from the encounter
- An example of a stage design that possesses these qualities

The encounters are: *Resonance, Gender, Ghosts, Angels, Demons, Communion, Pure Energy, and God/god.*

Resonance

The Lakota holy man said: "I hear the herd rumbling miles below..."

In a space, such as an old rustic building, you might sense a vibration from the past. It comes through and resonates with the presence of past emotions. It vibrates through its design elements like echoes of laughter and shadows of tears, all captured in color, texture, shape and line, etc. As you walk, you might, in mind and imagination, hear an echoed howl and feel the shaking timbers around you. You smell steam and see in your mind's eye a gaslight piercing the perforations in the flooring strips. It's a locomotive rushing along an ancient railway, cars carrying souls to some promised land, some grand dream in some mythic vision. And yet it is not real. It is a resonance that rises up from underground as the sights, smells, textures and sounds radiate in psychic waves. The space you walk buzzes upon a catalog of cultural strata. The space is a physical echo. You pause, close your eyes and contemplate all this sensation.

Your contemplation reveals to you that over time, a culture, as it evolves, lays down artifacts not only physical in nature, but also emotional and psychic. It places these reminders like the measures of a lasting song playing below the soil deposits on an eternal tape loop. And these reminders rise to the top as a profound story is told, not in words but in transcendent vibrations that stir your own core memory. It's similar to a monk's levitation at a moment of great spiritual enlightenment. The story lifts because it must. Something important below sets it loose and all that is built upon it has been designed for this very phenomenon. It seeks you. You perceive how the colors and shapes of the timbers and floorboards are perfectly logical outgrowths from the train trestles that reside (figuratively) somewhere below. The story is clear to you because something within you is part of that story.

If you are a designer, you learn from this encounter. You learn that meaningful spaces are built on a layering of defining strata, sometimes mythic and epic. You must put that layering down as you design a space. Research the history of emotion in the culture and design a base that holds an element of that history. If there was a past tragedy (real or poetic), weave a remnant of that tragedy into the substrata of that space. If there was triumph, be sure to equally implant facets of its celebratory jewels in the foundation as well. The profound and defining moments of cultural history should resonate through to the present surface.

A Design: My design for *Hamlet* is set in the industrial revolution, early in the nineteenth century. The show presents the inner workings of the mind of the lead character. And those works are rendered with the imagery of an enormous dismantled clock on the stage. The springs, gears, cogs, hands and face are strewn across an industrial structure made of stairs, platforms, bridges, gantries and ramps. It's a collage of a factory world adorned with the large clock mechanics. The space resonates with an ancient, creepy vibe. It also resonates with the ghostly elements of the play and certainly with the steady, calculating killer urges of the title character. The set employs a drainpipe with a regulated drip-drip-drip effect. This resembles the ticking pendulum of the clockwork. All these elements hold an air of troubling inevitability. It's like a machine headed for disaster. And brewing up from below is a stew of seeping gas that suggests a sinister intent and a vile aspect of human nature dating back to much darker times, in this case the time of Edgar Allan Poe. It's a space resonant with a cold, cruel world.

Gender

The good rabbi said to young Joshua at his bar mitzvah: "You will always walk with both parents, one in your ear and one in your eye...."

Swiss Psychiatrist and theorist Carl Jung (1875–1961) is celebrated for asserting that human psyches possess an aspect of the opposite sex that can impel behavior. He labels the masculine and feminine energies in our psyches as "animus" and "anima" respectively. I am a male. But I have a female side to me. That feminine side might, at times, drive my actions. It's a fairly acceptable notion in popular culture today. And its roots can be traced back to Taoism, where it its professed that a "whole" existence necessitates a balance of opposites such as with gender.

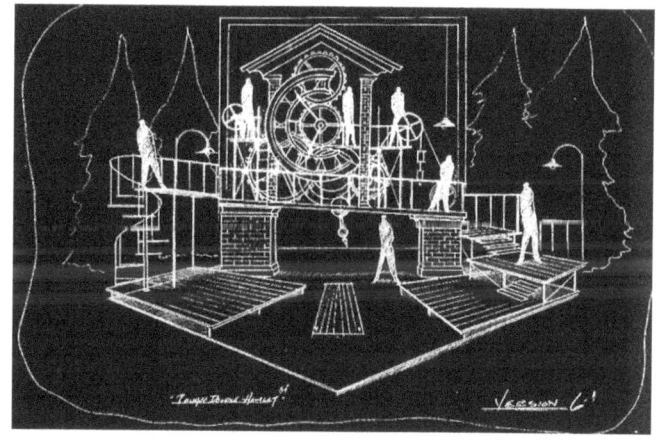

Thumbnail sketch of design for *Hamlet* by Shakespeare. Design by the author.

Following suit, it might be logical to say that each of us has an element of both our father and mother within us. Certainly, this is genetically verifiable. It might be psychologically evident as well. Occasionally one of these gender qualities is dominant in a person. And the nature of our feminine or masculine tendencies can be personally defining. I suggest that a space might also possess and deliver a dominant gender quality, one that you can encounter via a visit with the space's psyche.

You might be walking through a well-designed history museum. There may be several distinct galleries within the museum, each covering an important subject. The first one you enter may cover the topic of the holocaust. The designers, realizing the horrors inherent in this subject matter, may have intentionally relaxed the intensity of the space to generate feelings of sympathy rather than anger. As a result, the entry gives you a welcomed or invited sensibility. It may cause you to ponder your place in the world for a moment, allowing introspection. It may seem nurturing and deepening, drawing you in to explore its nuances. The walls may be concave and seem to hug you. It may have soft edges. And since the subject it covers is so profound, it might channel a regression in you, taking you back to your secret origins, your own foundation, and your own dark history. Obviously, these maternal qualities suggest that this is a feminine kind of space. The way it touches your psyche is by drawing you back in, to reconsider your deeper and perhaps truer self, to feel rather than act. This kind of spatial behavior is activated by its very composition, its arrangement of component parts. These include a concave or wrapping layout, deep niches, maybe a corridor that leads you to some profound experience.

You then might move on to another gallery, one that covers a subject more concrete and recognizable, such as the history of space travel. It is well lit. There is little shadow. It is honest and clear. The space acts forward, bringing the subject directly at you like the rocket on display in the center of the room. The facts and figures on the wall deliberately project outward from their bearings. The whole place channels a progression. In fact, the subject matter is all about progress and inspires you to dream of where you might go with your own frontiers. The surfaces of the space might be hard, sleek, aggressive and protruding. The impact might be to push you forward and to move you along. These somewhat cliché descriptions of masculine characteristics are fairly obvious signifiers of a male kind of space.

You may pause in each cell and contemplate what these sensations mean. Your contemplation may reveal the notion that the culture in a space is like a space's offspring. Either a mother or father figure within the space's makeup parents the behaviors, customs and objectives of the tenants. It could well be a union of both genders that commits the parenting. The marriage of the animus and anima of space can be balanced or imbalanced, each scenario having dramatic results. These gender qualities will push or pull the tenants, and at times hold them still.

It's interesting that space can have this significance. It can actually be a cultural parent. A designer can learn from this. He should ask: Should I create a world that embraces its tenants or one that propels them forward? Or is it a mix of both? In theatre design, he might ask if the set's gender quality projects toward his audience or toward the characters on the stage. He can control these choices. And they should be deliberate, rooted in an appreciation of the power of gender in design.

A Design: I am fortunate to have so many Shakespeare productions on my resume. *Romeo and Juliet* is one of my favorites and my design for it contains elements of spatial gender. The star-crossed lovers play out their tale in an open environment dominated by two large picture frames tilting and overlapping one another. These frames have sharp edges and no doubt represent the two feuding families. They also represent the tyranny of being grown-up. Adult life, with the uncomfortable realities of feuds and social restrictions, contrasts the impetuous impulses of youth and young love. This is at the center of the play. My set has bits and pieces of enchantment (stars, constellations, symbols of magic and romance) floating into and out of the picture frames, like young lovers darting through the stoic structures of society. The frames, representative of established order, are masculine, father figures that try to control emotional wandering. The pieces of enchantment floating in the space represent the feminine, a tie back to childhood, and the protector of uncorrupted human nature. It is a dance of both parents.

Ghosts

The old man said: "There's that knocking again... P'haps just the wind..."

You may walk in an aged fortress. The stone walls bear the blemishes of slow decay. You can sense that much has happened here and many a soul has passed this way. Your steps come slow. You move with slow respectfulness. As you go you might sense the approach of an odd specter, one that may try to reach your own inner spirit. In the highest reaches of the walls, amidst the darkened corners along a hall, and among the images that hang about the periphery there might seem to wander a quiet and vaporous presence that you feel is there, but do not readily discern. And it stirs your deepest memories, both good and bad. Its presence may be accentuated by the mood of the space and by the formation of the spatial attributes. These attributes comprise the portal that allows the spirit in. If you can temper your guttural fears, you might take a moment to pause and contemplate this encounter with the ancient dweller.

Your contemplation might bring about an epiphany with lasting value. You may have often wondered about these kinds of things, these ghost stories. Now you can claim that it is possible for there to be a invisible presence in a space, an apparition of a soul or a memory from a distant past. It might also be a premonition of something yet to be. And it is possible for this presence to arise, move about and make itself known. It can do this in the hollows of your own memory as you pass through the space. You can be haunted by your own past events, choices, actions and feelings. They can remind you of truths you'd rather forget. This kind of specter might arise if you allow it, or if the space allows it through its own design. By opening up the possibility for the manifestation of a haunting presence, you invite it. You may not want it but you may need it.

Designers can take a lesson from this. You can foster the presence of ghosts. When you design a space, be conscious to not expose all of the architecture. Retain some dark hollows from which these presences might emerge. Include some mystery. Don't provide all the answers. Don't tell the whole story. You can do this literally, with clever lighting choices and lots of dimensional relief. Or, you can do it in a figurative way, by somehow leaving the space incomplete, creating forms that suggest there is more beyond their tangible surface, forms that invite curiosity. And more than all this, you should provide passages for the occasional entrance of dark and latent memories to manifest. Don't design the present exclusively. Allow a channel for a bit of the past. This takes a little imaginative pondering.

A Design: S. Ansky's folk-legend play *A Dybbuk* is a ghost-love story. The subtitle for the play is *Between Two Worlds*, referring to mortal and spiritual realms. Two lovers meet at the boundary between material life and ethereal life, one a spirit and one a living human. It is rich with Yiddish history and myth. It poses a lesson on the power of love. My design for this deep play is comprised of a massive bas-relief wall, mostly in shades of grey and silver, leaving the coloration to the imagination. But it is carved heavily with the imagery used by Russian/French painter Marc Chagall (1887–1985). There are floating figures, animals, menorahs, candles, tablets, stars of David, etc. on the carved collage. It is life without gravity, a mythic landscape, impressed dimensionally onto stone walls, like spirits trapped and suspended in space and time. The wall divides the two worlds. At the climactic end, the wall breaks apart and the two lovers embrace on the boundary line. When people stand on the stage they all sense the same thing. They say to the director: "There are ghosts here Henry… Ghosts are in here…." If you can conjure those spirits appropriately, you've done a decent job.

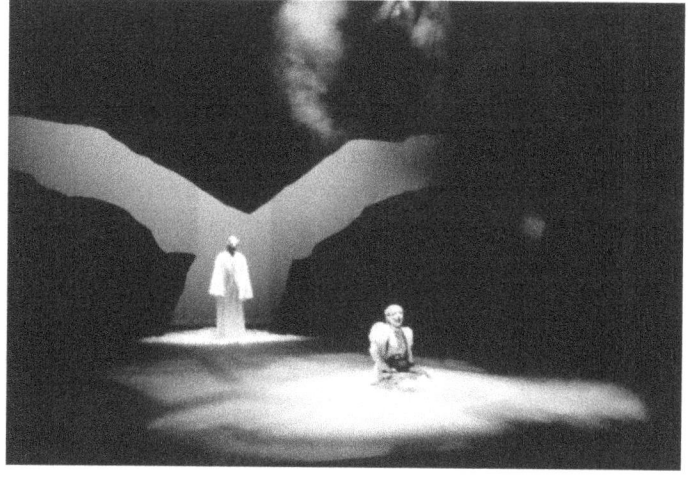

A production photograph of a design for *A Dybbuk* by S. Ansky. Design by the author.

Angels

Artist/Author Maurice Sendak spoke on the radio about seeing an angel float by his bedroom window as a child. A frustrated artist who was listening as he was driving said: "I wish I had an angel float by MY window." Just then, his rear car window exploded into tiny pieces. True story. Mine.

You may enter a large, white marble ballroom. It may be adorned sparingly with a few wall sconces and a pretty chandelier. Side chairs are neatly spaced along the walls. The doors are glass. There are windows along one side. It is a bright and pleasant place. Besides making you feel grand and proper, it also relaxes you. You feel you are safe and in the right place. You sigh contentedly. There may reside a benevolent and seemingly protective presence in the ballroom. It may be one that wraps around the space and offers a feeling of embrace. It may also seem to take a moral stance that might set you straight when you deviate. It might be sensed in the space's austerity, its coloration, the proximity of its perimeter, or in the arrangement of detail (orderly detail usually suggests protection as disorderly suggests abandon).

Now, some might feel uncomfortable here. They may be out of their element. But you are surprised that you are *not* intimidated by such a formal surrounding. In fact, you sense a strange elevation, as if a warden is carrying you through. You feel stronger, like an important figure. You feel the desire to maintain your manners and do no harm. You crave goodness. As this happens, you pause to contemplate.

Your contemplation may reveal the notion that a space can provide a conscience for its inhabitants. You can assess that there is a guardianship in such a space. And you believe that it is always present and reliable. Many inhabitants of the space want to run to it and be with it. They may willingly follow it. Something in there brings them back, and brings them out. And when they are there, it shields them and counsels them too. But, it is not tangible. It is sensed in the psyche.

From this, theatre designers learn that they should design *the container* of their show first, rather than the locale (see Chapter 4 for a discussion of *the container*). This means that they should put the show in a unifying framework that holds the life of the show together. The designer can give that container a power to enwrap ... or possess ... the inhabitants. I'll address possession in the next encounter. The container, or holding shroud of a space, really can give it angelic qualities. You might define an angel as an unseen benevolent presence whose purpose seems to be protection and guidance. You find yourself comforted and yearning to be near it. It becomes like a sanctuary. The surround, as a unifier of a dynamic space, gives it a conscious grounding, a trusted base. You can wander about while you are in it, knowing full well that it won't allow too much danger.

A Design: An actress friend of mine tells me that she loves to go and sit on the stage of my set for the musical *The Wizard of Oz*. She says she visits it in her spare time, just to be there and meditate, to feel like she is floating in the air. It's like she's an angel soaring in the clouds. I know why. The container for that set includes a vast sky, clouds and blue painted all over the floor, the portal, the side walls and backdrop. It's all sky. It's essentially a sky box. If you know this musical you know its many references to the sky: rainbows, bluebirds, tornados, flying witches, falling houses and hot air balloons. The sky is there throughout. This sky box gives my friend the feeling of sanctuary, and levitation. There is an angel in there, perhaps.

Demons

The drunk driver slurred to the policeman:
"I couldn't see ... there were flies on the windshield..."

If angels secure your footing, demons threaten it. And they are persistent devils, coming back again and again if they can, until they secure the object of their desire. What that object is, only they know. Those who are the pursued objects can sense all this. There is a story from the world of pop music about this. A famous singer warns her friends that a demon is after her. She doesn't know why. She is driving a road in a distant land and suddenly sees something in front of her; She swerves, hits a tree, and dies. Her passenger lives and testifies that there was nothing in the street to distract her. She just went off the road.

But something *was* there.

You might enter an old Cajun home in the bayous of the south. In it, you might notice its uneven floor, with creaky features and a sloping nature. It may be affected by the soft ground beneath it and perhaps by the unseen beings dwelling in the mud. It is not what it once was. As you creep around, you might sense a bothersome presence, perhaps one that threatens your stability, peace and equilibrium. It may reside in the asymmetry or unnatural angles of the space. And it may be embellished by an odd color or angle of light or by a specific, nagging image that hovers in the space, such as a vile painting or work of taxidermy. It's a presence that comes forth from a deep hiding place under the moist, unsteady earth.

And it may specifically target *you*. Something in there taunts you. You sense a personal danger. You have an uneasy balance. You don't feel like yourself. At a moment of pause, you stop to contemplate what might be going on. You wonder about voodoo legends and other such things.

These uneasy feelings are likely associated with your lack of proper footing. The world you are in is not at rest. All is not well. The ground you walk is not level and you teeter with vertigo. Your contemplation reveals the notion that any time you fight the laws of nature, known reality, and trusted convention, you risk ushering dark spirits. And there may be a reason a certain angle, image, shape or color bothers you. It may reflect something deep in your subconscious, perhaps a "demon" you've never exorcised.

Being in a space that taunts with discomforting reminders might stir that "demon." And if it stirs, who knows what may befall you? It may simply distract you. And that brief distraction might cause calamity. Distraction is one of the most effective ways to divert you from your safe domain. Once distracted, you could fall under possession, where the confusion overcomes you and you no longer are yourself. A demonic property in a space can do this.

A lesson for designers is that they have another power. In order to intentionally cause attendees in a space to experience these kinds of "demonic" moments, you can manipulate gravity. You can use tenuous rakes and angularity to throw the visitors off their course. Insert "traps" here and there and use unnatural angles and colors of light. Break the rules. This will suspend equilibrium. Dare to disturb. It can be quite effective. This all appeals to the sinister sides of theatre designers. If the play intends to move its audience to change, alarm and urgent action, you should design the space to offer them no rest.

A Design: I have a design for a play called *The Black Swan*. It is not based on Thomas Mann's novella, although it shares the same name. This play is about an aging woman who is confronting death and at the same time is trying to set her family affairs straight. There is a bounty of emotional tension in all this. The ultimate message is that the woman, who has sheltered her family and her own nature excessively through her life, is now trapped in a cage of impending death and is walled in by her own faulty tendencies. My design aims to reinforce the notion of a glass cage. I defy theatrical convention by placing the deathbed scenes behind glass walls, causing an oblique divide between audience and play. This prevents the audience from seeing the flesh of the character clearly. All is distorted, like looking through the sides of a specimen jar at a science project. This bothers the audience. It taunts and annoys them to a point where they have to think concertedly about it. They must confront what they are watching in an unusual way. Some audience members may find in this experience a disturbing truth about their own shelled-in lives. In other words, they may confront a demon within.

Communion

The evangelical preacher spit this out in his loud and raspy southern drawl: "we will-ah remove-ah the witch-ah that walks at the back of the church-ah! We will bring her up to face the lord-ah!..."
There are cheers, applause and then a charge to the back.

Sometimes it's good to join the crowd, to build community. Sometimes it can become a mob-mentality, or worse a blind conformity. But we can stick to the positive for now. Imagine that you have driven to an Ojibwa nation historical site. It is along a dirt road on reservation land. You are there at the invite of some new friends you met on your travels. It is a clearing in a wooded area. Pole pines surround a central, circular area with matted dirt and not much more. What follows is a gathering of forty or so Ojibwa people, all in dark sweatshirts and jeans. They stand in a circle. A very old woman wearing a long leather coat walks to the center, her head bowed. She cries out a word you have never heard and the people all shout back something else. What follows is an exchange of cries, chants, movements and interactions, all lead by the old woman. You may not understand any of it. But it grabs you nonetheless. You sense in yourself an urge to join the group or to dance with the group dynamic. You want to participate, join the "village" and follow the customs. You are drafted to interactive engagement, perhaps stimulated by the ritualistic layout of the space, its overall shape, and a central charismatic entity. In this case, the entity is the old woman. At a rest period mid-way through the event, you pause to contemplate what is going on.

Your contemplation may reveal that circles in spaces seem to affirm communal gathering. It is interesting that a square space doesn't have quite the same impact. There is an equality of participation in the circle. And the circle is magic. It makes for a powerful experience. Often, at the center of a powerful experience is a shaman. The shaman is the thread between the spirit and the people. And the shaman draws you in. The space facilitates the shaman. And so, the design empowers the group. The shaman could be a Catholic priest at Eucharist. She could be a storyteller, sharing legends with a group of schoolchildren. No matter what, the shaman facilitates a form of communion. The space fosters the gathering and the atonement.

From this, the theatre designer learns that his job is more than depicting. It is also more than supporting or reflecting. It is more than providing appropriate visual elements or imagery. The designer can also become a guide, sometimes a spirit guide. I urge designers to strive to bring outsiders to the shaman, to the story. Learn and practice the power of leading. Steer experience.

A Design: I have the pleasure of designing spaces for dance concerts at times. In my opinion, there is no form of dance more engaging than African dance. One design of mine for an African dance concert breaks the standard rules for audience seating. We bring the audience onto the stage and sit them on inverted paint buckets in a circle around the periphery. Even the most uncomfortable attendees clap with the music. Eventually they stand and clap. Later they shuffle around. By the end they are fully in the dance. The whole event becomes one thing, a communion. The liberty of the space, a space created by a circle of buckets, allows this.

Pure Energy

Mr. Spock said: "It's neither Jim. It's pure energy..."

Sometimes the thing you encounter is not supernatural. Yet it is a very noticeable and active, albeit unseen, presence that grabs your attention. You may walk alone into a modern foyer, the entry to a fine hotel. It is attractively lit with crisp shadows and reflections on its shiny walls. It is asymmetrical and curvy. It has tall walls with high ceilings. The ceiling has glints of reflective material like stars in the sky. There are stories about this place. They speak of great romances and passionate unions that were forged within the charming digs. You sense electricity and dynamism in the space. The seemingly static objects in the space seem to have a life to them. And sparks of energy, alive and glistening like jewels, even glowing, are in part charged by their material makeup and their color and light. Things dance about without mode or mechanism. It's motion without movement. This strikes you as strangely enchanting. You pause to wonder and contemplate its meaning.

Your contemplation suggests a compelling possibility. Each space tells a story and that story can be a reflection of past moments, moments of special significance. One can harness energy by injecting a certain kind of "magic" into the space. And that magic is rooted in the spirit of the story being told. A love for that story inspires a spark of magic energy. This means that love breeds energy.

What can a designer learn from this encounter? You learn to envision the things that won't be tangibly observed, but felt. A space should be felt, not filled. You feel energy. You can inject that energy into a design by making certain choices. And the only way to know what choices to make is to envision the potentials in your mind. You have to be able to tap in to your memories and your psyche to imagine what things will provide a spark of energy in the space. I will introduce the concept of *Metaspatial Design* in Chapter 12. Metaspatial Design refers to designing what is sensed more than seen. A designer needs to have a mechanism that allows him to enter that part of the creative process. It demands that you *know* the unseen worlds of spirit and psyche with some acumen.

A Design: Tony Kushner's adaptation of Corneille's *The Illusion* is a delightful play that discloses the heart and soul of the theatre. It also dabbles in matters of love. It is quite sweet. Part of its charm is its rendering of magic. The world of the play is a "cave of wonders." This is not a haunting or forbidding cave. It's a cave full of transcendence, energy and spark. My design for this play includes many of the structures that the plot demands, such as staircases and a large acting area. But beyond the vital needs are atmospheric inclusions. There needs to be a sensation in the space that energies beyond our familiarity are darting through the air like fanciful lasers. My design has long strings of colorful, reflective ribbon stretching over the heads of audience and performers, traversing the entire space. When lit properly, these lines look like beams of colored light, sparkling through the space. These ribbons, coupled with some other ornaments, give the space and the whole dramatic event a high sense of kinetics. Is it benevolent or dark? It's neither, Jim. It's pure energy.

God/god

> *The archdiocese at Fatima was interrogating an alleged seer of the blessed virgin. She was just a child. Little Santa Lucia said: "The pretty lady was there. You couldn't really see her face or body. But she was there..."*

Belief in the unseen. That is a central concern of this chapter. I suggest that space, my artistic medium, has many intangible qualities that are sensed rather than seen. And these qualities have distinct values. I even suggest that these qualities can be envisioned and designed. Belief in the unseen is also a central concern of religion. It is called faith. You may have faith in something beyond your immediate perception that you *just know* is there. You may have faith that it will provide what you need. For many, this is God; or in certain cultures/considerations it is god (with the lowercase g). To believers, God/a god is the ultimate unseen presence. Some might suggest that such a presence is sensed in certain kinds of spaces.

Anecdotally, here is how that might work. Imagine yourself at the bombing of France in World War II. You are seeking cover while you make your way to protected land. You stop in a bombed-out basilica. All that remain are a few buttresses and part of the rose window. There are other refugees huddled in the dark corners of the nave's remains. You join them even though they speak another language and you cannot converse. You feel a strange sense of safety, despite the proximity of bombs bursting nearby. And you find in your affinity for the others there and the awe of the gothic ruins' silhouetted magnificence, a connection to something bigger and more important than all the madness of the world beyond. You sense that in here is a far more basic reality. And in here you have a sense of hope that you will survive. That hope emits from within you and is triggered by something in the collective presence of everything around you, including the huddled refugees.

You sense the presence of an ultimate power. It might be a sense of glory and triumph, the radiance of the spiritual and the guiding light. It may also be much more simple, just a glimmer of light at the end of the tunnel. Either way, it's a force that emits from a central source. All things and beings have access to it, as it is rooted in all things. And you can sense it even in the seemingly mundane trappings of the space where you reside. As you gather with the foreigners in the rugged corner, you glance at the remnants of the old rose window and contemplate what you feel.

For some, certain spatial features can signify a god, reveal a god, allow a god, or even construct a god. And these features have a common connection, a unity. That unity itself can be defined as god, the omnipresent spirit. And that connection may extend to you as well. If it does, it should tie to the roots at *your* base (as a dweller in the space). It should connect to the experiences of your youth, your early learning or the corresponding base form of your culture. This suggests that the god stems from the base, from the beginning and from the root. The god may even be the root, the base, and the source. In that case, one must know the root to know the god and vice versa.

The theatre designer takes a lesson from this. Sometimes it's best for the audience not to see the force. Avoid the deus ex machina. Let the force be with the performance and not the spectacle. Create a space that allows for the sensing of the power source/force. Provide a unity in the design so that the diverse elements all relate. Give all things a common thread. Figuratively speaking, have everything be carved of one stone. Let all elements be clearly the offspring of a single origin. That origin might be called the "god of the space."

A Design: John Cameron's play, *14*, about "corrective" therapies for "curing" homosexuality at Brigham Young University in the 1960s, has powerful messages. It calls out the apparent moralistic arrogance of the Mormon Church, and that draws some controversy. But, that is a surface layer. Below that, is a study of the struggles of the human soul. It looks at how we defy our own sanctuaries and truths, how we often train ourselves to hate ourselves. It examines our cultural fear of deep realities, those things sometimes identified with God. The assistant director on our production of this stirring play is a practicing Mormon. It is easy to be surprised by this. One expects an LDS member, sealed in the temple, to reject or lash out against any endeavor that questions the teachings and beliefs of the church. She even makes claims of receiving intimidating messages on this subject from LDS authorities during her duty. But she has a repeated refute. She tells us, "God gave this play to me."

My design for this episodic play is a field of white: an angular white floor, a white backdrop with dramatic projections, abstracted white columns that flank the stage like pillars of the temple and white furniture. Many ask me why I use white, being so bright and reflective, stark and jarring. Sometimes I suspect there exists an unseen rulebook for design that reads, "You mustn't make a stage set white because audiences will find it too jarring." Oh well, rules are meant to be broken. One easy answer I offer is that white takes projections nicely. And this show uses a lot of projections. But the deeper answer comes from a life-influencing trip I made through the Great Salt Desert region years ago. The salt flats are insanely white. They are akin to snow, yet insanely hot. I came to realize that salt provides a powerful image when my car broke down on those flats and I had to traverse their sandblast furnace by foot. Salt is unrelenting. It is unforgiving. It haunts. Yet, it also purifies. I can attest to being physically "purified" by the end of my trek. The play holds the exact same idea: Those realities that we must confront, our deepest truths and the seemingly forbidden sanctuaries of our deepest dreams and desires haunt us until we face them, admit them, embrace them and then can be purified by them. In some teachings, God follows this exact same process.

The white of my set provides a neutral limbo-world where a lost soul in the play roams and eventually finds itself. It is white because white doesn't relent. It offers no hiding place from the truth. As a result, one might find "God" there. By baring oneself, stripping down to the core essence, one can face and commune with this theoretical God. I say to the young assistant director on opening night, " Perhaps your God not only gave you this play, but works on it as a collaborator. If that is true, His presence might be found in the spaces where we least expect, in the most uncomfortable places, the places where we think he shouldn't be." She agreed. He may dwell in both the blackest abyss and amidst the jarring white.

The Spirituality of Space

I often believe that some kind of governing spirit resides in a meaningful space. The designers and builders imprint it there. It is connected to its founding and expresses the deep cores of its attending culture. It is manifest in the spatial makeup and you sense it in many ways as you pass through. Considering such a presence is a practice similar to considering the psyche of space. Only this time it addresses the spirituality of space, a slightly deeper and more romantic concept. The governing/energizing spirit speaks with and through the soul of the space. And it speaks to the soul of the people involved. I believe that one may encounter it, contemplate it, and know it.

It is a powerful notion that one can interface with the spirituality of a space. And it is useful for designers. We have one of the few jobs I can think of where one is charged with "injecting" things like spirits, souls, and even a god, into a created world. Therefore, we also have a responsibility to weave that charge into our practice, to educate ourselves in these strange arts. For instance, it is our responsibility to know how a spiritual presence might function in/with and through space. We need to know the relationship and the potentials that relationship offers. The designer of a church has a practical requirement to include God in the walls, airspace, layout, colors and composition of the environment. This requires some advanced interpretation, imagination and experience. It also requires some foundational observations.

Imprinting the sense of a spiritual presence into a space can be achieved by first understanding how such a thing might manifest in traditionally sacred spaces. Three examples follow. I name them by their architectural descriptors: the temple, the cathedral and the "interior castle."

The Temple

A spirit manifests in and through space. This is evident in the temple.

A temple is a place for quiet, collected worship. It is also a place for meditation, prayer, reflection and learning. The temple implies a holy presence and the solemnity of a divine dwelling. It is an ancient concept. And it is nearly universal. Temples exist in the Middle East, in the Americas and in Asia. Nearly all predominant religions have some form of temple in their architectural canon. Temples also tend to be secret places, places where sacred or protected rites and teaching may occur. Supernatural events are also said to occur in temples, such as levitation and out-of-body experiences. Temples are frequently places for private and personal encounters with the divine. It is the kind of space that cultivates a "soaking" interaction with a god or some similar spiritual concept.

By soaking, I mean that the spiritual presence seeps through the walls and up from the floors and floats in the mist of the environmental atmosphere. As an attendant to the temple, you absorb its permeations. You leave benignly saturated. The architecture exudes the substance of the presence. And the architecture of the temple, if designed effectively, is devised to encourage that in every way it can. It fosters solitude and privacy by providing niched retreats and cleansing atmospherics. There may be perforations in walls, arched ceilings, dark hollows, reflecting pools, smoldering pits, mysterious lighting, places to sit quietly alone and meditate, etc. Each temple is spatially unique depending on its founding culture. This is the kind of place where the individual *person* encounters the spirit. It is a place of individual development.

Templar behavior can find its way into theatrical employments. A stage director can look at how the offerings of the temple interface with the quiet motions of the attendees. It's the use of the space that triggers the spirit presence. And the way temples afford introspection rather than collective actions can be explored by movement patterns and choreography in a performance piece. Maybe there is a character in a play who keeps going back to the same mirror in an intimate room on a stage. That action is personal and necessary. There is a desire to look inward at the self and the space provides a conduit to do so via the mirror. The behavior is like a repetitive chanting, a focused cycling toward deeper understanding.

The Cathedral

A spirit is expressed by space. This is evident in the cathedral.

A cathedral is the grandest of Roman Catholic buildings. We find its original versions still gallantly postured before the skies of Europe. It has its best revivals across the Americas. This is the vessel of High Mass, the prime ceremony of communal worship, with great pomp, circumstance, imagery and protocol. The architecture itself follows significant protocols. The Church requires many of the cathedral's sacramental fixtures and there are many architectural firms who specialize in providing these distinct spatial mandates. It is a reliable and expected structure that can serve each liturgical exercise in the dogma, remaining consistent from county to county, nation to nation, culture to culture. As all Masses have the same recitations, all cathedrals have the same base features.

It is remarkable how the floor plan of the cathedral so reverently reflects the holy cross. The nave is the base shaft of the cross, the longer end. The two transepts represent the perpendicular arms where Christ's hands were nailed or bound. The choir is the heads-piece and the apse is near the "top" where one expects the inscription "INRI" to be affixed. The buttresses, invented to counter the structural compromises of having so many lancet windows letting inspirational light in, bear the cross both literally and visually. At the very "top" of the cross is the lady's chapel, signifying the importance of the Holy Virgin in the Roman Catholic system. I can imagine the hope of the early architects, anticipating their Father, gazing down from the heavens, to be pleased to see this stylized rood anchoring the village landscapes across medieval Europe. Even more pleasing may be the image of so many parishioners flocking into the facades to celebrate the Holy Mass. This is because, therein, the architecture itself and the people interacting with the architecture express their God in a direct way.

The Mass is about the group communing with their Lord. While the temple provides a sanctuary for the individual person's connection to a guiding spirit, the cathedral is devoted to housing a mass of people's collective intercessions and praise. The event is not personal, save for occasional silent prayers. Hands are held among parishioners during the Lord's Prayer and there is a strong group dynamic to the rank and file processions during Eucharist. Instead of looking inward, where a spiritual presence glows deep in a personal envelope, cathedral attendees project their God image outward and upward toward the altar and kneel before Him. As I discuss above, He is elevated and expressed by the cathedral itself. The rows of kneeling faithful reinforce His structural position at the center of the event. God does not merely soak through the ether in the cathedral. The incarnate body is the central and whole expression. The group responds and sings toward it. It's all about the directional worship of the primary image. All the gothic majesty in the architectural surround buttresses that Imago Dei.

So, people use the cathedral to express rather than impress. As they act out to their exalted One, they move en masse both literally and figuratively, as the space becomes an echo chamber of common intonements. The result is a release of energy that can only be activated by the swell of the group. And that energy is the expression of the God figure. Cathedral behavior might be employed on the stage. One can envision a stage full of people with a common cause rushing to action in service of their collective passion. I keep thinking of *Birth of a Nation* and *Waiting for Lefty*.

The Interior Castle

Tapping into the soul of a space can call out a spirit. This is evident in the concept of the Interior Castle.

Saint Theresa of Avila is responsible for conceiving this metaphorical domain. Her mysticism involves a process of retreating into the deepest regions of one's own soul, emptying the vessel of all egotistical elements via an inward purging. She describes an interior castle of the soul, with many rooms or parcels that one by one can be explored through meditative prayer and the rejection of physical and material concerns. The objective is to move toward the castle's central chamber, that destination cell where Theresa suggests one can reach and embrace the inner essence of her central source. It is a deep place, a space that is far from the trappings of any real architecture.

Yet, in theory, it *is* a space. And the process of entering such a space is an act of deep and intense peeling-away. It is far more intense than templar solitude and directly opposes the noisy gathering of the cathedral Mass. You get to the heart of your matter by removing the surface distractions of daily life, including urges and worries. Theresa advocates a kind of descent and search, an exploration and a sacrifice. There is a linear passage to it. By conducting such a purgative passing, you yield your yoke of earthbound duty and begin to allow the release of a spirit within. This is the space of a spirit quest.

If a space can be a journey, it can engage new aspects of life. It can have a power and can lead to change or affirmation. The quest for a spirit, or even the quest for a deep truth, is an epic trek that demands a willingness to dare. If you can think of a space as event, like the arc of a hero's journey, then you begin to unveil the space's purpose and method. Theatre directors always think of the event and how the show happens, how the audience enters an experience, lives the experience and then leaves the experience. Ultimately, space *is* experience, and it could be designed as a spiritual experience.

Designing a "God"

Sometimes, a space can design its own form of deity. This is based on the presumption that environment can dictate a theistic choice. I'll try and illustrate how this can work. One type of definable space is the living environment where a group settles and develops (it could be a clearing on a waterway or the caves in the cliffs on dramatic plateau, etc). From that environment, springs the method for survival (instinct drives this). It could be agriculture, hunting/gathering, etc. From the method for survival is determined the culture. Because the group's focus is on survival first, it builds its ways around that focus. From culture springs the "god" concept. This is because the group feels it imperative to identify the provider for the culture. From the god concept, and the subsequent dogma, are made the defining choices of the people (including art, architecture, clothing, icons, morals, laws, ideology, ideals, dreams, love and hate, etc). These choices define the structure of the culture. The structure expresses and controls the nature of life. So, in the process, the space determines the nature of life. And it creates a "god" along the way. Awareness of this progression can inform a designer because it encourages the establishment of a unifying ideal. Everything is connected. One might design that connection intently.

And designers take note: You should design, at times, an appropriate place for the inhabitants and their higher power to thrive. Doing so allows a restful mindset among the culture's inhabitants and a flowering productivity in the space. But, at times, you might design a contradiction to the inhabitants and their higher power. This will stimulate a magnum shift in that world. All will not be at rest. Change can be induced. This teaches us that space can impact the balance of the world.

Designers tread on high wires.

The Soul of Space

To conclude, I'll reiterate the central point in all this discussion of psyches and sprits. I allege that from the depths, well below the epidermis and skeleton of space, exists an essence that is a far truer nature of its being. In the words of an old German folk poem: "...deeper, deeper, in the depth there is a light...." I suggest that we ought to try to know it. I suggest that such an essential entity converses with the individual souls of the dwellers. It is found during ethereal encounters. And it holds the deeper substance of existence. To know it means to know fully, as it is *the* core. And once you can identify it, you may act. If you are a designer, you may design.

But, design from the soul out.

11
The Anthropology of Space

The spiritual and psychological exploration of space leads to a *way of knowing*. By exposing your previously fortressed selves and daring to enter the spatial midst, you may enjoy encounters with essential spirits. You may sense primal energies. You may realize psychic ties. From these experiences, you might take pause and attend to what you perceive. And in contemplation, you might come to know some significant truths. These kinds of exercises entail personal exchanges with deep forces. What they do not entail is a dialogue with the tenant cultures in the spaces. This is why I advocate for another way of knowing, one that asks you to walk with the culture.

Space and culture are entwined. Space bears behavior and vice versa. People design and build based on their drives and inspirations. What they build spawns the evolution of their ways. Form and function follow one another in a design cycle that ebbs and flows with cultural fluidity. A space may reflect the collective, aesthetic sensibilities of its tenants and the sensibilities of the tenants may be markedly influenced by it. The tenants will design a reaction to the existing form and the use of the new form will stir new reactions that keep the reality moving. Anthropologists address this kind of cultural dynamic. I suggest that we, as designers and interpreters of space, embark on a similar kind of study to serve our own understanding. This is because approaching space in the manner of an anthropologist provides that other way of knowing.

Spatial Constructions

The spaces where we live take on many formations. Humans, in groups, manufacture these formations from a deep engine. The formations comprise a necessary exhalation of life energy rooted in the origins and myths of the culture. And these formations are centered on various kinds of recurring spatial constructions. These constructions are essentially key physical elements in a living space that are used extensively by the tenant group. When observed and experienced in a manner not unlike Anthropology, they tell the story of their culture(s). I believe it is very useful to discuss these as a way of illustrating how culture and space interface. The following are some brief descriptions of several significant spatial constructions we can find in the civilized world. I'll touch on the cultural significance of each based on my own experiences.

The Grid

A grid is basically a network of evenly spaced intersecting lines. It can be completely flat; can take a three-dimensional, or cubic shape; or be purely conceptual and metaphysical. You see grids everywhere in the modern, technological world. Digital data, the Internet, communication systems, utilities, navigation, roadways and land divisions are structured as grids. Modern and current architecture embraces the grid. American office buildings have a grid-based layout of cubicles and departments. The floors of the building are essentially stacked grids. The windows and even the plastic diffuser cells in the fluorescent lighting fixtures are all set up as grids. City streets are grids. Even the way businesses and other modern systems operate is grid-like. The grid is perhaps the most prevalent and dominant spatial construction in the modern world.

But what story does the grid tell us about modern culture(s)? Modern humanity cannot function efficiently without an easily comprehensible structure. Modern survival, as complex as it can be with inflated population and limited resources, depends on abundant production with little room for novelty. Many modern, western, and technological cultures neatly structure all aspects of life into the simplest organizational framework they can muster. By compartmentalizing life into a grid, the culture can keep up with and understand its basic outline. It cannot, of course, appreciate its nuances with this device.

So, the grid is a tool of culture, one that also reflects the culture's need for basic geometry. A culture that must devote most of its energies to rapid creation and maintenance of the created also has a desire for quick and clean amusements. A ninety-degree angle is quick and clean. A group of many such angles provides an easy-to-read foundation map for life. And the grid system allows easy passage for the delivery of fast sustenance and entertainment (cable television, social networking, season ticket packages, etc.). In turn, the grid as a form becomes nearly sacred, revered for its resemblance to the machine, the giver of life in this world. It represents progress and a thriving economy, hallmarks of the western way.

The Elevator

Another aspect of corporate culture is the onward-and-upward mentality. In times of economic stress, this is relaxed a bit. But the desire to "climb the charts" is evident throughout recent time. There is a glittery allure in rising to the top, be it the executive office or luxury penthouse. And we want to expedite that rise. The elevator carries us swiftly at the push of a button. It does via locomotion, not human effort. And when you ride, the elevator comforts with sweet and gentle music to calm your nerves (sarcasm intended).

The elevator represents civilization moving the people rather than the reverse. You could argue that we live in a big machine. If you stand back and look, the city comes across as a mechanical operation. Devices transport us and the spaces we reach all have specific gadgetry to get some job done. The elevator is a machine within a mega-machine and establishes its significance by lifting us to the motherboards of the operating system. By defying gravity, it trumps the lateral movement of sidewalks, buses, subways and cars. In space, it offers easy access to high domains. It does so until there is a fire or other catastrophe. Then the machine must halt and we must default to our own devices. We then must climb the stairs.

Stairways (The Ascent and Descent)

Like the elevator, stairs can lead us vertically. But unlike the elevator, these require an expense of personal energy. You can control the speed and style of your rise and fall in them. As a result, they have a different sort of impact. I will include various types of stairways along with ramps and slopes in this category. They each have commonalities and distinctions.

The Grand Staircase: The grand staircase, or central staircase, offers a grand entrance and exit. It is usually the main artery of a home or dwelling with a slow descent and rapid ascent. People get noticed on the stairs. It is usually a focal point and can provide some visual humor depending on its use.

It represents cultural fantasy in some ways. What lies at the top of the stairs can be a dream, a wish or a fear. When someone descends, they might reveal some trinket taken from the dream space above. Seeing the grand staircase in the center of Graceland, Elvis Presley's mansion in Memphis, you can envision the "King of Rock and Roll" jogging confidently down the steps with necklaces and chains tinkling and glistening. You might wonder about the treasures above. You'd love to sneak up and see. But as a mere "mortal," you cannot.

The Spiral or Winder Stairs: These offer circulinear ascents and descents. The spiral, in top view, is essentially a complete circle with pie-wedge steps. The winder looks more like a candy-cane from above. These stairways exist to save space, since wedged steps in unison have a smaller footprint than their rectangular counterparts. But they offer a dance-like motion when people travel on them giving them a great impact. The sweep of the curving form yields a romantic or spiritual quality. They are mysterious, sexual, and eloquent and draw curiosity. The have an allure. You want to climb them for the sake of *feeling yourself move* on them. They are found in grand halls, lighthouses, church belfries and backstage. All these locales carry an essence of mystery and so these stairways appeal to the curiosity of culture.

The Ramp, Slope and Switchback: You may ascend and descend on a grade without the mechanical aid of stairway treads. Wheelchairs must use these kinds of access devices. They are also common on roads, paths, sidewalks, and in industrial spaces. They are a convenience. Things can roll on them and so they expedite the carriage of goods. Culturally speaking, they offer change without mental calculation. You don't need to be conscious of the steps. They allow thought during the rise and fall. If ascents and descents represent going to and coming from dreams, these types of spatial transitions offer contemplation zones in the passing.

Switchbacks are repetitions of slopes in an alternating array. These allow you a manageable ascent by reduction of grade: lengthening the distance, but relaxing the slope angle. They are found in mountainous regions for obvious reasons. And they are very interesting motive devices in a designed space as well. You might see them in a parking ramp, at a ball field or in an airport (escalators). They are about moving a bounty of people with ease. People pass one another and can see one another in the passing. From a distance, the movement forms a visual "Z" pattern. This composition of human motion suggests a cultural metaphor: our lives are a on a constant series of overlapping rises in a gradated flow. We pass and exchange glances as we ascend (or descend depending on your stance) from cradle to grave, each generation a ramp ahead or behind, but all within sightlines of one another.

Ways

The lateral movement of humans in space is guided by various constructions. The path, road, bridge and labyrinth are some. These are the carriers of culture. They take us on planned treks to destinations or through vital experiences, on the grounds we adopt.

The Path

The path is not the road. It is not a forced linear journey, but one that follows what nature has given. It has rises and falls, turns and obstructions. Yet it is organized and implies a destination. It follows trusted ways of reaching places, perhaps originating with the movements of animals and/or early cultures. Culturally, the path establishes order and provides goals. It also functions as a marriage of nature and structure, a way of using the givens to reach the desires.

The Road

The road is an aggressive defiance of nature. It plows right through "as the crow flies." Its intention is to eliminate the spooks of the wild. It wants to get you there without worry. It is about speed and efficiency. It also avoids the nuances and poetry of the natural world. You "keep your eye on the road" and don't "stop to smell the roses." The rose fields are off the beaten path anyway, out of sight and reach. All you see are the guideposts, billboards and how many miles to go. It is a way designed for your ease. It connects the outposts of culture without the savage encounters.

The Bridge

The Bridge takes us over the dangerous currents. It is a common component of the path or road. In its grandest form, it joins two worlds and spans the previously insurmountable torrents between. It extends the culture to promised lands, tempering the troublesome gaps, filling the void of fear with the substance of cultural ties, bonds and communication. A bridge can be metaphorical. It can be any way of mending estrangement or disconnect. It is the construction of culture that provides unity, despite the trolls. I discuss two famous bridges later in this chapter.

The Labyrinth

You might overlook this one. It can be disguised as mundane and usual, a thing we negotiate day-to-day without completely perceiving.

The labyrinth is essentially a maze, a way that we must tactically engage and resolve. It does not have navigational aids. Thus, it teaches a lesson. A culture might implement its own lifeline challenges to force self-study and analysis. Neighborhoods are not always neat grids. Escape routes may not be clearly delineated. The place where you go may beckon you to explore it, not just rush in and out. It may be designed to force you to take some extra time. This can be a culturally based agenda. It might be set up as an exercise for your cultural indoctrination.

Passages and Dividers

Passages are access constructions, such as arches, doorways, and portals. They are transitional, acting as components of the dividers between worlds, while still allowing passage. They are similar to the bridge but do not possess linearity. Divides are the containment boundaries between segments of cultural space such as walls, fences and windows.

Culture sometimes compartmentalizes life. Private life is especially subdivided. There is usually a significant transition or transcendence between compartments. Your family life is separated from your spiritual life. Your spiritual life is separated from your work life. Yet, you can pass from one to the other, often with ease. By the same token, you might envision planes of existence: your physical existence vs. the existence of your soul, your dreams vs. your reality, etc. These are partitioned by dividers and accessed by passages.

Walls are usually opaque and prevent the permeation of sound and light. They shroud private acts and serve to protect and incarcerate. Doors in walls extend the opacity when closed but liberate the dwellers when open. Windows have the three-fold asset of enclosure, refraction of light from cell to cell and allowing protected visibility to the world beyond. Arches and portals are usually grand definers of transition. They carry an air of pomp and pretension. With no obstructions, they invite, even encourage, passage. The portal also functions as a decorative frame, capturing a picture of a person in passage. Fences keep the predators out and the progeny in. They are safety features and convey the culture's impulse to protect and control wild externals.

Spirit Access

I allude to the paranormal in Chapter 10. I suspect that there are important presences that exist below the immediate surfaces of a space. I am not necessarily a believer in literal ghosts, angels, demons and the like. I tend to be more interpretive. But I am fascinated by the possibility that spatial "holds" exist for carrying certain kinds of indefinable presences. Some spatial constructions seem to be ideal homes for these elusive mysteries and if so, become crucial elements for consideration by designers and spatial "anthropologists" alike.

These kinds of constructions tend to be vessels.

Hollows and other dark zones have a strange and deep emptiness. They seem to beg for a mystical hiding of spirits. Some of these are intentional: crypts, closets and cells devoted to silent deposits of the past. Some are accidental. But either way they seem to serve a function. On one hand, culture must have its sunny clearing, a space to convene and celebrate. This is a display table where a lofty god might view his flocks. Much the same, a culture must have a dark retreat, for its more solemn moments, and for harboring its hidden skeletons.

Towers can be these kinds of holds and they take interesting forms. Some are fortressed, perches for shadowed sentinels who protect the group. Spires point to the sky, reaching for the celestial gods. In them you find bells and symbols, great accompaniments for spirits. Vents and cupolas extend the height of the living space and serve to break the horizontal dominance at the tops of buildings. In each of these you might expect to find a transient presence with easy access in and out. The reason these locations have this quality is because mortals seldom visit them. They are difficult to reach. Their interiors provide a dark vessel for elusive spirits to dwell. And they may do so in our imagination. For that matter, these spatial constructions themselves might exist *solely* in the imagination.

Enthusiasts of the supernatural describe unseen "portals" or "windows" that allow the passage of spirits from their world to ours. They have no material substance. But they tend to be concave in concept. They can be located at a closet door or the corner of a room. A deep dig into the history of the space can expose the reason for their existence. I will address "deep digging" in the next section of this chapter.

General Construction

It seems that civilized humanity is heavily reliant on structure. We tend to build up neatly organized systems of understanding and interpretation to help us define ourselves, our origins, our beliefs, our actions and our mysteries with recognizable forms. This means that we have strayed from acknowledging our dependence on nature. Nature no longer defines our religions, our life systems and our expectations for life after death. Some Christian denominations even structuralize the layers of heaven. It seems that we cannot function without a perceptible framework. We must have a structural language in order to understand our own story. And the structures we build in and around our living spaces can be *read* as part of knowing that story. It is a *Deep Reading*.

Deep Reading

So far in this section, I suggest that we try to know ourselves by experiencing that which resides below the spatial epidermis. We should go within. We can enter like spiritualists, psychologists and anthropologists. In the case of the latter, we must dig deep for essential artifacts. This entails what I call Deep Reading. When investigating a place, a designer or interpreter must decode or decipher the language laid down below the cover. This concept asks one to appreciate the surface of a space but then to dig through (or in some cases, *look* through) the undergrowth, roots, soil, strata and eventually soul.

You are looking for the poetry and the narratives in the foundation. As you go, you map the depths, chart the movements and record the findings. Interpret them. Find the connections. See the patterns. Confirm the meanings. Read down and through. This is a task of intellectual and informed imagination. So you will find yourself doing some personal speculation along the way. But this is a natural part of a creative process. You can't, and shouldn't, remove yourself from the mix. Deep Reading is a useful exercise for beginning a design. In order to decorate your own spatial surface, you need to do some deep digging, deep knowing and even deep writing of the story your space must tell.

In design, much of this is conducted in research. Designers begin with an open mind and many open books. If you can't explore real spaces, you can certainly explore and read evidence of spaces in documental and archival research. You can dialogue with the founding culture of an extant space even without physical immersion. In doing so, you begin by approaching abstractly. Start with global themes, broad keywords. Find a book on the base topic. Adjacent to that, you will find related books on related subjects. Then, look deeper in each of these familial books. The evidence will grow exponentially as you proceed (more on design research can be found in Chapter 15).

Whether you find an inspiring image in a book or in material life, look into it. Look for its story. Imagine its precursors. Dig for its creation myths and fables of growth. Scan for the lessons, the teachings, the philosophies and the epitaphs of its heroes. These can all be found via deep reading, whether by looking at a photograph of an ancient stone wall, or walking through Stonehenge itself. You can begin to analyze your inspirational source by finding its repetitions and themes (many of these are visual). Follow the themes as guides when considering the next inspiring image/thing you come across. And keep going.

You will interpret much of what you find. This means that you will apply a bit of yourself to the "knowing." Knowing is about connecting yourself to the subject at a deep level. You can only do so by reading the "text" of the subject's entirety. As a designer, you can move to employ this research only if it excites you, only if it has become part of you, and only if you know it. Don't use research by merely regurgitating details and facts. Create from the deep meaning out. Or as I say in Chapter 10, design from the soul out. Every great historical site, building, living quarter and monument has a "library" of interpretive information within it. You can find the connection between history, governance, arts, religion, sustenance and all other components of cultural life in your study. And as you proceed, you begin to know how the surface details arrive from that life. With that base of knowledge, you build.

You have to establish *usability* of what you read. *Use* means to pull from and push to. The actual reading is only half of this anthropological journey. Intelligent, informed and poetically interpreted expression is the other half. But I won't preach this concept any more. Instead, I'll illustrate with examples. Below, I share some case studies of spatial deep reading that I have personally conducted. These are brief comparison-contrasts of archetypical places, each with descriptions of what they taught me.

Hopefully, you will deduce that these readings of space, architecture and locale expose the stories of their human connection. This is why I call it *Anthropology*. You immerse your imagination and personality into the subject you observe and soon begin to know its truths. You seek meaning of a place by entering it. That is deep reading in a nutshell. You may also notice that I express the nature of what I've read in what might be coined "deep writings," or poetic replies to my encounter(s) with a place. The creative transition from reading to writing is vital to the design process. Here are five examples.

Five Case Studies of Spatial Deep Reading

The Bridges: Brooklyn and the Golden Gate, Reflecting America

If you look beyond the basic silhouettes of two of America's most profound bridges, you come to know two faces of America. Readings of these two great American icons reveal an honest depiction of who we are:

The Brooklyn Bridge is relentlessly Gothic, with cusped arches on rugged stone towers and a tracery of guy wires that reinforces its haunting magnificence. It represents the ancient, the weathered, the wayworn and as much, the solid. It will not sway nor sink. It is as steadfast as the boroughs it connects. Its piers are mogul. Its towers vault like Notre Dame, with no less reverence. It is about a journey, the immigrant journey from squalor to the promises and demands of the New World. And these promises and demands directly echo the religious teachings (redemption through morality) of the faithful voyagers who settled in the early twentieth century and established one side of America with a rock hard fist.

You can read the story of the Brooklyn Bridge's pugilistic demeanor in the weight of its grand towers. Yet, somehow, you can also find a softer, maternal figure in the cables. The cables weave a graceful filigree, with a gorgeous delicacy that starkly contrasts the vertical masses. These cable web-works seem foreign to the sensibilities of the towers, yet they marry with them devoutly. They mate for life. Their offspring is the bridge's very motion, the passing of souls from one end to another all day and all night. This is New York. It's about brute force, elegance and a perpetual rush. The bridge is never still. People move energetically on it, nearly manic in their drive to take over the world. With this bridge as an inspiration, they definitely will.

On Interstate 80, 2915 miles west, and much farther in the American psyche, is another iconic American span. Connecting the quaint refinements of the Marina district with the muddy hippies of Marin, the Golden Gate Bridge is nearly beatific in its appearance, soaring over the marine layer like a heavenly host praising God and gold alike. Its name is perfect. "There's gold in them hills" and the "gates of Oz" beckon like an angelic seductress. This is California my friends. It is deco-sleek, forward thinking, tan and gorgeous and strangely synthetic. It is about dreams and desires and an honest chance. Often it is the second chance. Unlike its Brooklyn counterpart, it is not an old marriage, but a constantly flirtatious affair. Unlike the Brooklyn, it does not extend a punch but a handshake.

The towers rise to the same heaven as those in Brooklyn. But these are not cathedral spires. They don't represent pious devotion and tough grit. They represent allure and rapture. The Golden Gate Bridge, as a whole composition, evokes the frontier spirit. It carries the same curiosity, hope, excitement and attraction that is found on the sunny beaches, along the Sierra streams and under the hoods of the well-tuned muscle cars that cross it on Sunday. It is all about the curvaceous lines, clean shapes and a friendship with the whitest fog on earth. Its color is the perfect compliment to the sky and the landscape nearby. It is sweetly balanced, symmetrical yet dynamic. It is confident and sexy and stands like a trophy for its relaxed, yet eager home state. You can read all this in the deco armatures and the flowing suspension arms. While in Brooklyn you see an earnest, strong and matte portrait. Here you find a lusty, glowing and glossy pin-up.

These are the two quintessential faces of America, the work ethic and the dream. You see them emerge as the tugboats blare above their churning waters.

Highway 21, Two Roads:
Elemental Encounters During the Coming of Age

There is a two-lane highway running horizontally through the dead center of my home state. Generally speaking, it divides the wilderness areas from the agricultural areas and cuts through several miles of boggy lowland. It is a common, state-maintained paved road, about 150 miles long, mostly straight with only a few towns and Amish colonies to interrupt your impulse to speed. I remember driving it many times during my late teens and twenties. Here are two logs from my diary that if appropriately interpreted become deep readings:

Drive Log 1. February blizzard. Mid-afternoon. Age 21:

There really is no road that I can see here. Yet I keep traveling. I am going from one place to another. So that thing between must be it. The Amish nearby are wisely huddled around their wood-burning stove. I can barely see the grey-brown plumes wafting from their simple chimneys. They have it right. I have it white. It's white in all directions. I am confronting white today.

There is a line that stretches far across this land and I know it well. It reminds me of the icy wires stretching above, with their strange hum. I hear it when I pause and open my window, to try and get my bearings and avoid the ditches that promise certain doom. I must follow a line that I sense more than see. I am to ride it now in these conditions because I have been forced to leave all of my old stuff behind. The clock has turned. I must get to that other place. That stuff behind me is spent. The old, dead dreams are no longer there for me to cuddle. It isn't safe anymore. Something has betrayed me. Or maybe I betrayed it by reaching this very point. Now, I have my reckoning with the white road.

If I stop, I have no place for sanctuary. The Amish wont let me in. They embrace the black. I'm stuck out here in white. If I continue, I may likely perish since I can see no delineators. It's all guesswork. Unless there is some invisible guide among the hypnotic snowflakes, some "windego" perhaps, I am on my own. And cutting through the white on this road is a necessary evil, a painful circumcision. If I don't, I am in limbo. There is no more home. Only road.

I put it in drive and head toward what I cannot see.

Drive Log 2. June. Tuesday Night at 4 A.M. Age 21:

I only have one arm tonight (the other is injured). So it's a little hard to steer. And it's my guess that some deer are about to dash out as they sometimes do before dawn. So I am on as much alert as my sleepy eyes allow. I also have no cash, no means of securing a room for the night. So I sally forth and go. I've done this thing before.

It's fairly cool and there are traces of early morning fog. I slow down for the blinking yellow lights in each town. I see a cop driving down a side street ignoring me. There are no cars or even trucks on my passage as it's a tad too early for delivery and the drinkers don't come out so much in the middle of the week. Besides the silly talk on a distant station, I have the night and the pavement to myself. I can drive in the wrong lane and even do slalom curves between the center stripes for amusement. My only worries are the one arm and the deer. I can't well defend myself.

And then the clouds clear. I forgot that the moon is full tonight. But I am now reminded. I shut off my headlights and can see as clear as day. There are no streetlights for miles, and certainly no headlights. The cop is taking a smoke 30 miles back. No town for 20 more. Something else is out here with me tonight. I know it when I take a rare curve around a bend and come by a lowly bog. Driving in the dark, I see more than I've ever seen before.

I pull to the side and gaze out over the bog. There is a low mist in iridescent glow, thicker than that produced by the best dry ice machine in any ballet. It sweeps across the water. The cattails are silhouetted in a midnight indigo. The moon is a centerpiece between two oak trees.

It's a world without sorrow.

With wonder, I whisper to myself as I stand gazing beside my car. No one can hear me except that thing over the bog.

"...I am being enchanted right now..."

I travel on that pavement still. But I never will drive that road again.

This narrative recounts two experiences while becoming an adult. It represents the yin and yang of youth. We travel a road of confrontation and wonder as we come of age. The linear space of the road can be metaphorical for these key passages of life. But it can also be read on its margins. There is a bounty of deep meaning in those seemingly mundane moments along the shoulder. It's a good idea to stop once in a while and look to the sides. The following reading also deals with some very interesting objects on the side of a road.

Dakota, Tower and Train:
Reaching for Infinity in the Middle of Nowhere

Somewhere north of Fargo along a sugar beet railway that stretches in a straight line as far as an eye can see, is one of the tallest structures in the world, a television broadcast antenna with over three-dozen strobing lights. The railway and tower, two perfectly straight manmade lines, one horizontal and one vertical, make an arresting tandem statement that considers infinity. And they do so amid the most barren and flat landscape imaginable.

North Dakota, with its stoic and proud Lutheran farming culture, is exhaustively flat. And the wind doesn't relent. The cold stays around for 8–9 months and there are only a few remote outposts of civilization, usually marked by a grain elevator or water tower. It's the perfect place to approach infinity. As you roll down the interstate, you parallel the railway, often racing with the long locomotives riding its steel. At night, their headlamps stretch out and extend the train into forever. As you follow that constant horizontal, you can see the vertical sibling coming from many miles away, a line marked by dots of red light rocketing into the atmosphere. It's a dizzying height.

These two lines intersect at a place of no great significance. When they do, they form a cross that unintentionally signals the Christian roots of the local culture. And though this modest culture might resist the daring comprehension of an afterlife, its holy book forces the issue. These steel structures force it as well. They remind you that the ceiling really doesn't exist and the ends of the horizon go on forever. Only in this cold and arid landscape can you perceive such a notion. And the tower and rail drive the point home.

There is another consideration in all this that ties into the concept of infinity. Not far up the railway from the tower are remnants of cold war weapons silos that once held minutemen intercontinental ballistic missiles (ICBMs). For all we know there may still be some secret "live" silos on those plains.

The linear extensions of rail and antenna, thrusting outward and upward, become a little disturbing when flavored with this knowledge. They remind us that beyond our earthly reach, exists a greater potential to take things farther. And perhaps it's farther than we should go. Our advances occasionally flirt with infinite destruction. Maybe the self-imposed limits of the Lutherans who farm under the tower and above the silos are doing good service. Maybe those limits keep the Lutherans grounded on a proper soiled plane. Maybe it is good that these toilers don't get too starstruck by the dangerous stretches of the cosmos, or mess with the ends of the earth. They might say, "Don't look up at that thing; you'll get vertigo. Don't look out on those tracks; the light may blind. Keep your head down and attend to your work."

The reading of these two simple, yet expansive, structures on a vast plain poses a moral question: When we are given a glimpse of infinity so profound that it that toys with our equilibrium, how do we respond? The next reading examines moral questions as well:

Saturday Night and Sunday Morning:
From Club to Confessional, Rave to Regrets

It happens. It has for decades, maybe for centuries. Set your clock by it. Young people finish their workweek, take their pay, howl at the moon and run out for a wild Saturday Night.

As reliable as this ritual may be, the arrival of the midnight hour and closing time is equally inevitable. The sun also rises. The young ones groan as it slips through their blinds. And with the breaking dawn they pay their weekly tab. Here is a brief account:

Saturday 11 P.M.:
It's a club in Memphis, a living descendant from the cradle of dance music. It once was a warehouse. It now has the galleries above, the floor below and everything lives in a sizable cube of brick and steel. Laser lights cut through the haze, pulsating with the throbbing bass rhythms in vivid pink and green. The light shafts seem solid like one could grab and bend them. Their movement stirs frenzy. But the light is selective. There are shadows everywhere, places to hide, nooks and crannies to get lost and conduct impetuous acts.

The bar at one end is a clamor of exotically dressed souls with mixed agendas, many flaunting and all celebrating. They celebrate the end of the week. But they also celebrate the freedom to release their burdens. They can live tonight. They live in this spatial container with its dark escapes. They weave in and out of the dance, drawing stares. Some commune with strangers along the brick enclosure. Their intoxication swells as the music thumps and roars. The lights take off into a choreography all their own. It's impossible to perceive anything as substance here. Everything is glimmer, flash or glint. The participants lose their lucidity, becoming a swirling wash of instinctual drives and emotional release swallowed by the night.

Sunday 10 A.M.:
It's a church on Union. It is brick with choral galleries and pews below. It is a sacred cube, once a factory, and still a vestige of Memphis' industrious past. The organ drones as heads pound. Many there wear sunglasses. This is because the sun pours in from the eastern window onto their alabaster faces and crimson eyes. It is refracted by shards of a colored mosaic that paints a picture of a haloed figure in glorious radiance. This wakes up the participants. They rise and fall, rise and fall as the service plods on. The singing lifts and fills the space, like the lights of the sun spilling over the rim. They remember where they have been, recalling those secret corners in the dark surround. But now there is no escape from the flooding light and the devotional music. That music might be as inspiring as last night's song. But it is far from pulsating. Like the week before, this wakeup call draws them up to the altar to repent.

These two spaces are read by their light and sound. The impact of light and sound on behavior is remarkable, perhaps explaining the amount of attention they receive when mounting a theatre production. They carve the spatial experience. And more so than all the other attributes of a space, light and sound are devices that operate in the realm of time. Time is a key component of the next reading as well:

The Houses on Elm Street 1910 and 2010: The Evolution of Home Place

On one end of the block is the 1910 three-story. It is decorated with attempts at gingerbread and has classic clapboards and a symmetrical profile. The city registry confirms that many families have entered and exited its doors; many mothers have hung laundry outside while children played; many have lived and died between the walls. The oak molding has developed a burned patina and the plaster bears trowel marks, uneven from many years of patching. Yet it still stands viable as a living space. In fact it is desired, worth easily 20 times its original selling price.

It's atop a small hill, once standing alone among crops and fields. The large cottonwood in the back is fairly new despite its amazing height. It is the grandson of the original shade-provider. You can map the interior with a right triangle template. The front door opens to a center corridor and central stairway that leads up to the bedrooms. The center hall array is the spine and key feature of the house, the first thing entrants see. It allows access to all the arteries and destinations within. The kitchen is in back and churns like the machine of the home, providing necessary sustenance. It's all a spatial operation crowned by two showrooms, the parlor and dining room, set out front and split by the central hall.

This house is about efficiency and service. It is the keeper of the old American way. The two front rooms are the only touches of presentation. They are modestly comfortable, adequate places for occasional company. There are several bedrooms above, all small. But they provide the space for many bunks, once there to serve the farmhands and later the many offspring of working families. Some rooms have been shrines to offspring lost at war. The house has all the components to serve daily life, and death. And it does so with little offering of excess and luxury. It does not address the evolution of the modern psyche. It does not serve the current trends. It bears the face an honest layman. It bears the heart of a devoted mother.

On the other end of the block is newer construction. The 2010 multi-level has more bathrooms than bedrooms, a three-car garage and an asymmetrical layout. It revisits some of the architectural adornments from its up-street elder, but is much more clean. And its framing is much less sturdy: Joists are narrower and the walls are made of recycled chipboard instead of tongue-and-groove slats. Its not meant to withstand as much time. It is meant to save time and is well staged for an immediate sale.

The "great room" is the first thing you see. The interior is all white with lots of light. It doesn't have much warmth, but it is crystal clear. And there is an excess of height in the open space above. This gives it an air of grandeur, and an illusion that the dwellers achieved more than they really have. The hall winds around with twists and turns, a little counterintuitive for the older folks. The bedrooms are spread out and are all different sizes. The master seems huge. It seems to offer more comfort than anyone would have time to enjoy. The living room is tiny but the recreational family room is huge. Clearly it is planned for at-home amusement.

The 1910 architects would find this wasteful. Why are there no more bedrooms? Why isn't it a neatly stacked and optimal organization to provide for the largest family? Why are aesthetics prioritized over serviceability? Why devote so much space to amusement? Isn't this vain? Isn't it wrong?

The answer is no. It's really about spatial evolution. The house reflects the way the culture lives. As time pulls us away from industrious duty and technology provides us with leisure time, our work ethic changes. And the world doesn't need so many offspring to tend the fields and carry the blood. The planet is filling fast. Ironically, builders provide plenty of unused space in these new homes. That is because the owners want the feeling, the fantasy, and the castle. The feeling now trumps the service. Often, open space evokes that feeling.

You can deep read the evolution of the American family as you stroll down Elm Street.

You might ask how deep reading can service the practice of theatre scene design. For one thing, it reinforces the vitality and magnitude of design research. Designers must look deeper than the surfaces of their collected imagery and interpret visual evidence in a personal manner. Deep Reading also reemphasizes the importance of the connection between life, culture and their story to the places where they exist. It bolsters a way of knowing the story;

a way of knowing the play; a way of knowing the place where the event ensues. And the distinction of such ways of knowing resides in its connection to you, your personality, background and spirit. It validates you as a vital component in the creation of space.

The cases above regard the immediate, tangible experiences of existing places/spaces. You can find a great deal by digging through the reachable material. But, it is also important to consider the background of the space, its unseen origins and developments. This is a subfield in the study of spatial anthropology. I call it *the archeology of space*.

The Archeology of Space

A space can have an evolution. It may not always be what it always was. It can have varied transformations, triggered by its many tenants, owners or caretakers. A space may be built of meta-strata, layers of usage and meaning all housed in its basic shell formation. These layers communicate with and inform one another as the remnants of past usage bleed through.

As an interpreter of space, you ask how the current state reflects, echoes and expresses the imagery and voices of its past. In this, you conduct the Archeology of Space. The evolution of a space includes its transitional history. A space was originally a _____, then became a _____, then a _____, and now is a _____. What the space is now is what counts the most. But you should ask how much and what of the past emerges and impacts the now. Does a space resonate with its own history? Does the "chord" of its history ring with harmony or dissonance? Does the spatial evolution parallel cultural evolution or does it disregard it? Are there ghosts from the past and do they interact with the current dwellers?

This transitional history is another prime concern in the anthropology of space because it informs our reading and understanding of the space. And if we are designers, it helps us design the next incarnation.

* * *

I've spent a bit of time in the previous two chapters discussing the interpretation of "real" space, a way of knowing the found spaces of daily life. I'd like to return to my field of theatre design to wrap this up.

I assert that the anthropology of space is really the essence of scene design for the theatre. Scene designers create worlds. But in order to do so, they must first understand the relationship of people to place. This includes the audience for certain, but even more the characters in the play. This is because at the heart of the theatre experience is the story of the characters and their culture. The behaviors and movements of those characters can be studied at the textual level, revealing how the space should be planned. And as they analyze the script, scene designers should also continue to study the spaces of "real" life and how they impact behavior. When they do, they are better able to intelligently design a similar space that impacts a similar behavior among a play's characters. So, I suggest that scene designers not only be able to see space, but know space in a very distinctive way. That "scene-designerly" way of knowing is a central notion of my next subject.

12
Metaspatial Design

Design is a process of making. Purposeful making depends on knowledge. Knowledge is attained as we create. So, design is a process of coming to know. If we know it, we can make it.

As I've tried to convey in this section, there are different ways of knowing. There is the spiritual encounter, the psychic exploration, the immersion, the deep reading and others. Designers, especially the theatre scene designer, sometimes take a certain circuitous route to knowing. I call that exercise Metaspatial Design.

To begin my illustration of this, I'll offer up three parables.

The Parables

The Lamppost

A master teacher of design is observing his student's work. The student is designing a city lamppost for a street scene in a well-known show. He has his research, a series of magazine clippings showing photographs of a typical lamppost from the period. The student is diligently sketching away. The master teacher stops him saying, "No no no ... it's all wrong." The student looks up quizzically and protests, "But I am drawing exactly what I see in this research." "Never mind that," says the teacher. "You haven't captured the lamppostness of the lamppost."

The Peculiar Moon

A stage lighting designer (LD) with a very serious disposition is meeting with her show's scene designer (SD), a bit of a lunatic. The show calls for the image of a moon. She comments on his drawing of a large, round, ornamental and mechanical contraption. "So this is your ... moon? Tell me about it." "Yes well, it's all right there...It's the moon machine" says the lunatic. "I am afraid I see and don't see ... not the logic anyway. Why such a mechanical thing?" says the LD. "Life is an ever rotating wheel, you can't escape. Not with a moon anyway." responds the SD. "I'll devote my best equipment to it then," concludes the LD.

The Missing Tree

An opera diva insists on seeing the stage designs for her opera. "What's that?" she asks as she points at the ground plan. The designer responds, "That's the toilet in the dressing room, ma'am." "And where's the tree?" she continues. "You know. Act One." The designer looks around nervously because he knows that traditionally there has always been a tree in Act One. It's a convention started many years ago. "Act One really doesn't need a tree. Its not about that at all," he claims with Herculean courage. The diva mutters and asks to see the costumes.

We'll come back to these parables after a bit. For now, let's address the process of Metaspatial Design.

The Process

The following are steps in the process of Metaspatial Design.

1. *Observe (life).* As you begin a project, prepare by gathering all the concrete factors together: text/story, visual research, spatial parameters of your venue or site, resources, the world around you, etc. See what is there. Look at the tangible. Research and read.

2. *Sense (that which is beyond observable).* You need to step outside the box here. Contemplate, deep read and obtain knowledge of things you can't observe that still relate to your project. These things are "adjacent" to the things you can observe, such as objects, concepts and inspirations that are not central to, but seem to resonate with your work. This includes digging into inspirational imagery, encountering abstract research on period/style/feel, reading between the lines of the text, investigating the "soul/psyche/culture" of the spatial venue/site, appreciating the world around you, and conversing with your own imagination, etc.

3. *Refer (knowledge back to the observed).* Adapt the spirit of what you sense to what you observe. This enriches your understanding of what you observe. It reforms it and makes it deeper. It is a coupling of concrete familiarity and abstract awareness.

4. *Create (the new thing).* At this point, the circle is complete. You start by looking at the design problem, analyze it locally, project your self outside of it to explore, take your experience back to the problem and proceed with creation. Understanding is whole. You can design from it.

The following defines the term *Metaspatial Design*:

Meta-: Prefix with several meanings. The best is "beyond yet adjacent."
   —*Going beyond the observable*
Spatial: Relating to an area set aside for potential use.
   —*Attributes of space*
Design: Purposeful making
   —*To get to the essence*

Read those sub-notes in italics again and tie them all together: *"going beyond the observable attributes of space to get to the essence."*

That is the core of Metaspatial Design.

Metaspatial Design refers to a process, not a thing. It refers to how one responds to space and, importantly, how one might translate text into visual. Read, contemplate, refer-back, and design. You depart from expected reality here. You go out beyond the usual or typical. Once you step beyond the expected and observable reality you can begin to collect useful, albeit abstract, inspirations that lie on the conceptual periphery. You then take those inspirations and refer them back to the accepted reality, which they inform. In the course of events, you make the reality even more real. This is especially useful and effective in the theatre.

The Paradigm

How does Metaspatial Design apply to the theatre? Here is the basic layout: A design can look like _____, for a play that is about _____, because it does _____. Each blank in the previous sentence can be a completely different and seemingly unrelated thing. Yet it can work brilliantly. I've seen *King Lear* done against a wall of Plexiglas mirrors. I've seen *A Midsummer Night's Dream* done with little sparkling Christmas tree ornaments hanging all over an open space. The designs make sense once you see them in action, but who would have guessed?

In order to devise a design that is truly effective, you sometimes have to deliberately deviate from accepted norms or expectations. But you can't simply throw non-sequiturs around at random. Design always demands a process. Metaspatial Design takes you beyond the first, logical choice and charges you to explore unexpected, yet potentially successful alternatives. After you explore, you bring back knowledge of something beyond the rudimentary to inform your creation. And sometimes, it is obvious that the first logical choice is best.

The Products

And now, we can return to the parables. The following are examples of practical Metaspatial Designs for theatre referred to in the three parables above.

Guys and Dolls: The Lamppost

The young designer is working on the Times Square scene in the bold musical *Guys and Dolls*. His teacher knows that this musical is far from realistic. The music swirls and darts about in a jazzy fashion. That music, the dancing, the color and the broad shapes of the characters and the overall motion of the show set the tone for the design. It's a Warner Brothers' styled cartoon. And this cartoony style doesn't beg for a real lamppost. It begs for a realer lamppost, a lamppost with "lamppostness," a quality I would describe as "jazzed up." The lesson in this parable is that sometimes you need to honor style over substance. In this case the swirling music and movement of the piece dictate the style. You have to get outside the box of realism to sense it. The "swirl" of the music refers back and dictates the lamppost design.

Carmina Burana: The Peculiar Moon

This odd couple of designers is working on Carl Orff's famous stage cantata, *Carmina Burana*. The centerpiece of the whole show is the image of the wheel of fortune, most often rendered as the moon. But, why is the SD's moon so stylized and mechanical? And what sparked the LD's eventual resignation to artfully light the moon contraption? The LD knows her friend well. She knows his lunacy is born from earnest travels to outer limits. If he sees the moon as industrial gear, it is because he has found an association in the text that marries the powers of moon to mechanics. In doing so he ties together the omnipresence and regularity of the moon with humanity's continual urge to mechanize their existence. Such a symbol has enough importance to warrant artful visibility. The lesson here is that seemingly disconnected characteristics can find relevance if adequately explored and trusted. Give them a chance.

Norma: The Missing Tree

The diva is to perform the role of Norma in the eponymous opera by Bellini. The designer is a maverick. He knows the importance of tradition and realizes that a tree is appropriate to the libretto. But, he also knows that the emotional character of the piece transcends the literal demands of the story. Act One has "bigger fish to fry." The lesson is that sometimes you need to go out beyond the cultural expectation and find a higher mission to serve. Then you bring that mission back and allow it to trump the convention.

Creating these kinds of designs (all award winners by the way) requires an arc of a journey. You start at the text and in reality. You venture out to the edges of the realm of your work: beyond (yet adjacent) to the play's text, cultural convention and standard research. Then you return with your knowledge and apply it back to the original and observable reality of the project. Then you design. In a way, it's a hero's quest. And a huge component of any hero's quest is finding a way of knowing.

The Price (Once Designed)

The above represents one manner of design. There are many. But at the end of any design process, the work will be evaluated and assessed. It will be judged. It will be assigned a value, a price if you will. I call this *the appraisal of space*. In the next chapter, I address *how* we can appraise a spatial design, yet another way of knowing.

13

The Appraisal of Space

I love reading reviews of my work. Once in a while a critic "gets" my intended point. If he does, I ask myself if I've succeeded. My answer could be yes or no.

I can say yes. My point is made. The message is sent.

But then again, no. Only one point is made. And worse yet, I am noticed. A stage designer should not be noticed. The play's the thing. The spatial environment supports the play. It is part of the storytelling. It cannot upstage the other elements of the show. So, the best review is one that loves the show but doesn't mention the design. These are assessments.

One way to know space is to assess its value. And if I appraise space, as it stands alone, I want to be thorough. Too often, judgments on design focus solely on appearance, the way it looks in a book. I am a sucker for this. I love being awed by impressive stage photographs and lush design illustrations. But there is more. When one evaluates a spatial design, these are the things I believe should be considered:

- *Meaning*
- *Function*
- *Appearance*
- *Illusion*
- *Capture*
- *Spirit*
- *The Mix*

To illustrate these, I want to refer to a work of theatre that is near and dear to my heart. It is the show that cast a spell on me when I was in high school. I am a designer because of it. It is Tchaikovsky's *The Nutcracker*. This ballet has many incarnations, some great ones on film. Balanchine's version is a treasure chest of opulent garniture. Sendak's dazzles and haunts with exotic fantasias. The Milwaukee Ballet Company's version, designed by Oliver Smith, is the one that I refer to above. I remember it like a Christmas card coming to life, with blended colors that my synesthesia (see preface) relishes. *The Nutcracker* has recurring value to me. So, I will use it to break down the discernible values of spatial design.

Meaning—What it says. A design can teach a moral. It can convey an idea. It can stir thought, imagination and action. And it can have meaning. There is a design for *The Nutcracker* that includes an overbearing grandfather clock in Act One. The clock has the image of an owl at its crest. This is an appropriate part of the Bavarian setting. These kinds of clocks are traditional in central Europe during the nineteenth century. During the transformation scene, when reality breaks into a kind of nightmare for young Clara, the owl, a trusted and friendly timekeeper of Clara's childhood, morphs into the face of her uncle,

Herr Drosselmeyer. Drosselmeyer is the conduit for Clara's change from girl to woman. The clock's face-change represents the coming of age with all its troubles and delights. The clock, as a feature of the overall design, has a meaning.

Function—What it does. A design should be a participant in a show. Usually, a design has some mechanism in it that fosters the movement of action logically. It helps the show flow from scene to scene. I call that mechanism the "machine of the design" (more on the machine can be found in Chapter 15). There is a design for *The Nutcracker* that uses an ornate sleigh to transport the principles from locale to locale throughout the ballet. It sweeps across the stage each time the scene shifts. The sleigh acts as a mode of transportation for the audience's imagination. It keeps the motion fluid. As in this example, it is valuable for a design to be physically active.

Appearance—How it looks. As I say earlier, this is the basis for most appraisals of spatial design by the laity. The portfolios of aspiring designers usually focus heavily on the appearance of their works. If a design is masterfully presented, it can be candy for the eye. There is a design for *The Nutcracker* that is like a living book illustration. Each backdrop is lushly rendered, thick with rich detail and luster. In fact there are many of these. Such emphasis on visual spectacle is a long tradition of ballet design and justifiably so. People want to be swept away by what they see.

Illusion—What transforms. A design can represent or depict reality by using tricks that fool the eye or mind. Trompe Loeil is one example. But it can go farther than the craft of scenic painting. A design can create a powerful illusion of life and manipulate its perception by distorting or abbreviating reality. There is a design for *The Nutcracker* that uses a painted fabric cutout Christmas tree. At one point during the transition from reality to fantasy, the illusion of scale is manipulated by having this tree "grow." A Christmas tree is tapered, narrowest at the top. It looks like a two-dimensional triangle. But the angled sides of the triangle on this tree don't stop at the floor. There is additional fabric puddled behind the tree. When the top of the tree is pulled up by the fly system, the tree convincingly grows and expands at its base to double its original size. This simple trick transports us as an audience to a different perception of where we are. After the transition, the tall tree stands alone, with the walls and furniture removed. This abbreviation of reality further empowers the illusion of scale.

Capture—How it feels. A design can evoke a feeling. It can capture something in the audience member that triggers mood, emotion and impulse. This is often achieved with the use of light, color, texture and imagery. Something in the shadowy blue lighting of a cool, monochromatic forest scene that is covered in shimmering ice and the rotating image of swirling snow can stimulate a melancholy longing for the romantic winter's of youth or imagination. Such is the case with the "Waltz of the Snowflakes."

Spirit—What transcends. A design can move you in a way that exceeds emotion or intellect. It can strike a chord deep within that when experienced brings a kind of epiphany or transformation. There is a design for *The Nutcracker* that has the principles rise on a rotating elevator into the lofts of the stage during the apotheosis of the pas de deux. This moment, accentuated by projections of rotating light and haze, follows the swell of the music to a point where you realize a benevolent force in the universe, one that elevates love above the fretting of the world below. It can be an ecstatic moment.

The Mix. Design entails investing more than any one of the items above. These values mix together to form a composite worth. The worth is also influenced by the space's connection to its culture. Does the space tell the cultural story? Does it serve its cultural purpose? Does it become a world? A world is a series of living moments. You might have noticed in my descriptions of the values above, I do not describe the complete spaces. I describe spatial moments. A design of a space is a design of key, cultural moments that punctuate the cultural story. The next section encourages us to take what we have *seen*, inform it with the truths we have *known* and proceed to *make* compositions of our own, the composition of worlds.

PART THREE

Making

Spatial designers make worlds. Making worlds is about making experience. And making experience requires writing a story, the story to be told through the experience. The story has to have roots in the human condition it serves. And the design that follows has to be informed by deep understanding. Understanding begins with sight and knowledge, the subjects of Parts one and two in this book. Once you have accumulated a substantive understanding of the design problem and the kinds of things that can resolve that problem, you may proceed to activate the design. Design activation is a binary process of composition toward unity and reduction to the essence, a purposeful making that aims to result in a meaningful world.

Theatre artists abide by certain limits in the process of creation. They must engage with that which is laid before them. This includes the script/text, the stage and house, the resources and themselves. The intent of that engagement is to make a show. And for the scene designer, it's to make a space that is appropriate and effective for the show's purpose. This is similar to the missions of other designers, including architects, industrial designers and interior decorators, etc. What follows is a testimony on what I've learned about the design process and how it extends beyond its technical exercises and becomes a ritual of life. Chapter 14 addresses general engagement with a creative work. Chapter 15 addresses specific details of the spatial design process.

14

The Ritual of Making

Unlike other art forms, theatre has the goal of creating a live event, and a living world for that event. Film is great at preserving dramatic moments for posterity. But it is bound to its media and can't yet replicate the immediacy of live theatre (not even with high resolution/3-D devices). Music concerts are live events, but they don't usually entail creating an appreciable world on the stage. Installation art can be a live experience, but it doesn't include a set of living characters in its package, and often doesn't tell a specific story. I believe that live theatre has a unique place in the world, despite its strong competition. And I believe that theatre's process of making offers a variety of creative approaches you can explore, no matter what field you are in.

Theatre artists have a charge they treasure. Their job is to translate a text (a play) or an artistic idea into a tangible, purposeful, engaging and reflective event that *lives* on a stage. They go from inspiration to creation, abstraction to action, and dream to reality. It's usually a labor of love (The pay is poor, so they had better love it.). The scene designer translates literature into a visual and visceral world. And, of course, it's a world heavily reliant on space. The general process of creating that world is the subject of this chapter.

Before immersing in a discussion of the process, I want to share some more thoughts on the event. The world I discuss above is not fully realized until it becomes a living event, an occurrence in space and time. A living event that is shared between performers and audience requires a degree of spark, an injection of life energy. Life energy, to me, is a form of magic. And magic is one component of theatre that sets the art form apart.

If you watch a well-executed scene shift such as with a revolving stage and flying pieces working in precise coordination, the transformation can be magical. So too can be the orchestration of emotional moments, illustrated with inventive voice and movement by skilled performers. The immediacy of the shared experience between life onstage and the life of the attending audience is a magical link. These magic qualities allow us, as participants in the event, to surpass the limitations of our accustomed existence. The event transcends what is natural. It takes us to a higher awareness of ourselves and our place. The journey toward making such an event is an equally magical endeavor, one I describe as a ritual.

Waking

The theatre follows a ritual of making that is a process of growing collaboration. Like a rolling snowball, it's a journey that collects individuals along the way. Early in the journey, you, as the scene designer, join the collective as an important voice and contributor. You are responsible for the dramatic space, the physical environment. Your specific design process is a smaller version of the larger, theatre macro-process. You engage with more and more individuals who help you make the world. The basic sequence of that process goes like this:

1. First you are alone preparing to work
2. Then the author's voice is added (by reading the play)
3. Then comes the stage director and a concept is developed
4. Then other designers join in and things evolve
5. Then actors, then staff, then crew join in
6. Then audience. The group of world-makers has grown from one to hundreds.

You'll remember that composition is at the core of what designers do. This is another example. The process outlined above is a composition in and of itself. It's a grouping of hearts, minds, souls and egos all merging on a single purpose, put together in an artful way. My analogic take on the progression of that process is akin to waking up in the morning. Let me illustrate (analogs are in italics):

1. You begin solitarily, alone with the play.
    This is like being deep in slumber and dreaming. It's private and deep. You respond to the play impulsively and subconsciously.
2. More reading of the play. You begin to respond to it intellectually.
    This is like REM sleep, a more active and responsive sleep. Still private.
3. You then meet the director and other designers, develop ideas and collect research. The design is beginning to materialize. You aren't so alone now.
    You are collecting consciousness, becoming aware, emerging from slumber and the privacy of dreams. You hear others' voices. You begin to approach reality
4. You begin to work out the problem of the design. You begin to engineer it.
    You begin to move, you get physical, roll around in the sheets
5. You do rough design sketches, working out the actual vision based on ideas, research and engineering.
    You open your eyes; you begin to see what you have ahead of you.
6. You revise your roughs based on feedback from the artistic team and move to doing the final design presentation.
    You are up and out of bed; you are wide-eyed and can see clearly what is going on.
7. You begin to complete design documents, drafting, planning and specifications. The shops begin to get involved.
    You are alert. There are morning reality checks. You look in the mirror; you get naked and shower.
8. The design and show are realized, built, rehearsed and open for the audience.
    You are up, dressed and you can eat your breakfast.

So, the process of design is like the daily ritual of gaining consciousness. Much the same, the product of the design process IS consciousness. You add stimulators as you emerge from slumber. Or in design you add other people and refine ideas as you complete a project.

It's like coming from a private dream and entering a day full of cacophonous voices. At the pinnacle of the process, that point where you reach a honed reality, you enter the realm of enlightenment. You are fully aware. That is design. Design is awareness. Like all enlightenment, it is bred from a ritual. Within this ritual are four general phases of purposeful making:

- Imagining
- Collaborating
- Conceiving
- Creating

I discuss those in detail next. As I do, I will offer some advice on how to conduct these acts. This will be useful for theatre artists, but can offer some encouragement for creators from all kinds of fields.

Imagining

This goes back to the notion of beginning a creative process alone. This is the phase where you can convene with yourself. It's a rare moment of solitude. Starting the work with your inner being (or, "being in") means that the seed of creativity is essentially you. You begin with a kernel of yourself. And you allow that seed to develop as you carry a little bit of yourself through the process to the end. The seed is never lost. It is germinally fixed at the root as the work grows forward and others share in its fertilization. This is OK, because all creative work, no matter how collaborative or extensive, should bear a bit of its originator in the fruits.

This all involves trusting your exploratory impulses. You first become acquainted with the story, or text, you are trying to share with your audience. You will develop initial and raw impressions of what the text is saying. Trust those. And trust what you imagine the text might yield in its staging or realization. As you read it for the first time, trust your gut feelings from that early encounter. Trust your instincts, your training, your taste, and your ideas. And then allow time for imagining and dreaming of what might be. Nearly all good art begins with vision and the vision is usually personal. Because you are linked in to the collective of humanity, your impulses have merit and value. Express those impulses via sketches and doodles and notes. They are the artifacts of imagination, the residue of dreams. Keep them with you as you hone your work. Remember, the design begins with you and your dream and the time alone is brief. Soon enough others will join you and reality will "kick in."

Collaborating

That early moment of solitude and personal imagination is precious. But you eventually have to share yourself, your ideas and your work with others. Theatre, like many other modes of making, is about merging minds. You gather fellow enthusiasts, little by little, as you proceed. You work like you play, like little kids making a snowman on the playground together. Each one enters one by one, until its all a big mess of makers making.

It's a circle of souls around the work.

And it's a team approach. Each member brings his/her game. I'll share an example: In a theme park design studio I know, a project begins with a meeting of a mixed collective of equally ranked people. There are project managers, architects, designers, artists, engineers, producers, entertainment directors, businessmen, writers, illustrators, psychologists and even zoologists sitting around a casual room with couches and rockers and pillows and coffee talking and inventing. Each takes a turn at the chalkboard to doodle the vision. Each impulsively throws ideas into the mix as someone records it all, maybe on camera. The leaders of the project sift through the records. Then they gestate and document a concrete vision. What follows is the hashing out of details built upon that vision. The original founders of the vision complete the detailing. And, as such, they keep the spirit of that first meeting with them to the end. It's a lasting collaboration of individual dreams that meld in a collective consciousness. At least they can hope.

At its best, collaboration transcends a team approach. It becomes a family dynamic. Most of us can attest to the variability of family dynamics. There are dysfunctional families who cannot find their bonding mechanism no matter how the profess to seek it. There are passionate, highly functional, families who argue violently around the dinner table yet find love at the core amidst the din. There are families who claim to function healthily but in reality struggle with communication issues and getting to the heart of the matter. And there are perfectly good, tight-knit, happy families with well-behaved kids and loving parents. You can expect any and all the variables, from screaming to hugs.

No matter what the family's condition may be, there is in it a "blood bond" that cannot be escaped or denied. There may be difficulty in its functioning. There may even be dark memories, even horrors in its history. But, when a critical moment forces the issue, the bond usually manifests. The family recognizes a survival mandate. The group goes to work, sometimes spontaneously, to address the issue. It explores together. It tests things. It may fight or quarrel as it does. But the collaborative space becomes a house of action, an action of making.

In this family-style scenario, an informality usually emerges and with it a relaxation of well-defined roles. In a healthy way, the edges of "family" members' assignments or positions blur. It is more about an attitude of doing, even stumbling through, together. The house becomes a creative playground. And the synthesis of "blood bonds" neutralizes the egos and individual agendas among the players. The making takes over everyone's being and the collective group floats downstream as a unit, making what it must, solving the problems it must, by no textbook rubric, but by urgency and a bit of childlike inspiration. This is the best collaborative scenario imaginable.

As in a family, engaging with professional collaborators isn't always easy. There can be language or cultural barriers, interpersonal issues, personality clashes and deficiencies in communication skill among the group. Sometimes you, as a designer, need to be proactive and find creative ways to deal with the challenges. If you don't, it could hold up your work. I have to circumvent collaborative obstacles on occasion. These usually relate to someone's inability to converse effectively. A few examples of some solutions to those kinds of problems follow.

Engaging Via Imagery

Some stage directors, the first people you engage on a theatre project, can have difficulty articulating their desires for the look of a show. And they may have difficulty comprehending the language that designers use. If either is the case, you may find it more effective to engage using visual instead of verbal language. To avoid getting too specific too early, you should avoid sharing images that read like final designs. It is wiser to try and establish an overall aesthetic and share some very abstract visuals to see where things are headed.

You might do a set of doodles, maybe a couple of dozen small pencil drawings that show shading, lines, forms and general style. These are abstract. You then ask the director to rank them. I ask for five favorites and five least favorites. From these choices, which might arrive with no conversation at all, you can identify what kinds of visual qualities are appealing and what are not. The design can materialize by overlaying the five favorites and carving them into something concrete.

Engaging Without Direct Dialogue

When you have difficulty resolving a show conversationally with a collaborator, it may be because the collaborator is too caught up in specific effects and momentary details. And it may be inappropriate to confuse matters by using visual imagery as with the case above. In this situation you may opt to communicate by sending the person a series of written questions. These should be broad and general, trying to get to the heart of the matter. You try to find the center of the project this way. You ask for global themes and large impressions.

I have seen situations where the answers come back with no references to the original questions. They are just answers, just words. You may not even remember what they refer to yourself. Consider this a gift. You can take the words and arrange them in a document. Then you can read them like poetry. It really doesn't matter what the original questions were. The answers are here. They will convey the message you need and you can proceed to design by interpreting the poetry they present. It's a great way to begin.

Engaging by Shared Participation

There is no shame in exposing how you work, even in the sloppy, early stages of a project. You should sit down with a director and bring out the sketchpad and doodle in front of them as you talk. It's a way to create on the spot, to react directly to thoughts and inspirations as they come across. You might even offer the pen to the directors, empowering them with hands-on creation. You design together. This is the best way to make sure the designs are fresh and accurate because they materialize as the dialogue ensues. There is no filter. It's all pure and immediate.

Engaging by Listening

Frequently, good collaboration amounts to good listening. There are times when you simply need to shut your mouth. Sometimes a director has done the homework and knows exactly what the design must be. They may even hand you drawings they've done. These generally aren't in scale and don't have much detail, but they can be well-envisaged solutions to the problem of a show. Whenever a person has done that much preparation and has so much concern about the spatial design that they've ventured out of their own territory to resolve it, you can be glad part of your job is done. You know exactly what you must design. If you have some disagreement about what you've been presented, it is unlikely you will change their mind. If it is feasible, do it the way they want, help them achieve their dream, or leave the project behind.

These are just a few ways that you can engage with a collaborator. Sometimes people will want you to tell them what the project is all about. Sometimes they have it all figured out. Sometimes they need a little guidance. And sometimes they really want to mold it together. This is a dance of personalities. But that is exactly what makes design exciting. Each project is unique from beginning to end.

Collaboration is an art and not a science. There isn't a single directive on how to do it. Collaboration is also a composition of individual selves. And if there is a toxic presence in the composition, it can ruin the whole thing. A toxin in the collaboration usually means an unwilling partner, a person motivated only by power and control, or a leader without experience and with delusions of sufficiency. Or it may simply be an individual who aggressively advocates for a bad idea (a bad idea means an idea that deviates from the central truth and beauty of the thing being made).

You can neutralize the toxin by having the experienced folks in the party strategically and gently disarm it, finding value in the productive aspects of the toxin's offerings and weeding out the rest. Remain positive. It takes a village to raise the art. Trust is a necessary ingredient in the mix. So the group needs to eliminate that which isn't trustworthy and celebrate that which is. You hone that which you trust into vision. The vision morphs through the manipulation of many hands into space. All this is vital because in theatre and other similar enterprises, effective and expedient collaboration is the anchor of creation.

The objective of early collaboration is to establish the central spirit of the project that all can follow as they progress. This central spirit is known as *The Production Concept*. Collaborators engage together in a process of conceptualization prior to addressing the specifications of the product.

Conceiving

A production concept is the *way* you are going to tell the story. Storytelling is undoubtedly a key part of the theatre, and is also a part of architecture, attraction design, the arts in general and other fields. The concept is your angle of approach. And you need to plot that angle before you can begin to design. It can be almost any idea on how you frame, flavor and present the text. It's a method for making the spatial event interesting and accessible to its audience. It becomes the centerpiece of your creation, the thing you all look to as you embark. In order to solidify a concept, you need to craft a vision (that is why you start with imagining). These visions are theoretical constructions, things you build in your minds. As part of the construction, you often need to process your ideas and interpretations through some investigative or experimental exercises.

These exercises include *visioning, defining, activating and pooling.*

Visioning means to craft a visual image out of the text itself. You can cull words, phrases and literary symbols from the scripted language; ascertain visual equivalents or representatives for those literary components; and use them like jigsaw puzzle pieces to build up a collaged artifact. This can be deliberate and methodical. If the author uses repeated references to water and sleep, you might gather clipart with images in aqua blue, diffused forms and wavy lines. You can piece these clippings together to form an interesting visual collage that will stir imagination and lead discussions toward a concrete aesthetic concept.

As casual as that may seem, it is actually a momentous act. You are transfiguring thoughts from a concrete language to an abstract one. And the result is the transportation of the original idea from a known ground to a transcendent plane. This is a key aspect of conceptualization. If you can elevate ideas by refacing them through a transformational exercise, you are transmitting to receptors in the minds of the audience or visitors that otherwise go unstimulated. A space, by nature, speaks with an abstract voice and so the exercise of visioning is appropriate for its conception.

Defining means making concrete, intellectual interpretations of the meaning of the text. You deduce the messages from the written words and note them. Then you find a logical way to employ the meaning. For example, you might decide that a certain play is about a quest for some dark truth. Knowing that, you can decide what things distinguish *quest* (a linear journey in pursuit), *the dark* (the things that are generally unseen and threatening in our natures) and *truth* (that which is accepted as genuine). From this you might create a linear adventure into and through a mysterious zone that is somehow glinted with sparks of revelation. That linear journey can be the concept.

Definition is a common impulse. People seek to decipher meaning and crave a rational explanation. This is part of a larger desire to establish order from chaos. We abhor the unknown. We chase the stars and light up the dark. We have an urge to uncover truth because we expect truth to protect us. It is a survival instinct. Developing a design concept from an epiphany is a guarantor of substantive creation; but it doesn't necessarily foster transcendence or augmentation in the spatial experience. It explains the water, but doesn't push you in.

Activating refers to the practice of putting the text "on its feet" to test its potential. This might entail conducting a workshop. You can ask a group of people to read the story/play/etc. aloud. You mighty even ask them to rise up and move about in a room while they read to see what kinds of motions and patterns arise. This is usually quite illuminating. You can see relationships form, dynamics develop and you can select what things to emphasize in the storytelling.

This also helps you find the key moments in the text. Once you do, you can find devices to make those moments come alive. The devices you use might have common traits. And that common thread becomes the definer for the concept. For instance, you might imagine, as you hear a text read actively and aloud, that a rotating beacon of light would be the best device to visually punctuate the key moments in the story. Your design concept might be to place the entire event in a lighthouse setting, because the lighthouse offers you the recurring beacon you desire (and many other interesting things). You might not have arrived at this concept if you hadn't heard the text read aloud.

Activation is the incarnation of literature. And this is another huge step. No space is complete without life. And as long as there is life, there is motion. Activation means *to set in motion*. The space keeps evolving. This provides an astute model for visualizing your concept. You can see the words work and how they relate. You watch a rough draft of verbal choreography. This reveals the story in nuance and stroke. You then can choose what devices sponsor the movement best.

Pooling is the practice of opening up the table and having everyone throw their inspirations into a mix. Everyone involved in conceptualizing a project will bring his or her ideas, notions, research and inspirational imagery to the first meeting. Each will take a turn at presenting. All of the material is "pooled" into a group and the whole mix is examined collectively. This should expose certain dominant trends and themes. From those trends and themes can emerge a conceptual direction. This is usually more effective than simply sitting around and chatting about ideas.

Pooling usually reveals a collective unconscious. There are threads that tie us and ties that bind. And these often go without acclaim. Pooling is an exercise for exposing universals. Universal interpretations, tastes, desires and tendencies are rooted in ancient stories and myths, founding concepts for creation and existence that reside deep below our familiar sentience. By honoring universals you marry the story of your space to an ancient story of life. And you use the collective unconscious as a vow.

There are many other possible exercises to process your concept. The main objective is to help your audience "get" the message of the piece. The concept is the means to that end. In the theatre, there are some common strategies for conceptualizing a dramatic event that are repeated over the years. I think that some of these strategies can be applied to other disciplines as well. If you want to help an audience (or user) better appreciate the central meaning or message of a designed object, you might try injecting an unexpected zest into its substance. In the theatre this is often achieved by altering the reality or traditional context of a play.

You can change period and/or place from the original/written setting. By transporting the story to a vibrant period, you can give it a colorful layer of interest. You can also adopt a culture and apply it to a text. By taking a play written about the cultural life of a character in one domain, and reconsidering it through the eyes of a radically different culture, you can give it freshness. You can stylize, distort or abstract reality. This is often done by illustrating the world of the play in the manner of a graphic style or movement such as cartooning, expressionism and impressionism. You can simplify and abbreviate reality. By only including a few iconic elements in the design and only emphasizing the most basic qualities in the characters, you allow the text to come to the forefront.

You can choose to punctuate or accentuate things in a play using whatever devices best serve your needs. This allows you to create a series of moments rather than a single unifying premise. Sometimes you don't need to provide a parallel universe or a continuum in the design. It can simply be a montage of mini-events, contained in one larger event, using any services available to make those events interesting and understood. You can be blatantly theatrical, exposing the theatre and all its machinery for the audience to a see. There is no attempt at illusion or transformation. The show and the audience know they are in a theatre the entire time with no pretense. This eliminates the aesthetic concerns and forces a frank confrontation with the message. And you can try "environmentalist experientialism." This is my term for putting the audience into an experience. You surround them with the world of the play and allow them to feel the same things the characters in the play feel.

These are just a few examples of ideas that show up frequently on the stage. Conceptualization can be both the impetus to and the result of the act of creating, the next phase of making I discuss.

Creating

When you create, you should seek an empirical rapport with your work. That is, don't just "think it up." Play with it. Touch it somehow. Get your hands dirty. And make yourself part of the work. You should allow it to talk back to you and lead your progress. It's a conversation. Below, I suggest a series of modes for this kind of immersive creation. These are ways of making things. They are common in show development and can be applied to any creative endeavor. Because I am a spatial designer and an enthusiast of architectural design, I will use architectural analogies to help with their descriptions. I call these modes: *the mud hut, the handyman's shack, the well-made office, the grotto* and *the historic renovation*.

The Mud Hut

If you think about it, there is no way to plan the construction of a mud hut. Drawings and specification sheets are of little value because it is so organic. You just grab some mud and start making. It's possible to create beauty in it as you go, without following a preordained sequence. You avoid thinking it through, all for the better. This approach is not rare among musicians, studio artists and performers in their work.

The Handyman's Shack

Like the mud hut, this method is impulsive. You build it as you go. You build based on gut reactions and instinctual urges. And all your choices arrive from spontaneous reactions to sudden stimuli you encounter by chance rather than search. You discover some materials you have around. You say, "let's use this!" And you whip it all together from the found objects. It's about making with the resources in your midst, and avoiding the grander desires. It involves some thought, so it is not as raw as the mud hut.

The Well-Made Office

This is the opposite of the mud hut. It is an intellectual exercise, with things clearly thought-through from the start. There is a plan that is done as a response to a need. It employs a careful analysis of the processes it must contain. And it sets itself a goal based on function.

The Grotto

A grotto is made out of passion and emotion. You are driven by feelings rather than analytical thought. And it is created by embrace and devotion, hands-on and heart-in, crafted with care and revision from a personal quest toward an ideal. Like a shrine, the grotto is dedicated to the ideal you believe in your heart.

The Historic Renovation

This is making born of research and honor. It is a process of reaction to factual evidence. And it requires a willful study and the reverence for recreation and revival. Originality is not the main objective, but clarity, duty and respect for something you wish to reanimate because of its proven value.

So after you imagine what story you are telling, and you gather your fellow "makers" together and engage them in a process of conceptualizing, you can establish the mode of creation or *how* you are going to enter the process. Ask yourselves if you are building a mud hut or a well-made office. Once decided, it will lead you to a concrete starting point. And once you establish the direction, you step forward to design, the actual chiseling of the material world.

This whole ritual is not unlike the process of life. You begin existence alone and spend your life accumulating family, friends, enemies, mentors, colleagues, etc. And based on those relationships, you eventually decide on philosophies and priorities for living. You make choices. You establish your own living concept as you come of age. And you proceed to create things (and destroy some things) as you go. All the while, you usually have some aim, some desire, some dream or some wish that you follow. But somewhere along the line you might discover that the process of life (the steps you take with others and the experiences you enjoy) is in fact more important than your aims. The products of life (your achievements and gains) may be, in fact, very nice by-products.

So as I embark on the next chapter, one devoted to the specifics of spatial design, let me express that the very process of design, the constructive incarnation of the ritual of making, may hold more value than the material products you put out. Sometimes, the process is its own product.

15
Designing

The previous chapter addresses the poetry of the creative process. And poetry implies a bit of a leisurely enterprise. Early on, you spend time imagining, getting together with fellow artists to toss around ideas, conjuring a grand concept and eventually begin to materialize the vision. The dreaming is great. But there are pragmatic concerns to realized creation as well. Design is one part poetry and one part practical engineering. I find that a gorgeous duality. The practical part is no less creative and no less collaborative than the poetry part. It is just a more hands-on, "get dirty" and "get real" part. The poetry and the practical join to form the "doing." And such doing with a purpose, is design.

Below are the key procedural stages of practical theatre design. They are often followed as stages in architectural, event, attraction and industrial design as well.

The Source

Design is an active process that stems from a source. The source is an informant. It dictates the purpose of your making, presents the design problem and solves the problem. It is the beginning of the river, the headwaters of the creative process. All spaces evolve out of a central idea, a driving need or a design challenge. These impetuses have cultural roots. And in most cases they are expressed in cultural stories. The story is the source. In the theatre the source is structured as a text: the play script, score, libretto, choreography or something as esoteric as a movement study in modern dance or an improvisational exploration in performance art. It is communicated and recorded in some fashion and expects to be the root of a live event. The event is most often the telling of the story.

The source provides the context and the substance for the event. And it is the resource for finding all the answers to the design questions. You may ask questions such as, "What color? What shape? How big? What style?" It is best to seek the source for clues. These clues live in the flow of the language, the manner of the dialogue, the style, the music (if applicable), the ideas expressed, the themes, the characters, the intentions, the nature of the relationship of text to audience or visitors in the space, etc. Your reading of the play is "the thing." You might say that reading the source is another kind of "deep reading."

In the theatre, you visit the source early on and it is no casual visit. It can involve exploratory scrutiny. The aim is to analyze the breadth and depth of the story to be told. This can include literary deconstruction and even a bit of metaspatial engagement, where you go outside the source to look back in at it. Once you have done the analysis, you should be able to predict and presage answers to your design questions because you have come to know the text like an old friend, family or even foe.

Different practitioners have different approaches to this. Some count every word in the text; deconstruct every line, every measure, and every gesture. They miss nothing. Some open the text and allow it to do its job by its own device. They allow the text to penetrate them and then trust their gut reactions and personal interpretations from that penetration. Some go for the bigger picture rather than the microscopic study. But either way, artists must unpack the literary suitcase before donning the textual apparel and proceeding to the runway of spatial composition.

When a designer analyzes a text, the exercise should follow a rubric. You can start with a raw reading to get your impulsive take. The next reading can be more intellectual, where you interpret meaning and style. Then you can begin to write lists of the things the story is saying and the things the story demands of its spatial design. And finally you can read it with a design plan in mind to test your ideas. You imagine the movements and the use of the space by characters in the story. All this is done before designs are finalized. You read the text many times, see its methods and know its message and then make the appropriate choices to generate the best-honed design. You must read the culture of the story well. And after you do, you must conduct ample research that will reinforce the choices you make to inform the space.

Research

Theatre scene designers are dramaturges of space. You cannot simply make things up (unless it is a very peculiar project). You base your choices on evidence in visual research. Research informs, but not necessarily dictates, your work. You can be interpretive and selective as you arrange an informed composition.

Searching

You want to find two basic categories of visual evidence: inspirational evidence and detail evidence. Inspirational objects are those things that convey a sense of style, color, atmosphere, mood, density, ornamentation and overall feel. Detail sources are specific documented objects that you will try to recreate or stylize in the features of the actual design. You should concentrate on finding inspirations before details. This is because you need to establish the overall scope of the design and then decide what details need to be employed. Some of your detail research can be concurrent with the inspirational research because you do want some of the nuances of period details to play a role in that inspiration. Undoubtedly, you will go back and scrutinize details after you establish the overall direction.

Research can be historical, especially with period designs. But it can also be more abstract. You might look into works of art, photography, graphic design, technical drawings, etc. You can explore the history of the theatre for inspiration on how to solve a show's structure. You can look to architecture, interior décor, monument and industrial design. The list goes on. So, I suggest that designers begin abstract and gradually go concrete. Start with books rather than web-based search engines. There may be more opportunity to stumble upon useful, accidental research by browsing the shelves of a library and paging through books rather than trusting the search engine to decide what you should/shouldn't see. General overviews of art, architecture and interior design movements might be good starts. Then you can find some keywords, names and concepts that you can investigate deeper.

Choosing

You must conduct the research process with a firm grasp on the problem, the purpose and the context of the project. Research will directly serve those concerns. Research helps to define the design problem. It can pose as many questions as it answers, allowing you to see the way spaces work (or don't work) and exposing contradictions between your concept and the realities of what you can create. You may desperately want a pink wall in a staunchly period show. But research might reveal that pink was not used during that period. This forces you to resolve the problem. You might begin by asking why there is no pink and go from there.

Research must also know its project's purpose and intent. It should be directed with that purpose as the headlamp. If the purpose of a project is to stir social change, then you will want to find sources that offer catalysts for change. These could be emblems or symbols that you might employ to induce action. And research can reinforce the context of a project. It can inform by providing references for your design. The show may need an aesthetic unity. Research into an idiosyncratic painter's work, like Redon for instance, can give the whole show a ground on which to stand. The costumes, scenery, lights and acting movements can carry Redon's aesthetic. And as a result the space becomes "Redonic."

In the end, you choose things that advance creation with veracity. And you choose by always referring to the problem, purpose and context. Research conducts a dialogue with you as you proceed. It asks you questions and takes you to new charters. It is a collaborator in your design process.

Using

To make truly effective use of research, you should develop an intimacy with it. This can involve deep reading. You probe the sources you find, looking and seeing below their surface details. Under the crust of your found images may be substances that have a significant impact on you. You need to determine what in them offers such an impact.

Part of this is achieved by allowing what I call "design osmosis." You can hang the most inspiring images on the walls of your studio. As you walk by them day-to-day, you will begin to soak up their essential oils. They will be imprinted onto your sub-conscience and you will register them in your memory. This becomes what I call a "deep knowing." It's a great way to translate inspiration into conception without a lot of concerted effort.

From osmosis you can move to dialoguing with research by sketching replications of the details you want to use. You first try to copy what you see. Your pencil will respond to the lines, contours and nuances of the forms in the pictures. This helps you to understand the object because it can tell its story through the pencil's motion. After some initial replications, you can play with it, stylize it and adapt it to your needs while you draw.

At some point you will want to preserve the key elements of your findings in an organized collection. You can create a collage, a pool, a catalog or even a scrapbook of the primary images. This document can become a major inspirational influence in your process and those of others on the artistic team. With everyone glancing at your collection you can begin to establish a cohesive direction, a production concept and certainly the look and substance of the space. People will "pull from and push to" via this collection. It's a great tool. Once a research collection is confirmed and packaged, you are ready to conduct the material practice of designing.

Design

The Designer's Progress

The practical act of spatial designing is an architectural exercise, honing space to its essence. And if done right, it's the composition of a world. It employs myriad tools, techniques, trials, talent and taste. Your toolbox includes passion, understanding, inventiveness, energy, pragmatism and a poetic slant. It also comes with savvy, experience and a bounty of informational resources. Your process will generate a series of progressively more detailed documents, a gradation of commitments. Most of these will be graphic. Some documents (such as rough thumbnails) are only to be viewed by your immediate collaborators and you. Each one can be labeled a work-in-progress. Other documents will be lavish, complete and polished for the purpose of inspiring others to want to work with you and your ideas (such as perspective renderings and presentation models). There is a wide range of steps to refinement.

Design is a progress toward an absolute and ideal servant for the project. It seeks the best solution to the design problem. That is its function. It also has an aesthetic value. In the case of spatial design, you aim for an appropriate and effective sensory form. Much of the emphasis is placed on what is seen. The visual impression on an audience is generally regarded as the most important part of their engagement with space. This is because it beckons attention so assertively. You compel the viewer by appealing to their hunger for visual order, unity, balance and interest. Now, I will argue that a space is not complete until it has some design elements assigned to serve the other senses and the deeper psychic and spiritual perceptibilities. But we cannot ignore the power of the visual. It deserves significant attention by the designer. With a marriage of inspiration and logic, the designer's progress becomes, in part, a visual composition through *the alchemy of design*.

The Alchemy of Design — The Form

As you compose, you arrange basic visual elements in space to create a meaningful whole. These elements are the fundamental building blocks of graphic creation. They are *line, shape, proportion, color, texture, movement* and *light*. Line determines style, rhythm, direction and motion in a visual design. The quality and quantity of *lines* gives the design personality. *Shape* gives the design mood, weight, style, and character and establishes its overall aesthetic. *Proportion* gives a reference point for perceiving scale. The relative sizes of objects in a design can help with balance, rhythm and can give the design meaning. It also establishes the scale, value or status of the human figures within a space. *Color* is the most psychological element of design. It carries its own set of cultural definitions. And it gives the design a great depth of interest, meaning, atmosphere and style. *Texture*, the tactile modifier of form, gives the design a mood and a sense of dimensionality. It also tells a story of the history of a surface, where it's been and what it's been through. *Movement* can be real or implied. Real movement is found in a design that transforms itself. This is common on the stage. Implied movement is where the shapes and lines in a design seem to be visually dynamic and heading in some direction. *Light* reveals and conceals form. With the right balance of light and shadow, a design can gain unity, balance, and mood. Light also allows you to manipulate the focal point of the design.

Brewing these elements together at the designer's cauldron is one of your more artful endeavors. You take your early ideas, doodles, concept and research and pour them into the pot with the elements of design. With the right mix, you can achieve a golden result. With the wrong mix, you'll be stuck with molten lead. It's a fine line. Ultimately, your goal is to create a unified composition that is appropriate to the text. And, it should be visually interesting enough to compel the audience to engage. It shouldn't distract. It should foster the storytelling. It should seem natural and purposeful, not self-indulgent. You want the composition to be experienced, not watched.

This is really what composition is all about. Everything needs to be put together so that it seems natural enough to go unnoticed. Yet it should be so effective that the life of the world in it cannot continue if it changes. It should have (a) focal point(s) and these should be positioned so they emphasize the same thing the text emphasizes. All of the other elements reinforce the focal point(s). And if one of the reinforcements is taken away, the unity is diminished. There should be balance, whether symmetrical or asymmetrical. If the composition is rigidly symmetrical, it is formal and direct. If the balance is asymmetrical, it is more like nature, strangely logical yet not mechanical. In spatial design, composition is pointless without regarding the humans who dwell in it. A space must contain life to be composed. So, the designer must yield some of the space for that life to ensue. You must give the dwellers an appropriate place to live. The alchemical stew is not mature until life is induced.

Visual composition entails devising order from chaos and finding harmonious balance in a visual arrangement. There should be a good blend of unity and diversity and a logical "wholeness" to the completed design. While there is no science to this, it does follow generally accepted standards. There is a tradition of well-composed art that began in ancient Greece. It still is taught today, especially in graphic design programs. I would never suggest that all design for the theatre should abide by these standards, but it is worth noting that they have proven track record and are universally regarded as pleasing to the eye. You might want to look at art that seems pleasing to your eye and try to mimic its techniques.

You may recall that in Chapter 1, I introduce four basic forms of space: the organic, circle, square and line. Below I show illustrations of "good" and "better" scenic compositions for each of these forms. In most cases, the better designs are more visually interesting and more orderly. This comes from a process of trial and error and personal taste. While it is not morally "wrong" for a design to be imbalanced, poorly arranged compositions often become distracting and that is usually an undesirable result. I suppose if you are working

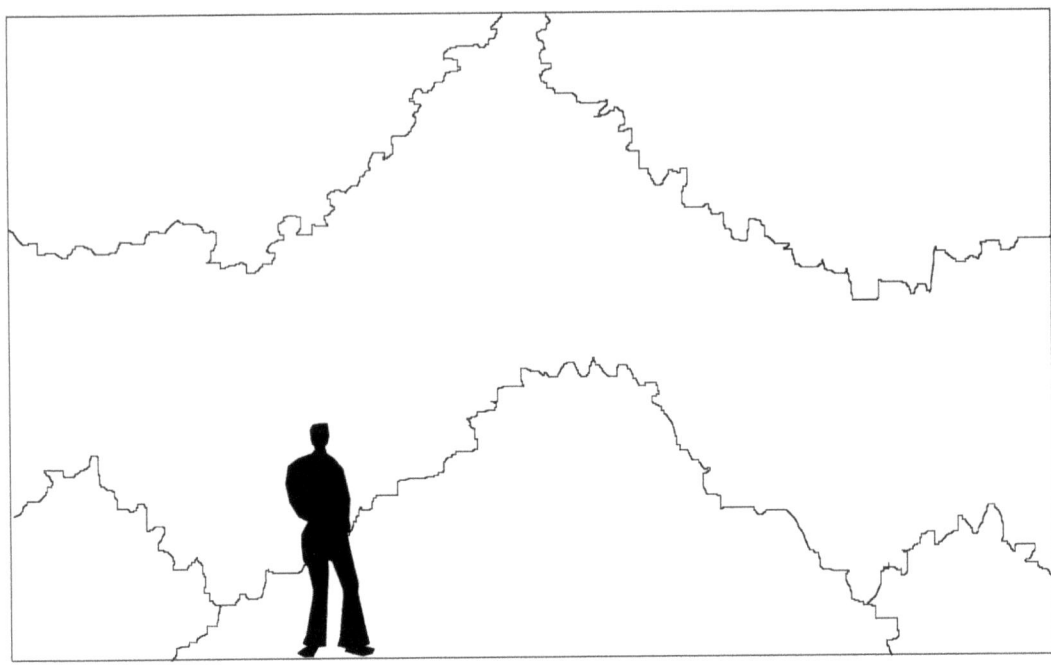

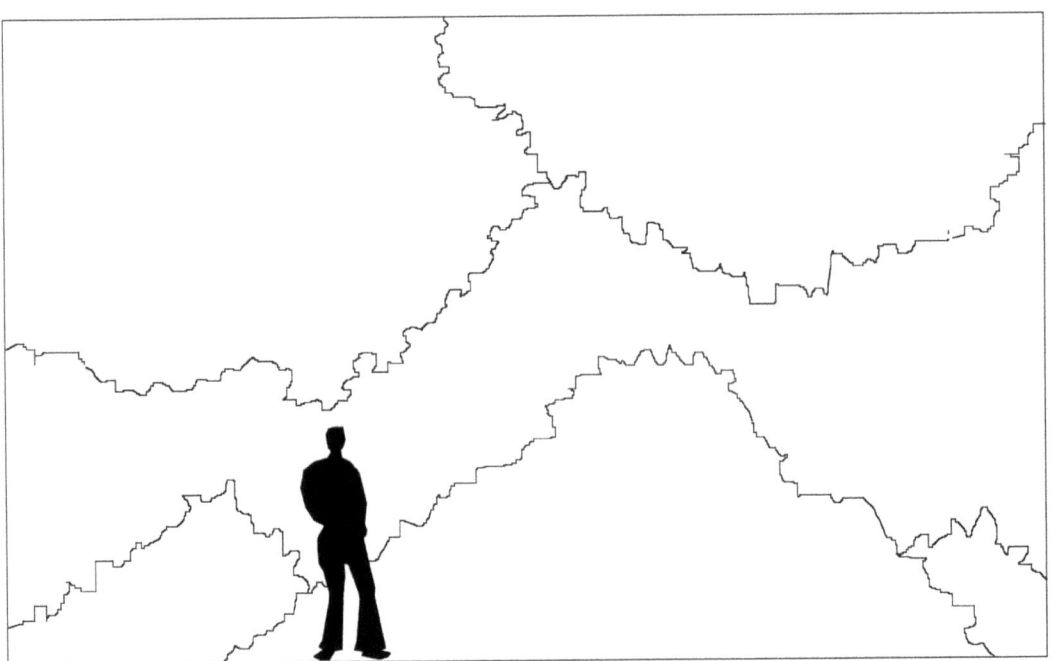

Top: "Good" organic space composition. ***Above:*** "Better" organic space composition. Some depth is created with a better ratio of positive and negative space.

on a project that intends to rebel against all of western convention, you might try to design against these principles. But either way, it's good to know the principles.

Revisions: It is important to note that the alchemy of design is never complete. Expect to hone and revise any visual design all the way through its realization. Too often, theatre administrators expect the scale model to be the final design, fixed and inflexible. The truth

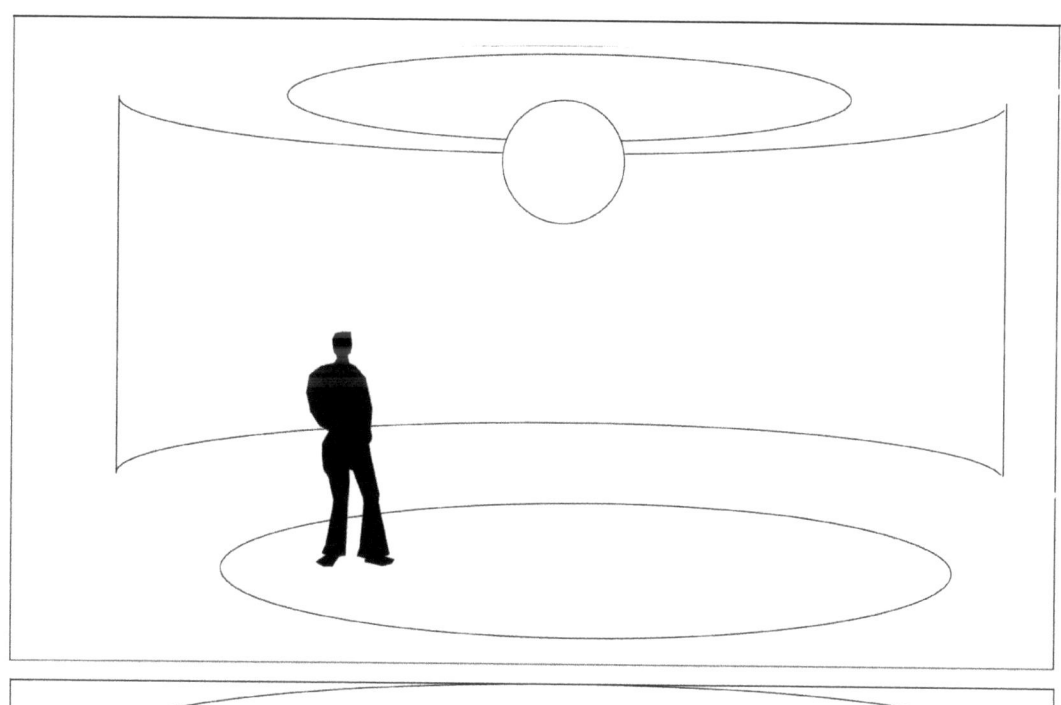

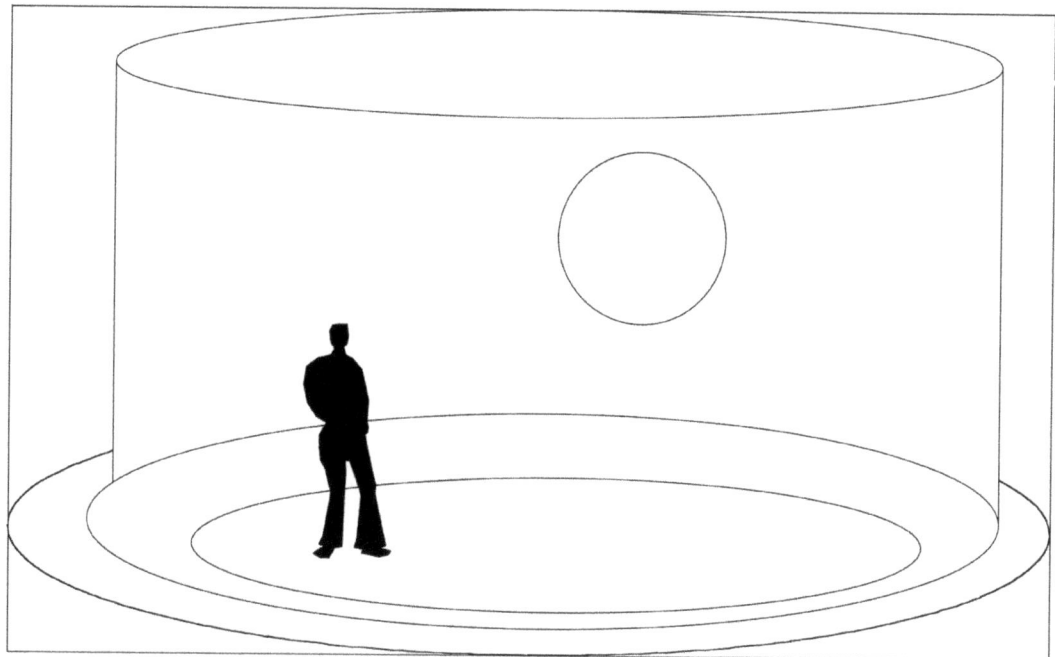

Top: "Good" circular space composition. *Above:* "Better" circular space composition. Here, separated parts are brought together and shifted to give a better sense of unity.

is, even on Broadway and at major opera houses with expensive crews and shop costs, revisions happen all the way to opening night (even beyond that). This is actually desirable. You must continue to design as the show accumulates its polished elements. The addition of actors, clothes and lighting reveals things that you could never foresee. That is why there is a dress rehearsal period. Continue to dream. Continue to make. Do so until the accountants peel you away.

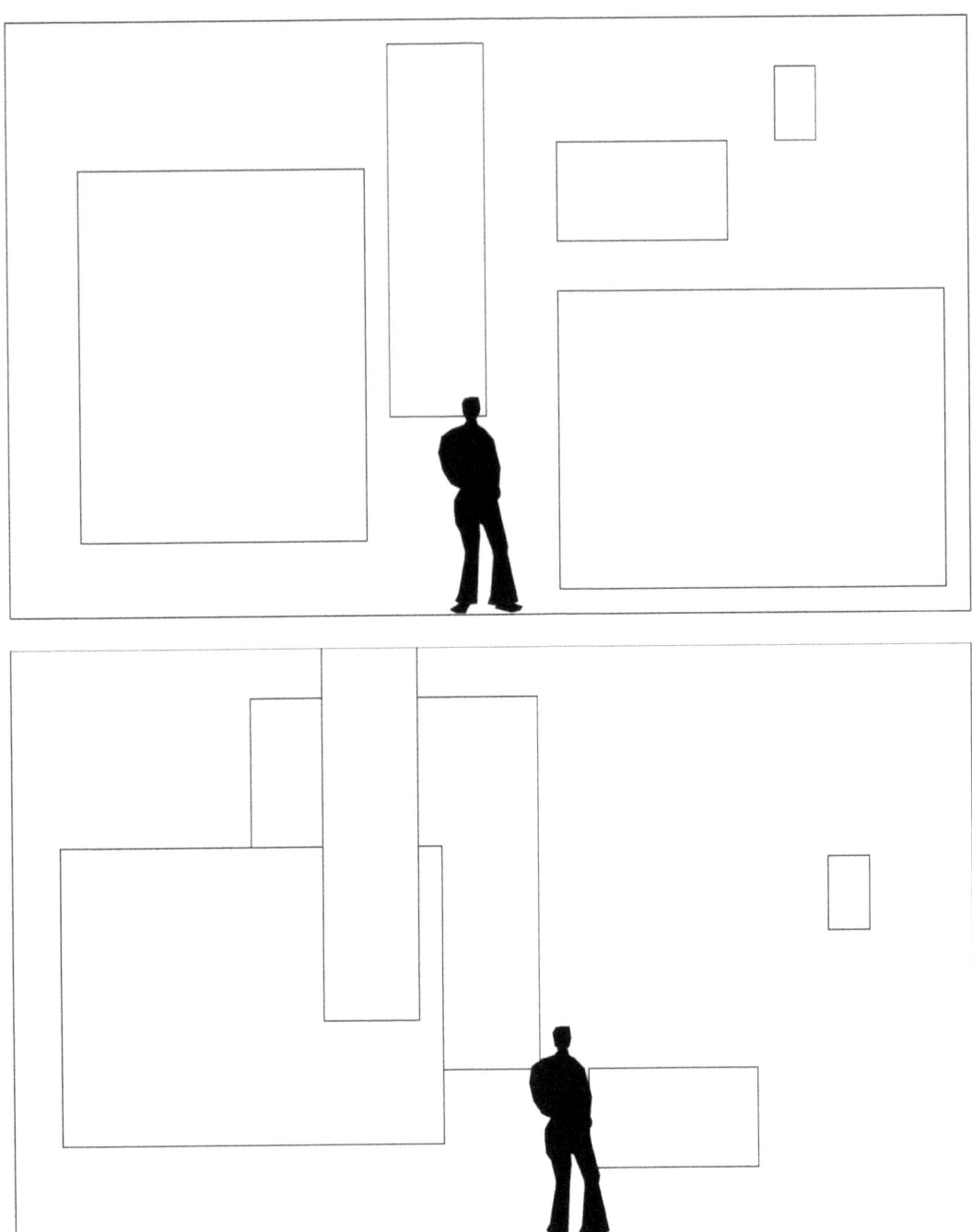

Top: "Good" rectilinear space composition. ***Above:*** "Better" rectilinear space composition. Here, the forms overlap and rearrange to create more asymmetry and visual interest.

The exercise of revision is healthy. It is necessary to reject some ideas and leave room for new ideas that you might not expect. Be open to explore; regard nothing as precious or perfect; and rely on collaborators to help you. Be willing to correct yourself. But keep mindful of the kernel of yourself, that seed you plant at the beginning. As you design and revise, it's vital that you know your base.

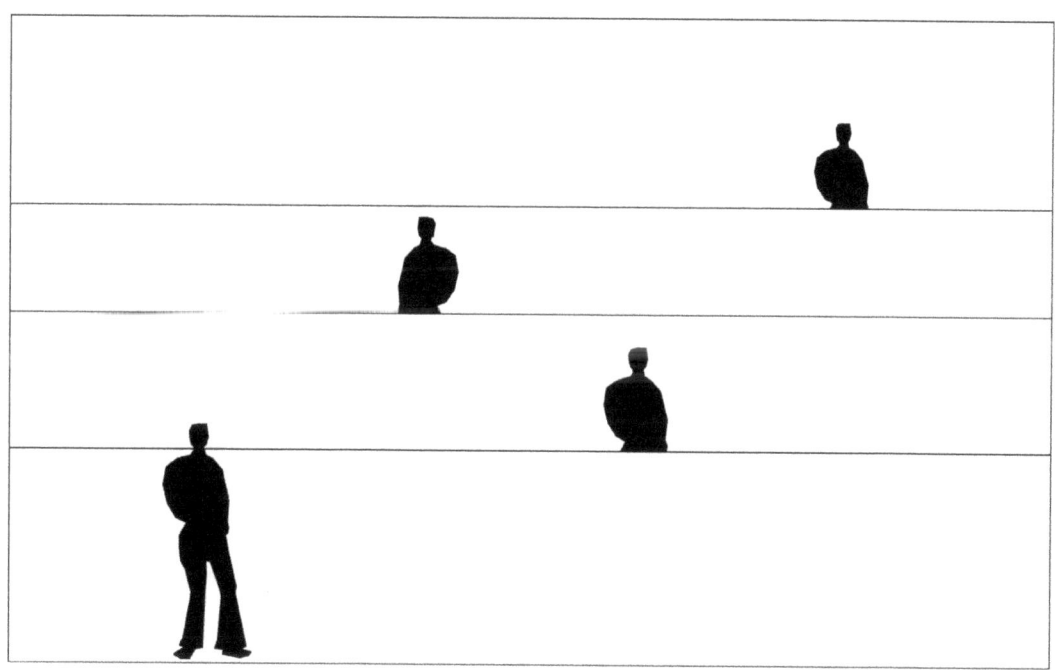

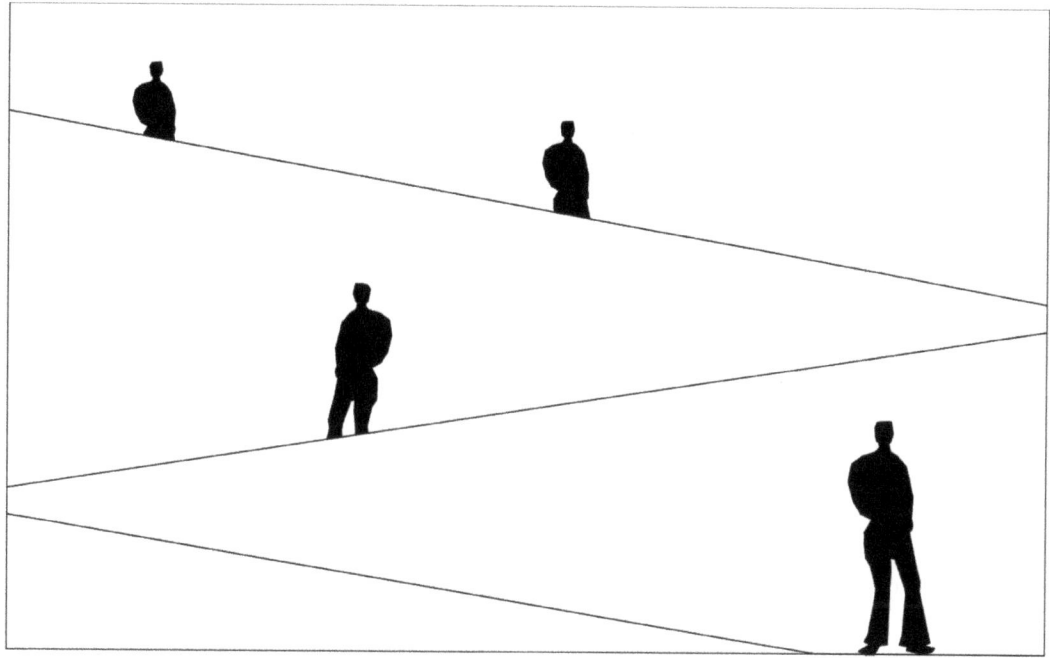

Top: "Good" linear space composition. A series of galleries all lined up. *Above:* "Better" linear space composition. The galleries become ramps, creating better linear movement with clear directionality.

In most cases, there are a multitude of compositions to address in a spatial design. For one thing, there are a multitude of points of view to consider. Your audiences, or visitors, have a range of vantage points and the design must be composed for as many of those vantage points as possible. You must compose dimensionally and rotationally and resist creating a single dominant viewpoint.

Also, the space is ever evolving. Since spatial design is about making an event or experience rather than a single static object, you need to design the key moments of that event as a series of individual compositions. You also need to design the flow of the moments and give them an arc, or some other unification. This creates a layered composition, or a matrix. One way to hold the whole thing together is via the engineering of design or what I call *the machine of the design.*

* * *

The Alchemy of Illumination

The revelation and concealment of space through light can have a dramatic impact on the perception, interpretation and understanding by its audience. Lighting should not be thought of as static imagery and a fixed presence. It should be honored as a dynamic force in space. Lighting has as much to do with flow and progression as it does with the look. When you compose light, you compose its visual attributes AND its action.

Lighting has its own set of visual elements, the things designers can control:

Color: Psychological influencer, mood setter, focus assister
Distribution: (the quality of the light; its texture, size, contrast and direction) Provides feeling, focus and drama
Intensity: (the relative brightness of light) Assists with focus, mood and clarity/perception
Movement: (the changes of light during a spatial event, the lighting cues) The dynamic element of light. It provides direction, range and brings the design to life.

Lighting has several functions that contribute to spatial design:

Visibility: The ability to see what you should see
Focus: The ability to be selective about what you see and don't see
Mood: The feeling and emotion of the space is established
Modeling: The visual forms of the space are accentuated and made interesting by the way they are lit

* * *

The Machine of Design — The Function

A good spatial design provides a machine for conveying meaning and accentuating essential moments. That is, it possesses a method to foster the flow of the action/life and allow the moments to be effectively experienced by the audience/visitors. It draws people to key dramatic points and punctuates them, allowing the meaning of the moment to transmit. And it functions in such a way that it carries a meaning/message in its own device. The machine is colored in the same palette as the story it tells.

So, you should evolve a mechanical operation in your design, concurrent with the visual composition, that serves the motion of the event by clever functioning. Look for a way to foster the flow of the event in the same manner as the story being told. In other words, make an appropriate choice. The machine itself could be a metaphor for the story. This is a way to pull everything together. Again, you need to start by knowing the story you are telling. And, beyond that, you need to know its structure and the quality of its movement. With this knowledge, you will disclose the design problem. And then you can proceed to solve it mechanically.

The machine of design can employ any means, but in the theatre it often utilizes some of the customary mechanics, traditions and devices we have in the facility. There can be shows that fly scenery, roll wagons, pop up props from the traps and revolve sets on a turntable. These are all machines. But, the best machines are more original. Caryl Churchill's sexually explicit play *Cloud Nine* calls for frequent shifting from the natural environment of the African veldt and the structured environment of Victorian England. Coinciding with these geographical shifts are shifts between the oppression of human nature by cultural structure and the subsequent release of natural urges.

My design for this play employs a machine that serves both dynamics. At the back of the main playing space is a wall of Venetian-type blinds. Behind the blinds is a translucent and glowing painting of an idyllic nature scene with trees. It is neutral enough to be Africa or a park in London. When the blinds close, they are painted with the image of a large union jack. When rotated open, they expose nature. The blinds are set up to rise and fall, allowing entrances and exits of characters. They comprise the main functioning apparatus of the design. The blinds also represent structure overpowering nature in an imperialist manner. The union jack closes out the trees and sky. This is because the play has moments where the stifling mentality of English manners impedes the human nature. The blinds then open and release the vision of nature during moments when human nature is set free. My machine both reflects the ideas in the play metaphorically and fosters its delivery mechanically.

Essentially, the machine of a design assists in conveying ideas and contains a flavoring reminiscent of the story's subject matter, style and language. There are many more examples. Renaissance stage designs use lavishly painted 2-D scenery that quickly and "magically" slides in and out of sightlines and transforms the space like the changing pages of an artist's sketchbook. This coincides with the spectacular nature of the plays and operas being presented. The machine can and should also transport the participants, cast and audience through the dramatic event. In the end, the key thing to remember is to make your engineering artful and as much of a storyteller, dressed in story-appropriate garb, as the visual poetry you compose with the elements of design.

The Network of Design — The Fusion

The third constituent of design, beyond form and function, is the capacity for fusion. A spatial design must "network" with its inhabitants or its characters and audience in the theatre. In other words, it should bond with its culture. Here is the spirit of design in a nutshell: *The form gets to the essence of the story. The function tells the story and the fusion connects the story to the people.* Devising the connector for that fusion is your next challenge. And this can be a little elusive.

Form and function ask you to refer back to seeing and knowing, especially regarding things like the physics of space and the anthropology of space. *Form* can emerge by considering the physics of space. You might begin your design by resolving the relief of the spatial section, or maybe by establishing the traffic patterns of the plan and sometimes by rendering the facial features of the elevation. You compose the visual nature of the space out from those initial constructs. On the other hand, *function* might emerge from a careful deep reading of the cultural myths behind the story's message. You might devise an operation that facilitates the manifestation of that myth. To establish the *fusion*, you need to go beyond sight and knowledge. You enter the realm of "being," the final phase of my book. In order to weave the connective tissue, you need to be able to put yourself (or your agent) into the experience.

It is imperative that someone involved in the design process personally activate the matrixing mechanism of the human collective. All people have in them access to the eternal. And by stepping forward and allowing your life, or the lives of trusted others, to "test drive" the article of your making, you can establish protocols of connection by accessing those deep commonalities. This can be initialized with masterful imagination and foresight. It can be advanced in workshops or by testing the project. You might even utilize a focus group to get feedback. This is a vital step. Test your connectivity. Put people, even yourself, in the space before you reveal the space in full scale.

Your goal is to find adhesives for fusing the hearts, minds, souls *and realities* of the people with the experience you design. I stress the word realities because you must go beyond touching the deep feelings and tendencies of psyche and emotion, etc. Sometimes you need to consider things as real as comfort, bathroom breaks, ease of movement and traffic flow, etc. You put all these considerations together and find the most effective (and reasonable) way to tie your story to the people. This might involve the use of a master symbol, or an engaging image coupled with a plan that fosters easy access and interaction by the participants. Your job as a designer is to bring the audience/visitors in. And once you do, you should let them be, and if needed, help them out. If you are good, you can impact their lives for the better. One way to do so is by *being* one of them.

Once you have form, function and fusion, you move toward completing the vast catalog of design documents. The purpose of these is communication. You need to get the point of all your thinking into the minds of others. At this point you depend a bit on technology.

The Technology of Design

The scene designer carries a hefty array of compositional tools. Of course, there are the simple drawing implements you use to hash out early concepts such as pencils, erasers, markers and paints. Then there are several, popular computer design programs including CAD, illustration and photo-editing systems that allow you to generate clear and modifiable specification documents. These offer great convenience. You can revise without losing the original version. They offer the ability to transport your vision with ease and speed. And you can create layers upon layers of detail in a drawing and retain the ability to peel away certain components whenever necessary.

These tools offer the flexibility for change and that is ideal. Spatial design is never complete because a space is never complete. As I suggest in my early chapters, space is an active and dynamic organism, always in regeneration. And it begins its gestation period with drawing. Drawing must be adaptable to evolution. Your tools should possess a range of duty. Your mastery of the tools should include an understanding of their flexibility.

A theatre designer also needs to be well acquainted with stage mechanics and machinery.

Since spatial design, especially scene design, is a design of occurrences, not of a static picture, you need to know the means by which these occurrences might perpetuate. There are a variety of high and low-tech mechanisms that foster change. Some of these are ancient. Even the old methods should be learned as a reference. Knowledge stretches the imagination. Knowing technology is a great liberator.

The Cinema of Space: One such technology, video projection/imaging, is enormously popular in theatre design today. It has, in part, supplanted scenic painting. In the past, scenic artists would render several backdrops for the different scenes in a play. Today, scene designers create an interesting array of projection surfaces onto which can be projected a near infinite abundance of changing imagery, including painterly illustrations, photographs, film and digital art. Some designers find this almost too liberating. Others don't care for the flattened look that these kinds of images often present. It's true that there can be a lack of lushness in projected imagery when compared to good scenic art. But that is improving. Like all technology, projections stretch our capabilities and our imagination to reaches we never dreamed possible in the last 25 or so centuries. The space is widening rapidly.

Digital Space: To piggyback on the notion of evolving technology, I want to address a new kind of space. Genuine tangible space, that which we encounter everyday, has immediacy. We can easily see and know it. And so this book addresses it in depth and detail. But there is another form of space that has emerged in the last twenty years with a remarkable impact, despite a lack of physical tangibility. As such, it is worthy of consideration in the practice of design. It is digital (or cyber) space.

Digital space finds itself a new subject in the anthropology of space. Cultural studies reveal that more and more people prefer to communicate without human touch. They communicate electronically via short, typewritten abbreviations that become a constant (and communal) cyber-dialogue. This is a dialogue devoid of visceral contact. It doesn't transmit body language including the subtleties of gesture and inflection. Therefore it is incomplete communication. On the other hand, social networking has a unique benefit. Due to the convenience of remote engagement, it allows perpetual communication, more so than ever before in history. And despite its lack of carnal contact, the emotional connections and impact are very real. People can be very convincing with simple text messages or posts on a digital board. Its potential is enormous. So is its danger.

We live in a world inflating beyond its material limits. You can reach out and connect with another soul, another idea, another dream and a ton of useful information all while sitting privately in your safe domain, alone. And digital space does not intrude on physical space. We can now stretch without actual displacement (at least we haven't observed the displacement, it *might* exist invisibly). That is a key signifier of our state in time. Humans have begun to master a new "final frontier" and I believe that is the threshold of a major evolutionary shift. If we are less reliant on physical space, our mind space coupled with digital space (the electronic version of mind space) will become a trend in how we develop.

The Web has approached a new eternity. We can reach the edge of the world in an instant. This expands space to virtual infinity. We embrace it because it offers the ultimate efficiency. It has speed, no need for tedious travel, and no material waste. Digital space also plays into the world of art. Interactive/cyber theatre can occur by allowing performances to be viewed and controlled by a distant online audience. The potential of its spatial content can extend to the reaches of the web; but the visual space must live within the aperture of the screen. So it still has limits. Designing digital space is fairly uncharted territory, a realm of creation yet to shift from peripheral into focused sight.

So, how do designers regard this kind of space? Below, I present three sets of questions and answers to address that regard based on recent conversations with some fellow designers.

How do designers describe digital space?

Response: It has several dimensions. It is expanding like the universe. It is absent of organic matter. But it is filled with signals of life, verifiable expressions that stand like persons on the screen, with enough of a psychological impact to provoke and evoke emotions. In that sense, it is a kind of "signal theatre." But it is incredibly interactive and the interaction is immediate.

How do designers define digital space?

Response: It is an embodiment of efficiency that circumvents the "wasteful" nature of human, carnal and sensory contact. Because it allows remoteness and independence, it can be curiously safe and detaching. As such, it can also pose danger. Either way, it creates new space in the mind that has yet to reach its potential. If liberated from the expense of time, mental effort and the distraction of human touch, it should free your mind to explore a new and unknown potential.

How do designers design digital space?

Response: It's done with the alchemy of spatial communications, back and forth and in and out. It's done by plugging-in infusory dispatches that will stimulate action. This makes it highly interactive for both designers and users. Designers stimulate digital action and digital design through signals. And the result is a grid of transmissions composed toward a purposeful engagement, without human touch, but with human effect. As such, it is definitely a viable form of spatial design.

All manner of space, hard or soft, can be manipulated by design. A designer should carry some kind of guidelines as work ensues. Below, I lay out an introduction to such guidelines. It is based on the work of one of theatre's earliest theorists.

The Poetics of Space

This is an outline of what a space should include, once designed. It's a "nuts and bolts" checklist for designers; a summary of what a spatial design aspires to be. Although it refers most naturally to theatre scene design, it is applicable to all spatial design. It follows the structure of Aristotelian *Poetics* and uses Aristotle's Greek terminology.

Mythos

The space must possess a structure that supports the beliefs, attitudes and values held by the group of people (characters) who inhabit the space (or intentionally and obviously contradict it for effect). The structure must not only allow, but drive, action. It should possess a motor, a means of propelling the action forward. The space has a motion that operates with the motion of the story. So the space should tell a story that arouses feelings in its audience.

Ethos

The space should be true to character. It should be true to the character of the story, the group of characters in the story and the individual characters in the story (there are differences between these). It should have a distinction in style, a level of reality, and an aesthetic quality that is consistent with the story (or deliberately inconsistent for a certain effect).

Dianoia

The space should communicate a theme, thought or knowledge in its own way. The space is responsible for radiating an idea at the appropriate level of volume. And it does so atop, within or aside the storytelling. And it should metaphysically argue its point with a metaphysical logic, in a metaphysically discursive way, or by whatever means that seem effective.

Lexis

The design can use signage and metaphor to communicate. It establishes its own method to communicate and writes its own language (diction). The space's language should reflect the character of the event within.

Melos

Besides its thought and its signage, the space should possess another aesthetic layer. It's one that connects more with intuition than intellect, a visual musicality perhaps, or a means of expression that gives the space a sensory identity, a feeling, mood or emotion that can de discerned, though not necessarily analyzed.

Opsis

And the space should have an appearance that is consistent with the story. It should have an appearance of substance, value and purpose, unified with a completeness that may be attractive, repulsive, or somewhere in-between, but ultimately interesting. There is no imperative that it look "good" or even polished. But if it does not, the reason must reside in the purpose of the project. A spectacle must suit its purpose.

In the theatre, spectacle has a long tradition as a contributor to the art. Theatre uses spectacle to attract and retain attention and to elevate the experience to a point where it awes, inspires or transforms, heightening the audience's appreciation of the story or gist of the experience. It is important to note that in theatre or any spatial design, *spectacular* isn't synonymous with *attractive*. In fact, spectacle can be quite disturbing. Ultimately it is about impact and the relevance of impact to intent.

The thing that is consistent among all these Aristotelian points is that they ask the space to connect with the story or the poetry from which they spring. They ask the space to relate to the text, reflect it, respond to it, refer to it and reinforce it. The hope is that in the process, the space becomes a *living world* consistent with its text.

Living

The injection of life into a space consummates the design process. A space comes alive once it is inhabited and interactive with its inhabitants. And when it has a story to tell and seeks to be heard, its life evolves around that story's text. The text comes in some registered form, literary or otherwise. When the conditions are right, the space becomes world. The ingredients that comprise a living world are equal parts of:

- Story/Text (usually one that allows a certain action)
- Space
- Culture
- Passion (a reason for living, for doing all this)

Informed composition makes the living world. The informed composer is nourished by sight, knowledge and life, and by a previous immersion in other worlds, past, present and even future. This nourishment is coupled with a creative willingness to allow the entrance of truths, seen and unseen. As stated earlier, composition is the process of taking many and making one, toward a unified and purposeful whole. That whole is life.

By seeing and knowing we make that which we live.

And in life, we make ourselves from that which we see and know (via observation, psychology, anthropology and religion, etc.).

In case you are wondering, the previous two sentences express the core thesis of this book.

In the introduction to this chapter, I claim that design is one part poetry (the dreaming) and one part engineering (the pragmatism). This is also the makeup of life. The duality of design could be reiterated on a grander scale as one part impetuous youth and one part maturity; one part formative exploration and one part industrious contribution; or one part vision and one part mission. So there is a parallel to be observed here. Design is like life. And life is an on-going composition. That is another core point.

I am proud to report that the theatre, my art form, makes life, at least a reflection of life, in part by the process of composition and design. And in that process may be found theatre's greatest cultural contribution.

Part Four

Being

Theatre artists get excited about opening night. There are cast parties and public galas and the crew can finally get some sleep. The scene designer relishes this moment because it means the space for the show has materialized and is now alive. These sentiments are similar to those of Dr. Frankenstein, I suppose. This kind of celebratory mindset is also present at the ribbon cutting of a new building, a theme park attraction or a public square. The space is inaugurated. It is not finished; but it is open for use and injected with life.

In the theatre, the space is not only the material surroundings of the event. It IS the event. A space is a composition of all design areas, direction, acting, movement, text and audience, together. And it is the story, action and message, together as well. The animation of a space, or its performance, is the life of the space. Life is generated and the switch turned on as the curtain opens.

As we enjoy the culmination of a spatial event design, we can reflect a bit. We might ask: What has happened? What brings us to this place? What process made all this? Creative design is comprised of the key phases I outline in this book: story, seeing, knowing, making, and being. Here is a summary of that process:

1. The *Story* is the first composition. We are storytellers in the theatre. And storytelling is a vital part of cultural life, especially with mythic stories. The first composition is made of characters, action and message. It is the "word and the law" in the creative process. It is a given, earthen, grounded and reliable. It supplies you with the answers you need. From it, you prepare your design.

2. *Seeing* is the study of the tangible toward a design. It is a composition of observations. You see the truth. It is visible. You witness that which you may use, such as the realities of physical material and the methods by which those are employed. From these elemental regards you can set the text into action. Through sight, you observe the substance of the earth, those concrete building blocks for your design.

3. *Knowing* is the encounter with the essence of things toward a design. It is a composition of realizations. It's about getting to know the spirit of the project and its story,

connecting you with the text. With knowledge, the spirit moves in you, and spreads with your design.

4. *Making* the new space involves the crafting of an event by a collaborative group. It's a composition of many souls. The collective breeds the event. It is a cultural imperative to create. Because you must, you gather together with others to conduct your design.

5. *Being* is the life of the thing created by collaboration. It is a composition of all elements as one, E Pluribus Unum. It is like a tribal village, the spirit united with the people. Life is brought to your design.

6. And with a *Passion*, the composition is complete. *The space is a world; life goes forward; you switch on your design.*

The above addresses the making. But, what is made?

Theatre is unique because it is a live art. It is a living thing and it also reflects life. Life is being. And Being and Space are bound. Cultural studies confirm this. "Being" in the theatre is The Event, or the live enacting of a culturally relevant story. With "being," the space is whole. When culture and space are together, the event is composed. So, the thing that is made is The Event.

The union of culture and space, as the event, is composed with the following conceptual "parts":

1. *The base structure of the event*

This is the foundation; the origins and strata of place and culture entwined. It is an impactive and observable firmament, a cultural ground. We can call it our world.

2. *The detailing and finish of the event*

This is the flesh and bone, the physical attributes. It is that with which we conduct personal interaction; it is that which arises to live on, in and beside us, our guide in space. We can call it our reality.

3. *The action of the event*

This provides the needs of the soul. It is the unseen energy that moves us; it is the marriage of humanity and space in motion, the unity, the being, and the message. We can call it our life.

4. *And us, the people who are characters in the event, the cast*

We are here because the event is our mirror to life. We can call it our story.

4A. *And us, the people who attend the event, the audience*

We are here because we all wish to participate in this ritual of being. We can call it our experience.

In summary, space and time unite into an event. And the event is made of structure, finish, action and culture. Beyond that, the event is *being*. And its very creation is part of its being, because the creation never really stops. Every time someone enters the space, the space evolves. The process is a grand, moving composition, with all moving things made whole. And the whole is the living, spatial event. This is especially manifest in the work of the theatre. Actors refer to this idea as "being what you are making." But its message is for non-theatre souls as well. To professionals in other fields and for the creative pursuits of everyday people, I offer the following points of advice on *being your making*.

In your endeavors:

Find relevance
   By Seeing: Anytime you look at something, you look for something

Express a truth
   By Knowing: All things go deep. Regard the seemingly mundane as profound and you might learn to know the magnificence of that around you.

Teach a lesson
   By Making: You make by living the thing you are making. And you share that life.

Expose life
   By Being: Being is a dance in space. It's immediate. Show life as you live it.

Clarify vision
   By Composition: The parts merge and gel because they wish to find a way to being one. Composition breeds understanding.

   And

Move someone
   In Space: You can find your way. But visit all of it, and make all of it as you go. Truthfully, it's everything. Engage that truth with others.

I'll close by saying this: Actors portraying life in a theatre space reflect "real" humans *being* in the spaces of life. So, all that I've said regarding seeing, knowing and making in the theatre holds true when considering the being of "reality." And I can validate this because, in more ways than one, *theatre is life* (it reflects life and its creation is a model of life, as creativity is the force and solvent of life).

Since space is a created event, it too is life. That life, that space, that potential, will not terminate unless overcome by the darkest forces. For instance, evils as black as the holocaust can truncate entire tribal lines. And targeted evils such as all forms of personal abuse can suffocate human spirit. In such atrocities, cultural and culturally rooted individual stories are ripped from the hands of their possessors and cease to exist. Here space can stop. But the halt is a pause. There is a deep vibration that can sustain as the smoke clears, a remnant of life. *Space is deep*. In its depth, it reconnects to life. The designer can offer the regenerative impulse.

Designers may be magic players in the cultural cast. They can spark and ignite. They can reform and reshape. They can save and restore. They can see and steer. They can write and tell. And they can slice the veil and dismantle the wall. Designers build the temple and then after the bombardment rebuild the temple. They plant a park on ground zero. They craft a memorial on bloodstained ground. They provide a sanctuary for innocents and havens for the dying.

They solve the problem.

This is the creative power. It's a power for service and not individual gain. And the service becomes an artistic practice. In the theatre, the artist practices the composition of worlds. She embraces the poetics of space, and welcomes a deep encounter with truth. The truth is that designing space means designing experience and not simply crafting goods. As such, she ultimately reaches her goal … the concluding composition.

Bibliography

Aristotle, S.H. Butcher, and Francis Fergusson. *Aristotle's Poetics*. New York: Hill and Wang, 1961.

Artaud, Antonin. *The Theatre and Its Double*. New York: Grove Press, 1994.

Austin, Robert, Lee Devin, and Eric Schmidt. *Artful Making*. London: Financial Times, 2003.

Barron, Robert. *Catholicism: A Journey to the Heart of the Faith*. New York: Image Books, 2011.

Bay, Howard. *Stage Design*. New York: Drama, 1974.

Beacham, Robert C. *Adolphe Appia: Artist and Visionary of the Modern Theatre*. New York: Routledge, 1994.

Brockett, Oscar. *History of the Theatre (10th Ed.)*. Boston: Allyn and Bacon, 2007.

Burian, Jarka. *The Scenography of Josef Svoboda*. Middletown, CT: Wesleyan University Press, 1974.

Campbell, Joseph. *The Hero with a Thousand Faces (3rd Ed.)*. Novato, CA: New World Library, 2008.

Dal Co, Francesco, and Kurt W. Forster. *Frank Gehry: The Complete Works*. London: Phaidon Press, 2003.

Hartmann, Rudolf. *Opera*. Minneapolis, MN: Book Sales, 1982.

Hawking, Stephen. *The Universe in a Nutshell*. New York: Bantam Books, 2001.

Ingham, Rosemary. *From Page to Stage: How Theatre Designers Make Connections Between Scripts and Images*. Portsmouth, NH: Heinemann Drama, 1998.

John of the Cross. *Dark Night of the Soul (Dover Ed.)*. Mineola, NY: Dover Publications, 2003.

Jones, Robert Edmond. *The Dramatic Imagination (Reissue)*. New York: Routledge, 1974.

Jung, Carl G., and R.F.C. Hull. *The Archetypes and the Collective Conscious*. Princeton, NJ: Princeton University Press, 1981.

Koltai, Ralph. *Ralph Koltai: Designer for the Stage*. London: Nick Hern Books, 2003.

Levi-Strauss, Claude. *Myth and Meaning: Cracking the Code of Culture*. New York: Schocken, 1995.

Merriam, Alan P., and Valerie Merriam. *The Anthropology of Music*. Evanston, IL: Northwestern University Press, 1964.

Oenslager, Donald. *Stage Design: Four Centuries of Scenic Invention*. London: Thames and Hudson. 1975.

Parker, Oren, R. Craig Wolf, and Dick Block. *Scene Design and Stage Lighting*. Beverly, MA: Wadsworth, 2008.

Parramon, J.M. *Composition*. London: HPBooks, 1987.

Rose, Rich. *Drafting Scenery for the Theatre, Film and Television*. Cincinnati, OH: Betterway Books, 1990.

Rosenthal, Jean. *The Magic of Light*. New York: Little Brown, 1972.

Sagan, Carl. *The Demon Haunted World: Science as a Candle in the Dark*. New York: Ballantine Books, 1997.

Sheppard, David. *On Some Faraway Beach: The Life and Times of Brian Eno*. Chicago: Chicago Review Press, 2009.

Simonson, Lee. *The Stage Is Set*. New York: Theatre Arts Books, 1970.

Smith, Ronn. *American Set Design 2*. New York: Theatre Communications Group, 1993.

Stein, Gordon. *The Encyclopedia of the Paranormal*. Amherst, NY: Prometheus Books, 1996.

Tharp, Twyla. *The Collaborative Habit: Life Lessons for Working Together*. New York: Simon and Schuster, 2009.

Theresa of Avila. *Interior Castle (Dover Ed.)*. Mineola, NY: Dover Publications, 2007.

Turner, Victor. *From Ritual to Theatre: The Human Seriousness of Play*. Boston, MA: PAJ Publications, 2001.

Whitehill, Angela. *The Nutcracker Backstage*. East Windsor, NJ: Princeton Book, 2004.

Index

Page numbers in **_bold italics_** indicate illustrations.

access 41–42
action 58
action of the event 164
activating the text 143
actors 16–17
aesthetic distance 38, 86
aesthetics 57
African dance 107
agression 61
alchemy of design 150
alchemy of illumination 156
allegories 68
Amish 121
The Anabaptists 95
analogies 68
angels 104
angular set **_49_**
angularity 48–50
Ansky, S. 103, **_103_**
anthropologists 114
anthropology of space 114
Appalachian Spring 76
appearance 132
Appia, Adolphe 14, 86
appraisal of space 131
apse 111
arc 73
archeology of space 126
arches 118
architects, architecture and architectural design 2, 9, 11, 21, 25, 29, 61, 84, 135, 142
architectural analogies 145
"architecture for moments" 11
area 36–37
Aristotle 160
art and artists of occurrences 11, 28
Artaud, Antonin 10
atlas 31
atmosphere 71
attraction design 142
audience 164
axis 33–36, **_34_**

Bach, J.S. 75
ballet 21
basic forms of space 12
Bauhaus 50
The Beggar's Opera 73, **_73_**
being 5, 158, 164
"being what you are making" 164
Bellini, Vincenzo 130
Between Two Worlds 103
Birth of a Nation 112
Bizet, Georges 66
The Black Swan 105
blood bond 140
The Blue Lagoon 60
body of space 19
bold strokes 88–90
book musical 21
box set 14
Brecht, Bertolt 58, 69
bridge 117
bridges 120
Brigham Young University 109
Brooklyn Bridge 120
Buried Child 21
buttresses 111

Cabaret 62
CAD 25, 158
California 121
Cameron, John 109
Candida 33
capture 132
Carmen 66
Carmina Burana 130
cartography 43–44
case studies of spatial deep reading 120–126
cast 164
cathedral 111
catholic 106
centerline 34
central power in the universe 96
Chagall, Marc 103
chamber music 11

changing points of view 40
character 18, 45
character actor 45
Checkpoint Charlie 41
Chekhov, Anton **_12, 36_**
The Cherry Orchard 35, **_36_**
choosing 149
chord progression 76
chorus 78
A Christmas Carol 71
Churchill, Caryl 41, 157
cinema of space 159
cinematic writing 14
circle 13, 85
circle of souls 139
circular movement **_73_**
circular space **_153_**
Cloud Nine 157
collaborating and collaboration 10, 16, 137–142, 164
collective unconscious 62
color 150, 156
coloration 70
comedic curves 51
coming of age 122
communication/contact 61
communion 106–107
companionship 61
competition 61
composition 4, 6, 8, 9, 16, 135, 151, **_152–155_**, 163, 165
composition of process 88
composition of the theatre artist 16
composition of worlds 150, 165
conceiving 142–144
conditions 83–84
connective thread 89
consciousness 138
Constructivism 98
constructivist theatre sets 98
container (of space) 31, 104
contemplation 99
continuum of texture 71
contour-meanings 43

Index

Corneille 107
costume 17
costume designers 17
creating 145–146
cultural forecast 85
cultural stories 147
culture 81–82, 114
culture of space 81
culture of the story 18
current conditions 83
curvilinearity 50–53
cyclorama 31

Dakota 123
Dalí, Salvador 63
dance 74
Dark Night of the Soul 23
day 48
Debussy, Claude 99
deconstruction 54
deep knowing 149
deep reading 94, 119–120, 126, 147
Deep Space Nine 7
"deeper thing to know" 95
defining 143
defining space 93
The Demon Haunted World 97
demons 105–106
departure 42
depth 26
design 9, 147
design influenced by fractals **56**
design process 5, 88, 150
designer empowerment 34
designers (stage) 17–18
designer's progress 150
designing (as part of the ritual of making) 150
designing a god 112–113
desire 61
detailing and finish 164
details 63–65
development 83
devil 64
"devil in the details" 64
dianoia 161
Dickens, Charles 71
digital space 159
dimensionality 23, 26
directors (stage) 16–17
disclosure 73
distribution 156
diversity 79
doodles 141
doorways 118
dramatic event 11, 28
The Dramatic Imagination 1
dramatic space 4
dramatic space historical cycle **87**
dramatic space through history 85
dramaturg 16
dreams 50
dressing 64
Durrenmatt, Friedrich 95
A Dybbuk **103**

E Pluribus Unum 4, 16, 31, 164
East 47
egress 42
elements (of visual design) 150
elevation **22**
elevation of space 37
elevator 115
emblems 68
enchantment 50
encounters 99–110
engagement 57, 140
Enlightenment 28
entrance 41
environment 57–58
environmental theatre 86
Epidauros 86
escape 42
ethos 161
event 28–29, 79, 137, 147, 163–164
evidence 148
exit 42
experience 29, 93, 97, 135
eye path 77

façade 21
faith 108
Falstaff 65
family dynamic 140
Fatima 108
fear 61
"feeling of the space" 59
feng shui 21
"the final frontier" 7
first dimension 19–21
flash highlight 70
focal point 77
focus 156
forced-perspective 27–28
forecast 84–85
form 78, 150
format 36
found textural materials **67**
14 (play by John Cameron) 109
fourth dimension 23–26
fractal 54–56
fractal — the Mandelbrot set **55**
Frankenstein **72**
Frayn, Michael **20**
free forms 53–54
front elevation 21–22
function 79, 132, 156
functions of stage light 156
fusion 157
future 82

Gay, John 73, **73**
Gehry, Frank 21, 54
gender 101–102
geographer 31
geometry 45
ghostly materials 66
ghosts 102–103
The Glass Menagerie 40
Globe Theatre 38
Go Lysistrata! 46
God/god 64, 108–110, 113
"god in the details" 64
"god of the design" 64
Golden Gate Bridge 121
golden rectangle 14, 56
gothic cathedrals 45
Graceland 116
gradation 42–43
grand staircase 116
The Grapes of Wrath 47
Great Salt Desert 109
Greeks 85
grid 115
grotto 145
ground plan 19–21, **20**
Guys and Dolls 129

Hamlet **26**, 100, **101**
hanamichi 47
handyman's shack 145
harmonious design **76**
harmony 75–76
Harnick and Bock (writers) 31
Hawking, Stephen 19
highlight 70
Highway 21 121
historic renovation 145
history 81
holocaust 165
horizontality 47–48
houses on elm street 124
humanism 28

Ibsen, Henrik 19
icons 68
"If it's not on the page, it's not on the stage" 19
illusion 132
The Illusion 107
images 69
imagining 139
immersion 58–59
The Importance of Being Earnest 63
industrial designer 29
inner-above 38
intensity 156
interaction 60–62
intercontinental ballistic missiles 123
The Interior Castle 112
intrusion 59–60

Johnson, Philip 21
Jones, Inigo 28
Jones, Robert Edmond 1
Jonson, Ben 28
journey 29, 77
Jung, Carl 101

Index

Kabuki Theatre 47
Kaufmann, Moises 66, *67*
Kaufmann and Hart (writers) 64, *65*
King Lear 129
knowing 5, 93, 120, 163
Koltai, Ralph 54
Kushner, Tony 107

labyrinth 117
"The Lamppost" (parable) 127
lancet windows 111
landmark designs 25
The Laramie Project 66, *67*
Laterna Magika 69
leading edge (of culture) 10, 28, 84–85
Lee, Eugene 40, 86
level 37–38
lexis 161
life 162, 164–165
light 150
light and sound 124
lighting 70, 80, 156
lighting design 82
lighting script 80
line 14, 150
linear space *155*
liquid 73
living organism 25
living world 162
local light 70
looking down 39
looking straight in at eye level 39
looking through 40
looking up 39
looking "way" down 39
love 60
Lutheran(s) 123
Lysistrata 46

Machinal 49, *49*
machine 115
machine of the design 132, 156–157
Mad Forest 41
magic 107, 137
magical repetition 55
making 5, 139, 164
making of worlds 4
mandala 13
Marat/Sade 67, *67*
Marisol 22, *22*
material 65–67
meaning 131
media theatre 85
Meisner, Sanford 16
melody 76–77
melos 161
Memphis, Tennessee 124
metaphors 68
metaspatial design 107, 127
meteorology 82
A Midsummer Night's Dream *51–52*, 53, 129

Mies van der Rohe, Ludwig 64
Milwaukee Ballet Company 131
"The Missing Tree" (parable) 128
Mr. Spock 107
model (scale) 23–26, *26*
modeling 156
modern dance 9
moments 57
mood 56, 70–*72*
Mormon Church 109
Mother Courage and Her Children 58
motion 72–73
movement 150, 156
mud hut 145
multiple axes 35
music 74
mythos 160

nave 111
network of design 157
New York 121
night 50
nineteenth century 86
Ninth Symphony (Beethoven) 76
nocturnal 50
Noises Off *20*
Norma 130
North Dakota 123
The Nutcracker 131

Ode to Joy 76
Of Mice and Men 66, *66*
Ojibwa nation 106
O'Neill, Eugene 19
opera 21, 65
opsis 161
orchestration 79–80
orchestration of light 80
Orff, Carl 130
organic 13
organic space 13, 152
organism 26
origins 83
ornamentation 63
Our Town 92

Pang, Cecilia 46
parapsychology 99
passages and dividers 118–119
passion 164
path 14, 117
"The Peculiar Moon" (parable) 127
perception 34
periphery 31–33, *33*
perpendicular *34*, 35
personality 57
perspective 26–28, *27*
perspective drawing 26, *27*
phallic columns 46
phases of spatial design 5
physics 19

Pinter, Harold 64
place 57
plan 19–21
Poe, Edgar Allan 100
poetic theatre 66
Poetics (Aristotle) 160
the poetics of space 4–5, 160
poetry of space 78
poetry of the culture 65
point of engagement 38
point of view 38–40
pooling 144
portal and portals 38, 118
portrait (as a subtle nuance) 91
positive and negative space 43
potential 9, 26, 29–30, 38
power 61
prehistoric theatre 85
present 81, 87
process 128–129, 137
process of life 146
production concept 142
products 129–130
progress 46
proportion 37, 150
proscenium theatre 86
psyche 95
psyche of space 96–97
psychological encounter with space 97
psychology 95
pure energy 107–108

ramp, slope and switchback 116
realism 19
recognition 62–63
rectilinear space *154*
Redon, Odilon 149
reflection 70
rehearsal 29–30, 73
relationships 60
relief 70
Renaissance 27, 86
Renaissance stage designs 157
research 18, 83, 119, 148–150
resonance 100
retail establishment 79
revisions 152
rhythm 74–75, *75*
Richard the Third 89, *90*
Rivera, Jose 22, *22*
road 117
Roman Catholic 111
Romanesque churches 13
Romans 86
Romantic art 98
Romanticism 99
Romeo and Juliet 102

Sagan, Carl 97
Saint John of the Cross 23
Saturday night and Sunday morning 123
scaling 37
scene design for the theatre 1, 126

Index

scenic scale model 26
scenography 1
The Seagull **12**
searching 148
second dimension 21–22
section 22–23, **24**
see 19
seeing 5, 163
Sendak, Maurice 104
Serlio, Sebastiano **27**, 28
Shakespeare 19, 23, 38, **51–52**, 53, 89, **90, 101, 102**
shaman, shamanism and shamanistic 79, 85, 106
shape 150
Shaw, George Bernard **33**
She Loves Me 31–32
Shepard, Sam 21
side section drawing 21–23, **24**
sightlines 37
signs 69
Simple Gifts 77
skene 86
sketch-model 25
sky box 104
"sky of many colors" 6
slope and scale 42
smell 92
Smith, Oliver 131
song of the space's culture 65
soul 95
sound designers 17
source 147–148
space (definition) 9
"space dictates experience" 29
space is potential 9
spatial constructions 114–116
spatial music 78
spatial psychologist 98
spatial theatre 85
spectacle 161
sphere of influence 59
spiral or winder stairs 116
spirit 74, 132
spirit access 118
spirit guide 107
spirit quest 112
spirituality 95
spirituality of space 110–113

Spock 107
square 14
stage carpenters 19
stage designer 17–18
stage director 16–17
stage lighting 80
stage lighting designers 17
stairways 116
Stanislavsky, Constantin 16
Star Trek 7
static and the dynamic 15
Steinbeck, John 47, 66, **66**
stone 67, **67**
Stonehenge 13
store 80
story 88, 163
storyboard 28–29
Strasburg, Lee 16
structure 119
structure of the event 164
stylization 63
subtle nuances 90–92
surround 31–32, **32**
Svoboda, Josef 69, 95
symbol 69
symbols and imagery 67–69
synesthesia 1

Taoism 101
Tchaikovsky, P.I. 131
technology of design 158–160
temple 110
text 147
texture 70, 150
The Theatre and Its Double 10
theatre art 10
theatre artist 7
theatre design 11
theatre space 11
theme park design 140
Theresa of Avila 112
Thespis 85
third dimension 22–23
3D model 23, 25
tools 158
topography 37
towers 118
tragic scene **27**
transepts 111

transitional history 126
Treadwell, Sophie 49, **49**
trompe l'oeil 22, 132
Twelfth Night 23, **24**
twentieth century 86

unity 79
usability 120
using 149

vantage point 38
vase-faces drawing **44**
vehicle of the event 11
vents 118
Verdi, Giuseppe 65
vertical space 37
verticality 45
vessels 118
vibrate and vibration 76
video projection 159
visibility 156
visioning 142
voice 77–79

Waiting for Lefty 112
waking 137–139
walk-through 25
walls 118
Waltz of the Snowflakes 132
way of knowing 114
ways 117
Weiss, Peter 67, **67**
well-made office 145
West 45
white (sets) 109
Wilde, Oscar 63
Wilder, Thornton 92
Williams, Tennessee 40
The Wizard of Oz 104
Wolff, Billy 46
wood 66, **66**
world 161, 164
world of the play 17

You Can't Take It with You 64, **65**

zeitgeist 83
zones 40

www.ingramcontent.com/pod-product-compliance
Ingram Content Group UK Ltd.
Pitfield, Milton Keynes, MK11 3LW, UK
UKHW051317161225
9608UKWH00036B/621